Love Isn't Quite Enough

Dr Maryon Tysoe is a social psychologist and award-winning journalist. An Associate Fellow of the British Psychological Society, she was formerly the psychology correspondent on the staff of *New Society* and the agony columnist of *Company* magazine. Her articles and reviews have appeared in such publications as the *Independent, Guardian, Sunday Times, Observer, New Statesman & Society* and *Literary Review*. Her first book was *All This and Work Too: the psychology of office life* (Fontana, 1988). She writes a monthly column on the latest psychological research for *New Woman* magazine.

Dr Tysoe lives in London.

D1510350

MARYON TYSOE

Love Isn't Quite Enough

THE PSYCHOLOGY OF
MALE–FEMALE RELATIONSHIPS

Fontana
An Imprint of HarperCollinsPublishers

Fontana
An Imprint of HarperCollins*Publishers*,
77–85 Fulham Palace Road,
Hammersmith, London W6 8JB

A FONTANA ORIGINAL 1992

9 8 7 6 5 4 3 2 1

A catalogue record for this book is
available from the British Library

ISBN 0 00 637766 1

Photoset in Linotron Meridien

Printed in Great Britain by
HarperCollins Manufacturing, Glasgow

For Ian and Gwen Hogg
my parents
who have been together very happily
for more than 50 years
and show it can be done . . .

Acknowledgements

Whoever said writing is a lonely business said a mouthful. But this can, of course, be greatly alleviated by masses of social support, which I have been lucky enough to receive. I would like to thank Vivien Green, my agent, and Mike Fishwick, my editor, for faithfully cheering me on as ever; my most excellent copy-editor, Juliet Van Oss; and Dr Graham Powell, for his comments on parts of an earlier draft and for his help with tricky points of statistical interpretation.

The staff of the University of London Library were unfailingly good to me, especially those in the psychology section. They always gave the impression that if they could have set up a camp bed and endless cups of coffee for me during the long months of research, they would have.

I am also most grateful to all my friends and family, who so kindly treated my book as a growing infant, about whose health and size they constantly enquired.

My thanks are due to the following for permission to quote from copyright material: Yukie Aida and Toni Falbo and Plenum Publishing Corporation for the items from a questionnaire in 'Relationship Between Marital Satisfaction, Resources and Power Strategies' published in *Sex Roles*; William H. James and the *Journal of Biosocial Science* for information taken from two tables in 'Decline in Coital Rates with Spouses' Ages and Duration of Marriage'; Routledge for the table from *Who Divorces?* by Thornes and Collard; David M. Buss for items from a questionnaire in 'Conflict Between the Sexes: Strategic Interference and the Evocation of Anger and Upset' published in the *Journal of Personality and Social Psychology*.

Contents

Introduction

LOVE: the perennial human obsession, clothed in mystery and magic. Its power is legendary. Love flashes like lightning across a crowded room, linking two strangers in a bond that will last for ever. For love we risk all. Great tales tell of derring-do for the beloved – glass mountains scaled, dragons fought, terrifying fathers defied.

Dangerous stuff. Very.

The emphasis placed in Western cultures on love and romance has been weighty indeed. This has had, in my view, an extremely unfortunate by-product. It has fostered the comforting belief that requited love really is 'all you need' to sustain a long-term relationship. Myth has endowed mutual love with the power of a psychological superglue. As a result, we are surprised and hurt – even devastated – when this turns out to be untrue. The rising divorce statistics aren't always enough to puncture our hope that divorce, the best-documented type of break-up, is something that happens to *other* people because they didn't love each other enough.

The binding qualities of love are not, whatever we like to think, entirely to be relied upon. Even those who are aware of, or reluctantly suspect, this are left floundering as to what other mysterious processes might be operating. The idea that we need to 'work at a relationship' is increasing in popularity, but it is still far from being a phrase on everyone's lips, and if pushed, people find it hard to say what this actually *means*. Yet for most of us in the West a central, loving relationship is of tremendous importance, as illustrated by the fact that the vast majority will marry at least once.[1]

In this book, I will examine why love isn't quite enough, and the implications for a more realistic – and hence potentially successful – way of conducting our relationships with the opposite sex.

What I have to say is directed at both women and men. The assumption that worrying about relationships is women's work, as we shall see later, is in itself one of the things that causes difficulties in heterosexual relationships. Men 'need to know' about relationships just as much as women do, and when men have asked me what I'm writing a book about and I tell them, they want a copy immediately. Yet I suspect that they'd don a false beard and sunglasses before risking asking for it in a book shop, just in case they were seen and labelled a wimp on the spot. Social pressures against men taking an open interest in the intricacies of relationships are weakening, however. And women aren't the only ones to suffer agonies if the loved one biffs off into the gloaming with a suitcase. Men may turn to drink and women to paper tissues, but neither sex has a monopoly on pain – at its worst, like having schools of piranhas make a light snack of your insides.

So this is for you, too, guys.

Courage can always be drawn, of course, from the fact that male songwriters, poets and novelists don't exactly recoil from the subject with a blush. Excluding Byronic cynicism of the 'Men love in haste, but they detest at leisure'[2] variety, they often let rip in a soul-spilling way. Take for instance P.G. Wodehouse's description in *Summer Lightning* of the reactions of Hugo Carmody to his friend Sue Brown's query as to whether Millicent Threepwood really loves him:

'Between you and me,' said Hugo confidentially, 'I don't wonder you speak in that amazed tone. If you saw her, you'd be still more surprised. I am a man who thinks before he speaks. I weigh my words. And I tell you solemnly that that girl is too good for me.'

'But you're a sweet darling precious pet.'

'I know I'm a sweet darling precious pet. Nevertheless, I still maintain that she is too good for me. She is the nearest thing to an angel that ever came glimmering through the laurels in the quiet evenfall in the garden by the turrets of the old manorial hall.'

'Hugo! I'd no idea you were so poetical.'

'Enough to make a chap poetical, loving a girl like that.'[3]

Sweet, no?

Squillions of non-fiction books on love have been written too. Many of them, however, are based on therapists' personal experiences with people in trouble or on interviews with unrepresentative samples. This one is not. There is a great deal of psychological research, conducted in a scientific manner, which is published in academic journals. My aim in writing this book has been to search for the latest state-of-the-art psychological themes and findings, and not only to make them accessible, but to use them to explore the questions of why love isn't enough and what else we need. This knowledge, I believe, might help people to cope with and flourish in their relationships. 'Common sense' is an unreliable guide. Not only is it full of contradictions of the 'opposites attract'/'birds of a feather flock together' variety, but also, if it is so jolly wonderful then why do human beings' relationships bite the dust so painfully in such droves?

I will be making generalizations, which is all one can draw from research findings. This does not mean that the subject isn't terribly complex; and obviously there are no rules and statistics that apply to all individuals and relationships! Research findings can make no predictions about individual cases. What they do is offer information which may be of use in managing one's own relationship. One can claim no more than that. Research is not a flawless exercise, and the growth of psychological knowledge is a continuous process. But there are lines of research that in my view provide the best clues we have so far as to what might be going on – and wrong – in heterosexual relationships.

I have chosen to concentrate on heterosexuals because they form an estimated ninety percent at least of all close pair bonds in Western countries,[4] and because there is another psychological literature on homosexuality which I do not have space to tackle. However, elements of what I have to say – such as how best to deal with conflict – should apply to homosexual relationships too.

To understand why love is necessary but not sufficient for a really successful long-term relationship, we need first to look at what it means. We tend to assume that everyone yearns for the divine state, and agrees upon what it is. But this is not so, and any mismatch between two people in their desire for or style of love can dish the whole thing. My first port of call, then, is a close look at love itself.

The next stop is an exploration of the early stages of relationships: selecting a partner, male versus female differences in attitudes to sex, factors that put the relationship at risk, different patterns and speeds of courtship. This is a tricky time. Shakespeare hit it on the button as usual:

> O! how this spring of love resembleth
> The uncertain glory of an April day,
> Which now shows all the beauty of the sun,
> And by and by a cloud takes all away![5]

Then we come to that crucial issue – once the relationship is up and running, how do you nurture it and minimize the chances of it collapsing slowly into a black hole? This is especially important now that expectations of relationships (in terms of, for instance, intimacy and emotional and sexual gratification) are higher than ever before, and people are less willing to stick with a partnership where love has disappeared. The barriers against leaving even the most committed of relationships are now lower than in the past. More women have financial independence, there is less stigma attached to divorce, and so on.

Much of the research relevant to nurturing relationships is on marital satisfaction, and so words such as 'marriage' and 'spouse' appear rather frequently. (Psychologists' measures of 'marital satisfaction' and 'marital adjustment' typically include measures of love and relationship happiness, as well as other aspects such as problems in the relationship.[6]) This is either because marriage is the focus of the research I am discussing, or because I am using it as a short code-word for 'long-term live-in committed relationship'. Obviously those need just as much looking after as those flaunting an official seal of approval.

Next comes the role of sex in relationship happiness, and the occurrence that can blow up a relationship like a psychological Exocet – infidelity.

Lastly I examine the question of how to try to repair relationships if they are already heading rather determinedly for the rocks, and make the point that life doesn't end if one's relationship does: one can apply greater knowledge to making sure one has a better chance of developing a stronger relationship in the future.

And developing stronger relationships is what this book is about.

ONE

What Is Love?

The notion that love is the only appropriate basis for a long-term heterosexual relationship is so deeply ingrained within our culture that it passes without question. Its delights, pains and complexities are explored in novels, plays and TV soap operas, maundered over in pop songs, celebrated in romance fiction. We are obsessed with it. Overheard gossip is shot through with analyses and angst over the divine state. 'Did you hear that Phil's fallen madly in love with Angela? Yeah, classic stuff. Saw her across a crowded room at Dick's party and next moment was the human equivalent of a homing missile. I'm saving my petrol tokens for a toast rack even as we speak.'

Cultural and historical perspectives

Yet the concept of love as a necessary condition for marriage is relatively recent. It is, too, a characteristic of Western cultures more than of the rest of the world.

The idea that there is such a thing as love, of course, is neither recent nor culturally bound. Its nature has been discussed and argued over endlessly from the ancient Greek philosophers to nearly-21st-century psychologists. The Greeks liked to divide love into types. *Eros* or lust was distinguished from the non-sexual *agape* or service to the ideal. The Greeks idolized the latter, 'sacred' or spiritual love, whereas passionate love was given rather short shrift.[1] As one modern expert puts it, 'The ancient Greeks . . . may have seen passionate love as providing wonderful material for drama, but they regarded it as madness

when it occurred in everyday life.'[2] Platonic ideas of love –
mixed in with Christianity – are thought to be the intellectual
predecessors of the mediaeval doctrine of 'courtly love' among
the European nobility.[3]

Courtly love is supposed to be the brainchild of Eleanor of
Aquitaine, reputedly fed to her wimple with the appalling and
boorish knights who used to hang around her castle when there
wasn't a war on. The general plan was that a knight should
love a lady passionately from afar, and go out at her behest
to brave dangers – marauding barons, dragons, whatever. In
other words, to do what they wanted to do anyway. As s-e-x
wasn't supposed to enter into it – the idea was that the man's
soul would be ennobled by his pure passion – the best target
for this 'love' was someone else's wife.[4]

Elements of this romantic love included falling in love at first
sight, being fated and uncontrollable, conquering all obstacles,
accepting no substitutes, being a consuming passion of agony
and ecstasy which transcended all social boundaries.[5] The
epitome of the 'loving passionately from a distance' idea has
to be the absolutely potty story of Dante and Beatrice, widely
lauded as one of the great romantic tales of all time. Dante and
Beatrice lived in fourteenth-century Italy. Dante saw Beatrice
first when they were nine, then not until they were eighteen.
They never progressed beyond the exchange of courteous
greetings (and she died at twenty-four).[6]

Brilliant.

A really mature approach to personal relationships.

Dante was inspired to write some pretty hot poetry as a result,
however, and literature of this kind has played a strong role in
embedding romantic love deeply into the Western world view.
And finally sex did, of course, worm its way firmly into the
concept of romance.

But it was still a long time before the idea that love should
be linked to marriage took a strong grip. Marriage was about
property rights and inheritance, wealth, health and social class[7]

rather than love, until relatively recently. Parents made the choices rather than the couples themselves.

This is not to say, of course, that individuals didn't sometimes try to marry the person they wanted even in the face of parental opposition. In early modern England, for example, neither Church nor State had imposed tight regulations on what constituted a valid marriage, still inclining to the mediaeval view that an informal contract between consenting partners (commonly called 'handfasting') did count, though the Church stipulated that it should be followed by a church wedding later.[8] This uncertainty could, of course, complicate matters somewhat. An English sociologist writes of Janet Barras of Whickham (Durham) in 1570: 'She had contracted herself to a man of her choice earlier in the year, in a ceremony held in the orchard behind the local parsonage. Yet at midsummer her father overrode this union and forced her into another match with a man he favoured. Both ritual contracts were performed with the correct verbal formula and witnessing of mutual pledges; but the first must have been her preference, for the man in the second had to bring a case against her to enforce his 'marriage'. Janet must have held out against her father.'[9] Good on you, kid. But, as the sociologist says, at this time 'free choice was a distinct luxury'. Parents during this period, while not necessarily forcing their offspring into marrying someone they actually disliked, would at least use their power to 'persuade' them into approved matches. 'Marriage and all personal affairs were still too important to others to be left entirely to the individual couple.'[10]

The idea that romance should be incorporated into marriage was first advocated in eighteenth-century Europe (though hints of this radical move were to be found much earlier, not least in the plays of Shakespeare), but it appears in practice to have taken off first in America.[11]

In America there was bags of land (making economic considerations less vital) and society was starting afresh (without, therefore, rigid class distinctions and other obstacles), so it is perhaps unsurprising that choice rather than arrangement in marriage took root earlier than in Europe. By the twentieth century, marrying the person you wanted to marry had become the rule rather than the exception in the West generally.[12]

But even marrying the person you choose does not necessarily incorporate the notion of love.

The first systematic study of the supposed connection between romantic love and marriage was carried out in America in the 1960s.[13] (Much of the research I shall be discussing has been done in America. This is inevitable given that it has by far the largest concentration of psychologists.) Over 1,000 college students were asked: 'If a boy (girl) had all the other qualities you desired, would you marry this person if you were not in love with him (her)?' Nearly two-thirds of the men said 'no', but fewer than a quarter of the women did so. (Nearly all the rest of the women were 'undecided'.) The researcher suggested that perhaps women were more concerned with economic security and status than men when they made their marital choices – a reasonable explanation given women's more powerless position in society. For men, however, emotional quality appeared to play a larger role.

But since the 1960s, women have been achieving greater economic independence. Theoretically, then, shouldn't love now be able to play a greater part in their choices of husband or long-term partner?

A group of psychologists from the University of Minnesota put the same question, about marrying a 'suitable' person in the absence of love, to college students in 1976 and 1984.[14] By 1976, the proportion of men saying 'no' had risen to 86 percent, and the number of women rejecting the idea had shot up to 80 percent. By 1984, it had evened out at men 86 percent and women 85 percent. As the researchers point out, with general improvement in economic and social conditions, positive emotional experiences have become increasingly important in determining *both* men's *and* women's decisions to enter (and their satisfaction with) long-term relationships.

The findings of this study echo the message that the media pump daily into our willing ears. By the 1980s, then, it seems fair to say that both sexes, in the main, were regarding love as the *sine qua non* of the married state. Nor is there any reason to suppose that this will change in the foreseeable future.

It is worth remembering, however, that this is still a culturally specific phenomenon. Among the Hamar people of south-west Ethiopia, for example, women are betrothed by parental arrangement when young. If, before the marriage, a girl or woman goes off with a man she likes to 'laugh' with him and then falls pregnant, rather than allowing her to marry that man if she wishes to, the foetus is aborted in secret and she is married to the man already chosen for her. No sign here of the power and precedence of the divine fire.[15] Indeed, anthropological studies indicate that in some cultures – Tahiti, for example – individuals cannot comprehend what the Western notion of falling passionately in love actually means.[16]

There is no doubt that cultures do still differ in the role they allocate to romantic love in the choice of a long-term partner. Arranged marriages occur to this day in collectivist cultures[17] such as India. The existence of polygyny (a man taking more than one wife) and the far rarer polyandry (a woman marrying more than one husband) in some cultures[18] are also marital arrangements where romantic love hardly seems to be given a leading role.

The importance of love for marriage, then, is a phenomenon that humanity has created in recent times in the Western world in particular. The trouble is that, having set up such a tricky requirement, we don't know what to do with it. In the days when all your kith, kin and wider community, plus the practical and economic exigencies of life, conspired to keep you in the marriage state, what you actually felt about it was hardly of major importance. This was particularly true of women, the more powerless ones, whose adultery – if risked – tended to be horrendously punished; male infidelity was not,[19] so men who felt deprived could get a bit of emotional and sexual gratification elsewhere, without upsetting the line of inheritance or their practical domestic arrangements.

Now it's different. But having gone to the other extreme and made a god out of Love, we have laid upon it all the weight of our deepest longings for intimacy and security. Love, not practicalities and outside pressures, is expected to play the greater part in keeping a relationship together. When a man and a woman gaze at each other and say 'I love you', each thinks 'Wow, at last, someone on the same wavelength. Surely, surely it'll be all right now.' That the rising divorce statistics argue otherwise, and that we all know that love can end, doesn't seem to stop us from longing for love to be enough and at least half-believing that it is – or that hell, it should be.

To explore why this is not so and, more importantly, what implications this has for the way we conduct our relationships, it is necessary to peer more closely at the concept itself. Not only have we endowed love with superglue qualities, but we tend to assume that we all know what we mean by the word and, what's more, that we experience it in the same way. Unfortunately, this is not true.

So what is love?

The question of what love is has been debated from time immemorial, and there is simply no agreed answer to the question at all.[20] Freud saw romantic love as 'aim-inhibited sexuality', the expression – or redirection on more socially acceptable lines – of sexual longing.[21] Such a one-dimensional (and much-criticized[22]) view of the matter is fairly typical. Broader-based conceptions, however, often end up sounding merely tautological: suggesting that love is 'an affectional tie that binds one individual to another'[23], for example, doesn't tell us much. The issue does, of course, provide a perfect platform for endless clever-clogs definitions that are no more helpful. Some are cynical: the journalist H.L. Mencken wrote, 'To be in love is merely to be in a state of perceptual anaesthesia – to mistake an ordinary young man for a Greek god or an ordinary young woman for a goddess.'[24] Or John Barrymore: 'Love is the delightful interval between meeting a beautiful girl and discovering that she looks like a haddock.'[25] Other descriptions are rather more lyrical, for example 'a spirit all compact of fire' (Shakespeare)[26], if no more illuminating.

Most of us have some sense of what it means. We appreciate that we use the term in lots of ways. We love our parents, children, best friends, lovers/spouses, and we love prawns – and in each case we know we mean something different. What I am concentrating on here is one specific kind of love – love for a heterosexual partner.

So what makes this kind of love different from other kinds of love? If pushed, we could come out with definitions, but they would probably be vague: 'Erm, well, I sort of feel terribly warm towards her – I like being with her . . . Gosh, it's difficult, isn't it?' Often, definitions sound very much as though they could apply to other categories of people whom we love – best friends, for example. Sexual attraction is the obvious ingredient that differentiates love for a partner from other loves – but it is not the only one, as we shall see.

To make matters worse, different people will describe love differently. In a study where students were asked to list what attributes sprang to mind when thinking about the concept 'love', the researcher found no fewer than 183 love attributes produced by 141 students.[27] Of these, 115 were mentioned by only one person. Of the rest, one attribute ('caring') was mentioned by 44 percent of the subjects; three ('happiness', 'want to be with other', 'friendship') by at least 20 percent of the respondents; and 13 attributes by over 10 percent of the respondents. These were: 'feel free to talk about anything';

'warm feelings'; 'accept other the way s/he is'; 'trust'; 'commit-ment'; 'sharing'; 'think about the other all the time'; 'sacrifice'; 'understanding'; 'honesty'; 'respect'; 'contentment'; 'euphoria'. While these students were not asked to *define* love, but to list its features, what these findings make crystal clear is precisely how idiosyncratic the notion of what love involves actually is. And this idiosyncrasy provides merely an initial glimmer of the problems human beings run into when they wish to rely on it as a relationship glue.

And aren't there different kinds of love one can feel within the same relationship over time (and for different partners) too? Surely the heady, dazed, 'madly in love' feeling isn't the same as the calmer, relaxed love for a partner of long-standing?

The world hardly lacks speculation on the matter, but actual hard research on the topic is a far rarer creature. Psychologists took a deep breath and started to examine the issue only in the late 1960s. Poking their heads above the parapet and remarking diffidently that they thought love was worthy of research brought an immediate hail of brickbats. When in the mid-1970s Ellen Berscheid of the University of Minnesota – now one of the most famous psychologists specializing in love relationships in the world – was awarded a grant to support her research, this triggered an attack from a certain Senator William Proxmire, which was widely reported with glee in the press: 'I believe that two hundred million other Americans want to leave some things in life a mystery, and right at the top of things we don't want to know is why a man falls in love with a woman and vice versa.'[28]

This attitude is idiotic. Given the immense role that long-term (or intended to be long-term) relationships play in the lives of human beings, what the hell goes on in our love lives is a profoundly important question. Ignoring the laughter, psychologists did start to study this most difficult of areas. What they have found, surprise, surprise, is that it's all very complicated, and they don't agree on a definition either. But what they have done is start to tease the concept apart in systematic ways which are open to observation and scientific test. Remembering that it would be risky to generalize what they have found beyond the present time in Western cultures, what have we got?

LOVE VERSUS LIKING

One of the earliest strands of research was the attempt to distinguish between love and liking. Social psychologist Zick Rubin at Harvard University was the first to try to devise a measure of love. He made up around 80 statements about feelings towards others, and asked friends and acquaintances of his to sort them into a 'love' pile and a 'liking' pile, according to their sense of what those words meant. Refining and shrinking the number of items, he next gave them to undergraduates, and asked them to rate how applicable each item was to (a) their current girlfriend or boyfriend (if they had one) and (b) a platonic friend of the opposite sex. Using complicated statistical techniques, he came up with two clusters of statements, one which appeared to measure liking and the other love. In its short form, the Rubin Love Scale runs as follows:

1. I feel that I can confide in X about virtually everything.
2. I would do almost anything for X.
3. If I could never be with X, I would feel miserable.
4. If I were lonely, my first thought would be to seek X out.
5. One of my primary concerns is X's welfare.
6. I would forgive X for practically anything.
7. I feel responsible for X's wellbeing.
8. I would greatly enjoy being confided in by X.
9. It would be hard for me to get along without X.[29]

These statements, Rubin says, capture the three elements which he thinks comprise love: attachment (needing to be with or cared for by the other person, e.g. item 4), caring (being as concerned about the other's needs as one's own, e.g. item 5) and intimacy (having a close bond with the other, e.g. item 1).[30]

If this is love, what is liking? The short form of Rubin's Liking Scale is:

1. I think that X is unusually well-adjusted.
2. I would highly recommend X for a responsible job.
3. In my opinion, X is an exceptionally mature person.
4. I have great confidence in X's good judgement.
5. Most people would react favourably to X after a brief acquaintance.
6. I think that X is one of those people who quickly wins respect.
7. X is one of the most likeable people I know.
8. X is the sort of person whom I myself would like to be.
9. It seems to me that it is very easy for X to gain admiration.[31]

Liking, then, seems to be more an attitude of admiration and respect for a person than the intense feeling of a specific person's importance in one's life.

But what is the relationship between love and liking? Is love just a superconcentrated form of liking? Are the two attitudes (as Rubin regards them) quite separate? Rubin's results implied that neither of these hypotheses is true. Love and liking, as they emerge from his studies, appear to be separate but overlapping entities. There is a moderate association between them. So though people can like without loving (which we know) and love without liking (which we also know, though it sounds weirder), on the whole, if you feel a lot of love or a lot of liking for someone, you will endorse some statements from the other scale too.[32]

One might at this point say, huh, these are just questionnaires – how do we know they measure anything real? Zick Rubin was concerned about this himself, and devised a seriously cute experiment. He put some dating couples (one couple at a time) who had both scored high on his love scale, and other couples who had both scored low, in his laboratory, and asked them to 'wait for the experiment to begin'. Observers hidden behind a one-way mirror recorded precisely when the couples looked at each other. The results showed that the 'high'-scoring couples gazed into each other's eyes significantly more than the 'low'-scoring couples – thus proving that the love scale was certainly on the right track . . .[33]

But if you give people lists of statements and ask them to respond, you can only get out what you put in. Rubin's scale identified components of love which he already thought might be there; that does not mean that love does not have components which he did not ask about. For example, Rubin's love scale doesn't refer explicitly to the aspect which most obviously differentiates heterosexual love from, say, parental love or platonic love for a friend – sexual attraction. Passion. Palpitations in anticipation of seeing the loved one, excitement, breathing funny – in the early stages of a relationship, at least.

In one American experiment devised to explore this aspect, male college students were told either to read an explicit description of a woman's sexual behaviour and fantasies, which aroused them sexually, or to read a tedious account of the mating and courtship activities of herring gulls, which left them completely unaroused. When they then filled in Rubin's scales about their current girlfriend, the sexual arousal was found to boost their love scores, while hardly touching the men's feelings of liking for their girlfriends.[34]

But is sexual arousal the defining characteristic of heterosexual love compared with, say, platonic love for a friend? Might love not have a central core, a 'general factor' which is present when we feel love in *any* relationship? After all, some items on Rubin's love scale could apply just as well to one's best pal.

The dimensions of love

The evidence is that there *is* such a general factor in love relationships. The American psychologists Robert Sternberg and Susan Grajek gave several love questionnaires (including Rubin's) to men and women who were 18 or over, who reported having had at least one love relationship and who described themselves as primarily heterosexual. They were asked to fill in certain scales with respect to their mother, father, sibling closest in age, best same-sex friend and lover or spouse (too few of the subjects had children to make this part of the analyses).

The results showed that there is a general factor of love which applied to all these relationships. 'The factor seems well identified,' the researchers write, 'as one of interpersonal communication, sharing, and support. Its aspects include especially (a) deep understanding of the other, (b) sharing of ideas and information, (c) sharing of deeply personal ideas and feelings, (d) receipt and provision of emotional support from and to the other, (e) personal growth through the relationship and helping of the other in his or her personal growth, (f) giving help to the other, (g) making the other feel needed and needing the other, and (h) the giving and receiving of affection in the relationship.'[35]

As should be clear from this description, this general factor is not 'an indivisible glob' of positive emotion, but a set of interlinked bonds, which 'yield the global feeling (and factor) that we identify as *love*'.[36] Nor is love the equivalent of turning on a light – being on or off. It appears to be more like a psychological dimmer switch. Sternberg and Grajek found that individuals differ in the amounts of love they display although, as they point out, it is not clear from this whether this is a personality difference or due to some individuals finding themselves surrounded by less loveable people. As low love for one member of the family tended to go hand in hand with low love for other members, and not to bear so much relationship to the amount of love felt for non-family members, this implies that at least some part of the difference between individuals is due to the circumstances in which they find themselves. If your family is a quarrelsome pain in the posterior, you're not going to be glowing with love for them like an emotional heat lamp.

Not only can individuals differ in the amount of love they report overall, but the 'quantities' of love can vary across relationships too. Lovers are reported as being loved more than family members; best friends more than siblings (poor lambs).

But even if there are elements in common between feelings of love for different people in our lives, we know damn well that it *feels* different. Sternberg and Grajek argue that their results are not inconsistent with this. '[The results] do suggest, however, that whatever the differences may be among relationships, they are not primarily in the nature of the core of love that forms part of their basis. Thus it is not the love, but rather the concomitants of love, that differ the most: the relationships may well differ in subjective experience because of differences in feelings of responsibility, sexual desire, perceived permanence or impermanence, competition for affection, kind and degree of communication possible, and the like.'[37] That 'core of love', however, sounds to me remarkably like a specific cluster of concomitants which happen to occur across a wider range of love relationships than purely heterosexual ones.

The latest conceptions of love have now faced squarely the fact that global definitions of love don't get us anywhere. What psychologists argue about now is the number and kind of elements which add up to make a human being feel that he or she loves another. Only by understanding at least some of the ways in which love can differ between people, or change over time within an individual, can we hope to have an initial grip on the potential for misunderstanding and later disappointment when two people tell each other that yeah, this time it's love.

THE TRIANGULAR THEORY

It is clear that the 'core' components of love, the ones identified by Robert Sternberg and Susan Grajek as applying to a variety of love relationships, are not the only elements involved in heterosexual love. Realizing this, Sternberg has gone on to develop the most promising theory so far on the components of love for a sexual partner. This theory is particularly adept at providing insights into why two people can say they love each other – and genuinely mean it – and then find that this apparently basic building block of a long-term relationship turns out to have the solidity of a blancmange.

Sternberg's theory is that love for a partner can be divided into three basic components. The first is *intimacy*, roughly equivalent to the 'core' of love identified in his work with Susan Grajek. The second is *passion*, which needs no definition. Or if one must have one, I rather like 'a state of intense longing for union with another'.[38] The third is *commitment*, which Sternberg sees as having two elements: in the short term, the decision that one loves the other person, and in the long term a commitment to maintain that love.[39]

One of the satisfying aspects of this theory is that it captures the fact that love is not just a matter of emotion. The word 'emotion' implies some physiological arousal; while it's true that in the early stages of feeling passionately in love we have a lot of trouble with our heart rate, steadiness of knee and so on, it's obvious that we can still feel that we love someone even with a normal heartbeat and rock-solid legs. The passion component does reflect both the emotional strand of love and the sexual one, which other theories of love (such as Rubin's) often play down. But the intimacy component refers to the actual attitude that one holds towards the partner, *and* some of the behaviour that love involves – such as self-disclosure, being supportive, expressing affection. The commitment component reflects the fact that to feel in love, you must decide that you are. Love is a cognitive (involving thought) as well as emotional experience.

Sternberg's triangular theory not only makes it clear that love involves emotion, thought, attitudes and ways of behaving, but it can also be used to capture some of the different flavours of the rich experience to which we give such a terribly over-simplistic label.

The three elements can be shuffled to form eight combinations. In their most simplistic form, these are:

1. *Non-love.* None of the elements present.
2. *Liking.* Only the intimacy component is present. Sternberg is using 'liking' in a non-trivial sense here, to mean the feelings involved in true friendships. 'One feels closeness, bondedness, and warmth toward the other without feeling intense passion or long-term commitment.' This sounds to me like what we mean when we say we 'love' a close friend in an entirely non-sexual way.
3. *Infatuated love.* Good old love at first sight. Feelings of passion gush like a geyser, in the absence of any intimacy (as you don't know the other person from a bar of soap) or commitment.
4. *Empty love.* Commitment to the decision that one loves another, but without the intimacy or passion components. 'It is the kind of love that one sometimes finds in stagnant relationships that have been going on for years but have lost both the mutual emotional involvement and physical attraction that once characterized them.'
5. *Romantic love.* Intimacy and passion combined. 'This view of romantic love seems to be similar to that found in classic works of literature, such as *Romeo and Juliet* and *Tristan and Isolde*.' (If complications hadn't intervened, perhaps the poor ducks would have got around to the commitment bit . . .)
6. *Companionate love.* A blend of the intimacy and decision/commitment components of love. 'It is essentially a long-term, committed friendship, the kind that frequently occurs in marriages in which the physical attraction (a major source of passion) has died down.'
7. *Fatuous love.* Passion and decision/commitment without the intimacy component. 'It is the kind of love sometimes

associated with Hollywood and with whirlwind courtships,' writes Sternberg severely. 'A couple meets one day, gets engaged two weeks later, and marries the next month. It is fatuous in the sense that a commitment is made on the basis of passion without the stabilizing element of intimate involvement. Although the passion component can develop almost instantaneously, the intimacy component cannot; hence, relationships based on fatuous love are at risk for termination . . .'

8. *Consummate love.* Yes, the big one. The result of all three components combined, and what most of us yearn for in a love relationship.[40]

What this theory does, quite starkly, is make the point that people can feel love which, because it lacks an essential element, has a good chance of being doomed. It also makes clear exactly how it is possible for two people to love each other and for them not to mean the same thing.

If one imagines an individual's 'love triangle', where each of the three components forms one vertex, one can see how the shape of the triangle might be different for each of the two partners. The greater a particular component, the farther that vertex lies from the centre of the triangle. The area of the triangle, which Sternberg views as representing the amount of love, might differ too. So not only is there potential trouble if two people's love triangles are of different shapes and sizes, but further complications are added by the fact that people also have 'ideal' triangles – how they would *like* to be feeling, and how they would like the other person to be feeling – and 'perceived' triangles, or how they reckon the other person feels about them.[41]

What's more, love can, of course, change over time. The American social psychologist Elaine Hatfield, one of the first psychologists to try to investigate love scientifically, believed that early passionate love would either fade to nothing or be transformed, over time, into companionate love (Sternberg's love number 6).[42] What little relevant evidence there is does support the idea that passionate love does diminish in intensity to some extent at least[43], and the general concept that passionate love can shift towards companionate love makes a lot of sense intuitively. It seems to capture what people mean when they start off by saying, 'Oh wow, I'm in love. I can't sleep, I think of nothing but Nick, I keep putting cat litter in the fridge and Sugar Cornpops down for the cat to poo on. I seem to remember eating at some point, but I think it was last week.' Later, two things can happen when one asks how it's going. There's the 'Nick who?' type of response, or there's the 'I really do love him, even though he does keep leaving his horrendous niffy socks in the bath' kind of answer.

The view that passion fades with time is one that Sternberg, too, agrees with. It's thought to happen because people become 'habituated' – that is, they become used to the situation so that the same level of stimulation gradually evokes less of a response. (This does not mean that passion is doomed to disappear altogether, but that it is unlikely to remain as intense as it was in the beginning.) Commitment, Sternberg argues, follows a different time course, being low at first, and then speeding up. It then remains level if the relationship is successful and, obviously, may drop to zero if it is not.[44]

Sternberg also agrees with the psychologist Ellen Berscheid's view of the time course of intimacy as being a rather more complex affair. The theory is that intimacy increases steadily at first, then more slowly, and finally reaches a plateau. To understand what happens next, Berscheid distinguishes between manifest intimacy, which can be seen, and hidden intimacy.

'As two people come to know each other better,' Sternberg says, 'each becomes more predictable to the other, and they are no longer aware of feeling as close to each other as they once did. But, as Berscheid points out, one of two things may actually be happening. On the one hand, the relationship may truly be dying – the two may be evolving separately and growing apart. On the other hand, the relationship may be thriving, with the two growing closer, but because of the smoothness of the growth, they are hardly aware of their interdependence.'[45] So in a successful relationship, the amount of hidden intimacy will be increasing while the observable intimacy is decreasing. In an unsuccessful relationship, the levels of both will be declining. Unfortunately, as the amount of observable intimacy is similar in each case, it may be a bit difficult for some couples (not all, I'm sure) to know which kind of relationship they have. It may take a serious interruption to their lives, perhaps a crisis of some sort or a period of separation, to show them how they really feel.

What all this means, then, is that the shape of people's love triangles – just to make things even more complicated – will shift over time. And, of course, they may not shift in unison for the two people involved.

It's important to say at this point that all this theorizing is relatively new, it does not yet have a strong body of research findings to back it up, and there is room for development. But the triangular theory has not been plucked out of thin air, and subsumes or is compatible with many earlier theories and associated research.[46] Although work directly on the theory is in its early stages, results are promising. For example, Robert Sternberg and a graduate student, Michael Barnes, gave rating scales to 24 couples. The couples were asked how they felt about their partner, how they thought the partner felt about them, how they would feel about an ideal person, and how they would wish that ideal person to feel about them. The results suggested that in general, the closer in shape and size were a person's real, ideal and perceived triangles, and the closer the match between the two lovers' real triangles, the more satisfying was the relationship.[47]

The theory's most valuable function at this stage in our knowledge is, in my view, to point out how people can declare love to each other and yet how, before we even start to consider the true day-to-day practicalities of running a relationship, there might already be serious inherent difficulties – in the shape and size of the triangles, in the way these relate to people's ideal triangles ('gosh, I do love him but I wish I *fancied* him more') and to their perception of what the other's triangle is (a lot of potential for trouble here – does 'I don't think you love me,' 'Oh yes I do' sound familiar at all?), and in the way that love is dynamic and the triangles can change over time.

This is not meant to be pessimistic, but realistic. If any of us are to achieve successful relationships through judgement rather than luck, we need to face the complexities. By developing ways of understanding them – which psychologists are now struggling to do – we can increase the chances of creating the relationships that we want. (It is, of course, possible to work on our own and other people's triangles, and I will be looking at ways of nurturing relationships later.)

On top of recognizing the ways in which two individuals' feelings of love for each other might differ, another facet of the complexities of love is the possibility that certain 'types' of people might characteristically differ in the ways they experience love. The most obvious and alarming possibility is that men and women experience it differently, making it apparently miraculous that men and women manage to form any relationships at all which manage to last more than a nanosecond. There has been lots of talk about 'men who can't commit' and a general impression given that for a man to be able to spell the word 'love' you'd have to give him a dictionary.

But is this fair?

TWO

Attitudes to Love

It is *not* fair to get heavy and cynical about men's views of love. There are some interesting sex differences in this area, but they are not the kind to make women fling their hands in the air in a despairing sort of way. They just point to some potential dangers.

Sex differences in love attitudes

The first, and comforting, point relates to how important it is to someone to have a close, sexually exclusive and (relatively) secure relationship. The stereotypic view is that this matters less to men than to women. The evidence is that it matters to both. As an example, in one study of American university students[1] (a rather common choice of subjects, as students are the most easily accessible population for research psychologists to try their theories on), the researchers found no difference between the sexes in the value they placed on 'dyadic attachment' in a romantic/sexual relationship. Such attachment is reflected, they say, in 'seeking security and permanence in a relationship, wanting to have many joint activities with a partner, valuing sexual exclusivity, and wanting to share personal feelings'.[2]

Zick Rubin, too, was interested in whether there were any sex differences in response to his Love Scale, but 'the average love scores of men for their girlfriends and of women for their boyfriends were virtually identical'.[3]

Findings like these serve to remind us that however much members of the two sexes occasionally wax cynical about each other's motives for entering long-term partnerships (someone to cook the dinner, money, easily accessible sex . . .), there is no reason to think that one sex ranks higher than the other in yearnings for love and companionship.

But there appear nevertheless to be some differences in the approaches of the two sexes. We have seen already that in the 1960s, men were far more ready to disagree that they would marry someone with all the qualities they desired if they weren't in love than women were, although by the mid-1980s this discrepancy had disappeared.

Nevertheless, even though women might now agree with men on the importance of love in marriage, the implication that women are rather more pragmatic in their approach to love than men appears still to be true even now.

As part of the general struggle to get to grips with the concept of love, a Canadian sociologist, John Alan Lee, categorized love into six 'styles'.[4] Any person can theoretically experience a mixture of these styles.[5] (Although Lee himself believes that one style will be dominant in a particular relationship, others, as we'll see later, reckon it's more complex than that.) But you can measure differences between people – and between the sexes – on each style separately.

Psychologists Clyde and Susan Hendrick of Texas Tech University and their colleagues have found fairly consistent sex differences in a number of studies.[6] To start with, women appear more inclined to *storge* (friendship love) and *pragma* (logical, 'shopping list' love) in their conceptions of love than men. To understand clearly what this means, it's important to see the questionnaire items these researchers used to measure the six love styles. Subjects (university students) had to indicate how much they agreed or disagreed with various statements. They were to answer with their current or most recent love partner in mind or, if they had never been in love, to say what they think their feelings would most likely be. The wording varied slightly from study to study, but the items below are from one of their more recent studies.[7]

The items to measure *storge* were:

1. It is hard to say exactly where friendship ends and love begins.
2. Genuine love first requires *caring* for a while.
3. I expect to always be friends with the one I love.
4. The best kind of love grows out of a long friendship.
5. Our friendship merged gradually into love over time.
6. Love is really a deep friendship, not a mysterious, mystical emotion.
7. My most satisfying love relationships have developed from good friendships.

And *pragma*:

1. I consider what a person is going to become in life before I commit myself to him/her.
2. I try to plan my life carefully before choosing a lover.
3. It is best to love someone with a similar background.
4. A main consideration in choosing a lover is how he/she reflects on my family.
5. An important factor in choosing a partner is whether or not he/she will be a good parent.
6. One consideration in choosing a partner is how he/she will reflect on my career.
7. Before getting very involved with anyone, I try to figure out how compatible his/her hereditary background is with mine in case we ever have children.

Rather strange, that last one (and the item both sexes tended to disagree with, but women less than men[8]).

There was no explicit item on the question that cynics are always raising – to what extent a man's income is a factor in a woman's decision. It seems a reasonable guess, however, that as women's financial independence increases, any need to make that much of an issue will decrease. As the Hendricks and their colleagues say, 'Traditionally, women have been socialized to marry both a love partner and a potential provider . . . [this]

would require careful consideration (*storge*) and perhaps a shopping list of attributes (*pragma*).'[9] But they wonder how long such sex differences in attitudes to love are likely to remain.

What is most interesting about females' greater agreement with storgic and pragmatic items is not so much the greater emphasis on practical and child-related considerations. This one might expect from all the classic stuff about 'it's women who get pregnant' and the traditional (though fortunately starting to weaken a little) view that childrearing is 'women's work'. Rather, women's greater emphasis on storgic and pragmatic love seems also to reflect, in my view, a more realistic idea of the factors likely to make a love relationship last (such as friendship, similarity, compatibility of lifestyles). It is in this area of male–female differences in attitudes to love that the greatest potential danger lies. We have already seen that people can use the word love in very different ways. What these findings imply is that for men more than women, feelings of love may not always be accompanied by components that bode well for how long the relationship will last.

Other recent evidence is consistent with this view. If asked to place a bet on which sex was the more romantic, I reckon most of us would plump for women without a second's hesitation. You only have to listen to women discussing their male partners – 'He never brings me flowers, never struggles through my fourth-floor bedroom window at night to bring me chocolates, never . . .'

But it transpires that it is men who are more romantic than women, not the other way round. In one American study, for example, researchers asked over 300 psychology students – men and women aged from 19 to 47 – about their attitudes to love.[10]

To measure romanticism, respondents were asked to say how much they agreed or disagreed with statements like 'Romantic love often comes only once in a lifetime', 'Somewhere there is an ideal mate for most people', 'Love happens swiftly, without warning', 'I can't concentrate on anything but my partner when

I'm in love', 'Love doesn't make sense; it just is', and 'Love at first sight is often the deepest and most enduring type of love'.

Surprisingly for the stereotype, the results showed that the men had significantly more romantic beliefs about relationships than the women did. This does seem at first sight extremely peculiar. After all, it's girls who are brought up on romantic fiction and boys on tales of tough guys whose only contact with women (if any) is to rescue them when they scream.

The findings suggested that men are more romantic because they are more emotionally dependent on love relationships. This greater dependency could be, the researchers speculate, because 'their relationships with women are much more intimate than their relationships with their male friends'. So for men an opposite-sex relationship is even more special than it is for women, who already have a number of psychologically close and meaningful relationships with female friends.

Highly romantic views of relationships, lovely and slushy as they sound, are actually not terribly realistic. But both the men and women in this study scored higher on the pragmatism than on the romanticism scale, both sexes agreeing with things like 'It takes effort to keep a relationship exciting' and 'Shared interests are an important factor in choosing romantic partners'. So men are not completely befuddled by a romantic haze.

The fact that there were no differences between the sexes in pragmatism in this study might seem superficially to contradict other findings showing that women are more pragmatic. But more detailed analyses showed no basic contradiction. The results implied that with increasing age, men become a bit less romantic, but no more pragmatic. Women, however, appear to lose more of their romantic notions than the men do and become significantly more attuned to the realities of relationships. Though not a very strong effect, the signs were that men seem to learn less from their experiences in love than women do.

But I don't want to overstate the case of women's greater realism. Differences in degree between the two sexes do not, of course, imply that one sex lacks the capacity to be storgic or pragmatic – that is clearly not so – and generalizations make no predictions about individuals. What such findings do offer is pointers to the psychological quicksands. If men have a slightly greater tendency than women to believe that love can arrive with a whoop and a holler with nothing much to base it on, then here is one source of potential heart damage. He gets disappointed when he discovers she's not as he thought; if that coincides with her slow discovery that she really likes him, she gets disappointed. Frankly, if anyone tells anyone that they love them pretty swiftly after the initial encounter, it's prudent not to rush out to order the wedding-reception garlic dips quite yet.

The Hendrick and Hendrick research finds other sex differences too. First, women tended to be more *manic* (possessive, dependent love).

To measure *mania*:

1. When things aren't right with my lover and me, my stomach gets upset.
2. When my love affairs break up, I get so depressed that I have even thought of suicide.
3. Sometimes I get so excited about being in love that I can't sleep.
4. When my lover doesn't pay attention to me, I feel sick all over.
5. When I am in love, I have trouble concentrating on anything else.
6. I cannot relax if I suspect that my lover is with someone else.
7. If my lover ignores me for a while, I sometimes do stupid things to get his/her attention back.

Women's apparently greater proneness to manic love could, however, just reflect their greater willingness to admit to such symptoms . . .

Second, the men were significantly less likely than women to disagree with items measuring *ludus*, or 'game-playing love', reporting on average fairly neutral responses. (I would think it'd be hard to own up to agreeing with some of the statements below . . .)

The *ludus* items:

1. I try to keep my lover a little uncertain about my commitment to him/her.
2. I believe that what my lover doesn't know about me won't hurt him/her.
3. I have sometimes had to keep two of my lovers from finding out about each other.
4. I can get over love affairs pretty easily and quickly.
5. My lover would get upset if he/she knew of some of the things I've done with other people.
6. When my lover gets too dependent on me, I want to back off a little.
7. I enjoy playing the 'game of love' with a number of different partners.

It seems to me that if men are more prone to ludic love than women, it should be no wonder if women did have more manic tendencies in this department. At its worst, being kept in a state of constant insecurity is the best way to reduce someone to a mass of quivering ganglions who never goes anywhere without her indigestion tablets.

However, both ludic and manic behaviour sound to me more characteristic of the early stages of a relationship than of a longstanding one. Clyde Hendrick, though he hasn't researched the question directly, feels the same: 'The consistency with which women report higher mania may be true only early in the relationship, when they are more uncertain of where they stand and are more dependent on the etiquette of male initiative for dates. The greater ludic qualities that males manifest may occur mostly prior to entering committed relationships.'[11]

But why should men behave like this in the pre-commitment stage? It can't simply be that 'playing the field' increases the chances of finding a suitable relationship, because that is true for women too. It is, Hendrick and his colleagues think, down to the way men are brought up to behave, which society and the media reinforce. 'The instrumental quality that is ludus' trademark is consistent with sex attitude research that shows males to be more liberal and less commitment-oriented in their attitudes than are females. The popular media stereotype exaggerates male ludic qualities with an emphasis on male-fostered one-night-stands and superficial sexuality.'[12] Men, they reckon, have been socialized to seek out sensuality in an instrumental way, whereas women have not.

But other research does fit the idea that game-playing may not be a permanent fixture in male approaches to love. There is some evidence that men fall in love more easily than women, who are more cautious about entering relationships. Once the men are involved, these studies found, they are less likely to initiate a break-up, and find it harder to remain friends afterwards.[13] And obviously men *do* enter committed, monogamous relationships, which is not terribly compatible with the description of ludic love.

The big media hype about 'men who can't commit', although such men do exist, has been greatly overblown, undoubtedly partly because so many women have experienced male ludic behaviour in the early stages of a relationship – watching the telephone grow huge and throbbing in its silence, wondering why he hasn't phoned when he said he would and what does this mean; does he still hanker after this blasted ex-girlfriend Caroline he keeps mentioning; who was that redhead I saw him sharing his lunchtime sandwich with last week? And all that. But if it is true that this is more characteristic of early stages, there is no reason to start castigating men as permanently hopeless; nor, as we shall see in the next section, do women always find it so easy to commit themselves.

It really is too easy to overplay the gaps between the sexes in love attitudes. The Hendricks' studies on Lee's love styles found no difference between the sexes in *agape* (all-giving, selfless love) and no consistent differences in *eros* (romantic love).

Eros:

1. My lover and I were attracted to each other immediately after we first met.
2. My lover and I have the right physical 'chemistry' between us.
3. Our lovemaking is very intense and satisfying.
4. I feel that my lover and I were meant for each other.
5. My lover and I became emotionally involved rather quickly.
6. My lover and I really understand each other.
7. My lover fits my ideal standards of physical beauty/handsomeness.

The statements to measure *agape* are as follows, though I must say that each item has such an obviously 'right' answer that one wonders how honestly they are answered:

1. I try to always help my lover through difficult times.
2. I would rather suffer myself than let my lover suffer.
3. I cannot be happy unless I place my lover's happiness before my own.
4. I am usually willing to sacrifice my own wishes to let my lover achieve his/hers.
5. Whatever I own is my lover's to use as he/she chooses.
6. When my lover gets angry with me, I still love him/her fully and unconditionally.
7. I would endure all things for the sake of my lover.[14]

At the very least, both sexes seem to be equally aware of what the 'right' answers are . . .

It is important to say again that we're only talking about general tendencies here, and that it's possible that an individual may have a mixture of styles in any one relationship.[15] We have no evidence that a person has one particular dominant style which they retain throughout life (although I'm sure we've all met the odd soul who seems irredeemably ludic, and should have a government health warning stamped on his – or sometimes her – forehead).

It has been suggested that it might be better to view the six love styles not as types of love but as attributes or dimensions of love relationships.[16] The other major theory emphasizing the multidimensional nature of love, Sternberg's triangles, is not incompatible with Lee's love styles. Sternberg himself says, 'The relation of Lee's . . . complex theory to the present framework is itself complex. Eros would be regarded in the triangular theory as fairly close to infatuated love (passion), whereas mania would be regarded as infatuated love gone berserk. Ludus would not be viewed as a kind of love in and of itself but, rather, as a style of interrelating that people can use in various kinds of loving relationships. For example, infatuated lovers, romantic lovers, and companionate lovers, as well as lovers of other kinds, are capable of playing games with one another. Storge would be viewed as close to companionate love. Agape would be viewed as a concomitant to the love that characterizes the loving relationships of people with an altruistic disposition in their personalities. Finally, pragma would not be viewed as a kind of love at all but, rather, as a pragmatic style of search for a lover, as its name implies.'[17]

Both the Sternberg and Lee theories carry within them two potentially painful implications, which I think worth re-emphasizing here: first, how rash it is to assume that when two people say they love each other they mean the same thing, and second, the potential risk if in fact they do mean really rather different things. Sternberg talks about the importance of matching triangles. Lee, too, is concerned about which love styles 'match'. But although his categories have been found fruitful by researchers (though they're certainly not thought to be the last word on the matter), the actual implications of what happens when two people have different styles do not appear to have been studied yet. Lee's comments, though, are interesting – as long as we remember that we don't know if he has got it all correct. He says: 'One obvious match is with a partner of exactly the same love-style – but the lovers may find their definitions of love so similar that the relationship eventually loses interest. Many love relationships require a certain amount of conflict to prevent boredom.' Another suitable match, he says, is with a partner of a conceptually 'nearby' style. 'For example, the definitions of "love" held by a storgic lover and a pragmatic lover will have enough in common to make their relationship satisfying for each of them. By contrast, a manic lover and a storgic lover will fill their days with mutual misunderstandings and accusations that each other's behaviour is "not love at all!" The storgic lover will argue, "If you loved me, you'd trust me like a friend, and not be so possessive, always asking where I've been," and the manic partner will reply, "If you loved me, you'd show more jealousy, and worry about me when I'm not around." '[18]

Ooof. Nasty.

Add the problems of some sex differences in attitudes to love, and we can see even more clearly how the phrase 'I love you' may not always be interpreted as the speaker actually means it.

The evidence on sex differences in love attitudes, taken overall, implies to me that the issue of concern is not the media image of men trying to avoid commitment and women trying to pick them off with grappling hooks. This is misleading because greatly exaggerated. The difference that matters is that men's conceptions of love are slightly weaker on the elements that are likely to maintain it (similarity, friendship and so on). It is a risk both sexes might watch out for . . .

There is one more potential danger in relying too heavily on what you think someone means by the word 'love' which I want to discuss here. That is, the possible influence of childhood on the way people approach their love relationships.

Effects of childhood

The idea that how we are as adults will be influenced by our childhood experiences is, of course, not new. But I don't want to talk here about psychoanalytic notions which don't lend themselves easily to being proved or disproved by research. I am interested in ideas which are far more testable – they're explicit, sophisticated, make sense and have a growing body of actual research evidence to back them up. This research, investigating in what ways our relationships as adults may be influenced by our childhoods, *is* new. It serves to emphasize how, when a person tells us he or she loves us, it may turn out that their whole approach to love relationships is significantly different from ours.

The starting point was developed by a famous psychoanalyst who wanted to make psychoanalysis scientific, John Bowlby.[19] Not for him a lot of talk about infant sexuality in the Freudian mode. Rather, he suggested that the reason childhood experiences were important for later relationships was that in childhood we develop mental models of ourselves and of what relationships are like. With those models we form expectations of the rewards and dangers of personal relationships – for example, how trustworthy people are, how deserving *we* are of care and love, what relationships between men and women are like.[20] These, in turn, are likely to affect the way we behave.

For Bowlby, the most important relationship was the one children have with their mother. Psychologists have now realized the extreme importance of the father, too. But early work on Bowlby's ideas focused on the mother, and the crucial next stage in the development of these ideas was done by M.D.S. Ainsworth and her colleagues, who closely observed mothers and their tiny offspring.[21]

Bowlby argued that, in infancy, we need to form bonds with those who look after us. From an evolutionary point of view, keeping close to mother serves to protect infants from danger. What Ainsworth's research found was that there are three main patterns of attachment. Although she looked at mothers, what follows applies to anyone who serves as an 'attachment figure' for the child.

First, there are the securely attached infants, whose mothers are consistently sensitive and responsive to their offspring. These children gain the confidence to explore their environment from this secure base. If frightful whiskery Auntie Flo arrives and frightens them to death, they know they can run to Mummy. (This doesn't mean that the mother or caregiver has to be constantly physically available, but he or she needs to be psychologically so.)

Second, 'anxious/ambivalent' infants have mothers who respond to them inconsistently. Sometimes they're unavailable or unresponsive, at other times intrusive. So these children become preoccupied with their mother's availability, and this interferes with their exploration of the outside world.

Third, mothers of 'avoidant' infants are rejecting, and tend to rebuff their children's efforts to get close to or physically touch them. So when these children need comfort, they carry on playing with their toys, squashing their cuddly mutant turtles, doing anything but run to mother. (They don't try things out in the truly interested way of the securely attached, but as a means of avoiding rejection.)

In 1987 two American psychologists, Cindy Hazan and Phillip Shaver, were the first to test the idea that perhaps romantic love in adulthood is an attachment process like the forming of bonds between infants and their parents.[22] They found evidence that adults did seem to relate to their lovers in ways that parallelled the three categories of infancy. 56 percent seemed 'secure', having love relationships characterized by happiness, trust and friendship. Anxious/ambivalent lovers (around 20 percent) had relationships marked by jealousy, emotional highs and lows and obsessive preoccupation with their partner. 'Avoidant' lovers (about 24 percent) reported being afraid of closeness. The percentages were similar for men and women, so there is no evidence here that men are more prone to avoiding commitment than women.[23]

There were some signs that attachment style in adulthood was linked with the relationships which the respondents remembered having with their parents, but it was not a strong link, memory isn't 100 percent reliable and the nature of the link isn't yet clear.[24] As the researchers point out, your security or anxiety in a particular relationship is also affected by factors unique to that relationship. What's more, any expectations of relationships you build up as a young child aren't necessarily set in stone for life. Friendships and love relationships in later life, for example, give you the chance to revise your mental models. Or again, thinking about and gaining insight into the workings of our mental models makes it possible to change them.[25]

You might also think, well, Hazan and Shaver thought that adults' approaches to relationships fell into these three patterns, and therefore they asked questions in such a way as to make sure that they did. However, whatever is discovered in future about the complexities of the patterns, other researchers too have found that adult attachments do seem to fall into three broad groupings.[26]

Hazan and Shaver, in fact, wanted to demonstrate that the three patterns of attachment in adulthood hadn't been somehow imposed by themselves. If this is a genuine phenomenon, not the product of certain kinds of questions, then it should affect other areas of life in ways that the theory might suggest, but which would not be at all visible to the subjects they were studying. If attachment styles as an adult fall into the same major patterns as in infancy, Hazan and Shaver wondered, perhaps they influence exploration as an adult in the same way that attachment affects exploration when in nappies. Looking at work as a major arena for our need to explore and master our environment, perhaps our attachment style could affect how we approach our work.

And indeed, in a more recent questionnaire study,[27] it does seem that ways of working and loving are connected. Respondents – women and men of all ages – had to say which of three alternatives best represented their feelings.

The 'avoidant type' agreed to this description of their love lives: 'I am somewhat uncomfortable being close to others; I find it difficult to trust them completely, difficult to allow myself to depend on them. I am nervous when anyone gets too close, and often, love partners want me to be more intimate than I feel comfortable being.' These people, the researchers found, were more likely to say they felt nervous when not working and that work left little time for close relationships. (In fact, they seemed to want to make quite sure it didn't.)

The 'anxious/ambivalent type' said: 'I find that others are reluctant to get as close as I would like. I often worry that my partner doesn't love me or won't want to stay with me. I want to get very close to my partner, and this sometimes scares people away.' These respondents, the researchers say, 'preferred to work with others, reported feeling misunderstood and underappreciated, were motivated by approval, and worried that others would not be impressed with their work performance or would reject them.' (This focus on trying to please others with their work – as a means of 'satisfying unmet attachment needs' – did appear, ironically, to interfere with their productivity.)

The 'secure type' said: 'I find it relatively easy to get close to others and am comfortable depending on them. I don't often worry about being abandoned or about someone getting too close to me.' They evinced a relatively positive approach to work; they were least likely to put off work and have difficulty completing projects, they were least likely to fear failure and rejection from their co-workers, and they reported 'not allowing work to jeopardize their relationships or health'.

This research is in its early stages, and no one is saying that there are simply three distinct types of human beings. The categories aren't rigid boxes. People are complex, can react in different ways to particular types of childhood experiences, are affected by what has happened since childhood as well as current circumstances and are capable of personal change. If your mother never wanted to play with you and teddy, this doesn't mean you're absolutely doomed to fleeing from love (and hiding yourself in a mound of work).

But it does look as though these ideas about patterns of attachment are powerful. After all, the evidence that how we go about our love lives and our work might be related in meaningful ways is really very surprising, and in my view points to these researchers having hit on something potentially extremely informative and useful. The more we understand about how we and others tick, the greater our chances of navigating through the rapids of life without spending quite so much of our time falling unpleasantly and damply out of our canoes.

What we need to know next is what happens when two people fall in love and they are or are not of similar 'types' in these attachment terms. Initial signs are that even if a person is some mixture of types, one type is likely to be dominant, and that although people's approach may be affected by a particular relationship – for example, if a secure person falls in love with an avoidant one he or she could pretty soon be made to feel anxious and insecure – their dominant style may be relatively consistent across relationships.[28]

Even though the research on matching types is only just beginning as I write, I'm going to make an educated guess as to what might happen in the six theoretically possible combinations.

Secure/Secure: Least likely to hit the rocks either because of a mismatch in approaches to love or because the approach itself contains potentially destructive elements. In fact, there is

41

some evidence that those who are comfortable with closeness are more likely to be with a partner who feels similarly, and less likely to be with one who worries about being abandoned. For women, interestingly, irrespective of their own attachment style, when their partner was comfortable with closeness they were much more satisfied with the relationship.[29]

Secure/Anxious: The danger here is that the anxious person's insecurity might drive the secure one up the wall. (Regardless of a person's own attachment style, early evidence suggests that men in particular are much less satisfied with relationships where their partner is anxious. It may be that men more than women see a partner's lack of trust, jealousy and dependence as restricting and a threat to their freedom.[30])

Secure/Avoidant: Oh boy. The avoidant one might get away unscathed, especially if male – there is evidence that the more avoidant a man is, the less he suffers when a relationship breaks up (though this doesn't seem to apply to women)[31] – but the secure one is in danger. They may well be made to feel anxious ('he promised to ring me today, oh dear, why hasn't he, oh oh oh,') and, if the other is afraid of commitment, they may indeed be let down with a deafening thump even if the avoidant one has declared that he or she is 'in love'.

Anxious/Anxious: Interesting one, this. Perhaps it could be OK – they have the same approach, so at least that would increase the chance of them understanding each other. Perhaps, too, feeling insecure yourself and having the other person worried about how you feel about *them* might, paradoxically, make you feel a bit more secure. However, Hazan and Shaver have found in one of their studies that the relationships of anxious/ambivalent and avoidant respondents 'lasted little more than a few years' on average.[32] What's more, another American study finds that anxious types were more likely to choose avoidant partners: 'Men and women who were anxious did not seek partners who shared their worries about being abandoned and unloved. Rather, by choosing partners who were uncomfortable with getting close, they appeared to be in relationships that confirmed their expectations.'[33]

Anxious/Avoidant: Potentially ghastly. The one who's already anxious about relationships finds their worst fears come true – they're treated in a rather rejecting way. But as we've just seen, there may be a tendency for people to want to confirm their 'inner working models', and to create their social environment to bring this about. Research is in too early a stage to be sure of this, but it sounds plausible to me.

Avoidant/Avoidant: With similar approaches, that should mean that they have less power to devastate than if they tangle with one of the other types. Even if neither really wants a long-term relationship, they might manage all right for a while.

Obviously these are generalizations and are predictions made in advance of the necessary research. But they do serve to reinforce the point made throughout this chapter and the previous one: if we are to try to understand why love isn't enough, and how this is to be dealt with, we have first to grasp how differently love can feel for different people.

For each of us individually, a clear-sighted view of what our partner means by love – and what we want them to mean – is the first step in the process of guessing what chance this relationship has, and what might be done to preserve or improve it. If, of course, that is what is wanted. Equally, we cannot automatically assume that our partner understands what *we* mean by 'I love you'. After all, we might mean 'I love you until, er, next week probably' or 'Darling, I'm just off to be measured for my wedding trousers'.

Time should eventually clarify matters. But much pain and misunderstanding might be avoided if people were more aware of the various types of ambiguity which lurk, trip-wires at the ready, in that so-enticing L-word.

In the next two chapters, I will look at the early stages of relationships, that time when love may or may not yet be burgeoning and uncertainty abounds. So *exhausting* . . .

THREE

The Initial Choices

A sparkling, new relationship, apparently full of promise, can, unfortunately, stub its toe before the laughing love god in any form has even had a chance to get a grip. Everyone knows that a relationship we enter with high hopes can in a few months disappear down the plughole, leaving us with enormous bills for Kleenex or whisky (according to taste), but it might help us to avoid this scenario if we are more aware of factors which operate in the early stages.

Selecting a mate

At first, the only thing two people can really be sure of is that they are sexually attracted to each other. The mystery of 'sexual chemistry' is still just that, a mystery. Psychologists cannot yet explain why your friend Susan might, having caught sight of a small weedy man with a nose the size of the *QE2* and ears like batwings, promptly fall into his arms with a faint gurgle.

Sure, we know some general things. Physical appearance is important for first impressions, and in every society there tends to be some overall agreement on who is attractive and who is not. The evidence is that couples tend to be made up of partners of about the same level of physical attractiveness (a significantly less physically attractive partner would probably have something heavy to 'compensate' – like wealth and power . . .)[1]. A possible explanation of this is that everybody would like the most attractive partner they feel they can get. But if someone isn't very stunning (or thinks they aren't), they

44

won't aim for a very attractive person and risk rejection – they'll go for someone not too devastating. As a result of this process, we are likely to end up with someone roughly at the same level as ourselves. Obviously, people who are less attractive than others still find long-term sexual partners. And, fortunately, how attractive we look to others in general depends on more than just what features we were born with. Those who are likeable, for example, are seen as more *physically* attractive than those who are rather cold,[2] and happy or neutral expressions are seen as more attractive than sad ones[3] . . .

However much we may dislike the idea and regard it as unfair and irrational, attractiveness is a highly valued 'commodity' in the social marketplace. And, research shows, more so when men are weighing up women than the other way round.[4] Evolutionary explanations suggest that this is because attractiveness in women equals youth and fertility, which is what a man needs in order to produce lots of offspring. Whereas women, the theory goes, need strength and status in the father of their offspring so that he can safely protect them from ravaging mammoths. But whether the fact that attractiveness is more important to men is due to some evolutionary hangover is a matter of some controversy. Certainly, since these days people in the West don't seem to want more than a couple of children and can use family planning, and since women can go on having babies into their forties, citing men's need to produce offspring as a reason why female attractiveness is so important to them just doesn't work as an explanation. (Nor do I find it convincing to suggest that boys are brought up to believe an attractive girlfriend is a status symbol much more than girls are brought up to believe the same about attractive boyfriends.)

The reasons why men seem to place more value on female attractiveness than women do on men's, even if connected with biology back in the mists of time, certainly don't serve any useful function for men now in the way evolutionary theories imply.

Although there may be a still-lingering sex difference in the importance of attractiveness, this doesn't mean that attractiveness has *no* psychological significance for women. Research shows that there is a 'what is beautiful is good' stereotype: that when we first meet someone attractive we tend to assume they will be more 'poised, interesting, sociable, independent, dominant, exciting, sexual, intelligent, well-adjusted, socially skilled, and successful'[5] than the less attractive. This is a most unfortunate tendency, since the evidence is that physical appearance actually has very little connection with personality and behaviour. The attractive tend to be socially more self-confident and skilled,[6] but if everyone is nice to them on first meeting this is hardly surprising.

So here lies the first potential pitfall in anyone's search for a romantic partner. We equate attractiveness with having bags of desirable qualities (which may or may not turn out to be true). Even more irrationally, we make deductions about character based on facial features. People tend to make 'metaphorical generalizations'. For example, having a coarse skin may be seen to imply you're a coarse or insensitive person. As John Liggett, a British psychologist specializing in physical appearance, rightly points out: 'Popular novelette writers often use their readers' susceptibility to this kind of false inference in order to add colour and life to their characters; their books . . . are full of men with firm, strong jaws who invariably display exactly the same firmness and strength in their characters.'[7]

People also draw analogies based on the functions of various parts of the face. For example, people with thin lips ('tight-lipped') may be seen as reticent, and those with high foreheads (more room for the brain) must, presumably, be more intelligent. Sometimes, too, structural features can suggest facial expressions – for instance, people whose mouths permanently curve upwards at the corners tend to be rated as friendly, easygoing, good-tempered and kind.

It's a pity we're not a bit more aware of what we're doing, as evidence indicates that the idea that you can predict the details of someone's personality from his or her facial features is just a mite over-optimistic. To illustrate the point: in one experiment, photographs of women students were shown to friends and to people who didn't know them. The friends largely agreed with each other in their assessments of the person in each photo. The 'strangers' agreed with each other in their ratings, too – but their personality assessments were quite different from those of the people who knew each woman personally.[8]

So here we have all the ingredients for starting off on the wrong foot. Of course, as we get to know someone over time, the truth will gradually be revealed. But the danger is that, because we are not very conscious of what we are doing, we feel more confident of our early impressions than we should. When we first meet someone, how they look is one of the few pieces of information we have, and in our search for certainty and predictability in life we immediately start drawing conclusions. Once we've got our theory about another person up and running, we tend to pick up on things they do that seem to support it and blank out any contradictory evidence. For a while, at any rate.

Add to these tendencies a strong dose of sexual chemistry, and we have a prime reason why a burgeoning relationship might go terribly wrong. Our human inclinations to want to understand and exert some control over what's going on, which lead us to draw premature conclusions about others, can lead us severely up the garden path.

But we won't be deceived indefinitely. One of the main factors that will become important is how *similar* the other person is to us. Forget all that 'opposites attract' stuff. They may attract all right, but they're less likely to stay the course than 'birds of a feather'. (That's the wonderful thing about relationship clichés: for every example you can find another that contradicts it.)

The evidence is that similarity is far more likely to be attractive than dissimilarity.[9] That doesn't mean that we want a partner to be a psychological clone of ourselves; that would be boring. But we do want the other person's major attitudes and values and views of the world to be like our own. (And we do tend to choose people of similar age, intelligence, interests, and social and educational background.[10])

Psychologists think this preference for similarity is partly because human beings need to feel that their view of reality is correct. With physical reality, there isn't a lot of doubt. Either Uncle Richard has just been pulled into the canal while out walking his savage, water-loving Rottweilers, or not. But with social reality, there is no such clarity, and we rely on the validation of other people to make us feel that we've got it roughly right. Someone who thinks similarly will do that for us. Having similar views may also be desirable because, as evidence shows, we feel uncomfortable if we disagree with someone we like.[11] In addition, we may feel that people with similar attitudes are more likely to like us.[12]

When we meet a new person that we're attracted to, we tend gently to make attempts to 'check them out'. Those who are very obviously dissimilar may be weeded out fast, leaving the more similar ones to be investigated more slowly.[13]

Most of the research on the importance of similarity of attitudes for attraction has been done in the laboratory, but there is enough evidence to confirm that it really does matter in real life. The American psychologist Donn Byrne and his colleagues, for instance, gave an attitude and personality questionnaire to 420 students.[14] They then leapt boldly into the outside world by forming 44 'couples' to go to the student union for a brief date. For half the couples, both people had made very similar responses on the questionnaire; for the other half, they had evinced very different responses. When they returned from the date, the experimenter took an 'unobtrusive measure' of how attracted they were to each other by seeing how close they stood together in front of his desk. (Always a significant sign . . .) They also had to rate each other on several scales. And lo, those matched for similarity of attitudes were more attracted to each other than were those who were dissimilar.

These 'couplings' happened pretty quickly, but the danger is that areas of fundamental disagreement (or even insufficient similarity) may take a while to emerge. It might be quite some time before you realize that the reason you never see Jemima on Sunday mornings is that she's running an infants' Bible class, whereas the only thing that ever drags you screaming into church is a wedding invitation.

Unfortunately, our emotions and our brains aren't always in synchrony. So there might be a painful process of relationship damage as a lack of similarity on important issues emerges. Even if you both feel 'in love', that doesn't guarantee that the seeds of major difficulties are not already present.

Of course, nothing is going to stop human beings falling in love before they know the other person properly. Sometimes we even think we've 'fallen in love at first sight', an overdramatic label we give to a strong surge of sexual attraction across a crowded dance floor.

Talking of dance floors, this brings us to one reason why we may sometimes experience surges that are actually stronger than they would have been under other circumstances – and which may therefore be a bit deceptive for a while.

One of my favourite psychological studies of all time (well, it always gives me a laugh) is the one where psychologists compared the reactions of young men crossing one of two bridges in North Vancouver.[15] One was a suspension bridge, 450 feet long and five wide, that swayed alarmingly over a 230 foot drop to rocks and rapids below. The other bridge was farther upriver, solid cedar, 10 feet above shallow water, and safe.

As each man crossed the bridge, an attractive woman (actually a confederate of the researchers) approached and asked him to fill in a questionnaire. She then offered him her phone number so that he could call if he wanted further information (ho ho). What transpired was that the men who'd been on the terrifying suspension bridge were significantly more likely to ring her – nine of the 23 men who'd filled in a questionnaire on the suspension bridge did so, but only two of the 22 who'd done it on the safe bridge.

There has been some argument about the correct explanation of this finding – for example, perhaps the men misattributed the physiological arousal induced by fear as sexual arousal. However, the latest suggestion is that if someone is aroused physiologically, their 'dominant response' to a particular situation will be enhanced. So if a man feels some attraction towards a woman, and is also aroused for another reason altogether, he'll feel even more strongly attracted.[16] That other reason could be – rather than fear of falling to your death from a wobbly bridge – something like dancing, for instance. It's no wonder discos are so popular.

Obviously, such an encounter is just a first encounter. But our abilities accidentally to deceive ourselves, plus the length of time it normally takes to come to know another properly, does bring danger. People may commit themselves prematurely, before they understand their partner and before they have truly seen how well they function as a couple. Whether this commitment is through marriage, having children together or buying a house together, it simply makes any break-up that much worse.

Of course it's true that two people can have a 'whirlwind courtship' and remain happily married for 50 years. Bloody lucky, I'd say. Or else, perhaps, old enough and with enough knowledge of themselves and relationships to know what they want and need, combined with an intense period of togetherness to investigate this fast. Plus, I still reckon, a dose of good fortune.

But apart from feeling sexually attracted and having similar attitudes, what else are people looking for? Both sexes are very similar in reporting that they want a partner who is kind, considerate, honest, has a sense of humour and is faithful and reliable.[17] But there appear to be a few sex differences. In one American study, men and women were asked what qualities they would want in an ideal partner.[18] Women preferred an 'expressive' partner more than the men did, where expressive meant aspects such as 'affectionate, compassionate, expresses tender feelings easily, and romantic'. Women more than men also wanted an 'ambitious' partner, where ambitious covers 'ambitious, accomplished in chosen field, outgoing, and self-sufficient'. What men wanted more than women did was an 'attractive' partner.

These researchers point out that men desiring an attractive partner more than women did and women preferring an ambitious partner more than men did fits an evolutionary perspective. As I've argued already, any biological purpose in men having an attractive partner is no longer applicable, even though social pressures (whatever their origin) may still apply. The evolutionary – and, for many centuries, practical – reason for women wanting men with sufficient resources to look after them and their offspring is also far less valid nowadays. Many women are returning to paid work after having children and are creating their own resources, thank you very much. So dependence on men for survival is hardly the issue it was in Palaeolithic times, and what women look for in a partner is unlikely to be as seriously bound up with practicalities as once it was. This is not to say practicalities have yet entirely vanished as an issue – in many cultures, women still apparently value being a 'good financial prospect', ambition and industriousness in a potential mate more highly than men do.[19]

Yet other issues are undoubtedly coming to the fore, as shown by the other major finding of this study, about 'expressiveness'. 'We suggest,' the researchers write, 'that experience has taught heterosexual women the importance of having an expressive male mate, despite or perhaps because they have not been led to expect this quality in prospective mates. Heterosexual men, on the other hand, are likely to expect expressive partners as a matter of course.'[20] This would lead to the pattern of apparent sex differences in preference for an expressive partner. So it's not that men don't want it just as much, it's simply that they assume they're going to get it anyway.

The truth about love between adults – and this can be hard to face – is that it isn't unconditional, as it is between parents and children. You can't assume its presence, or its continuance. This must be why expressiveness is important to both sexes: because what is expressed is love. We don't want someone who marries us to cease to make any gestures of affection and then say in shocked tones, 'But of course I love you, I thought you knew that' as you head for the hills with a steamer trunk.

This finding about expressiveness illustrates a fundamental point. That is, our partner's qualities are most important in terms of how they emerge in his or her *behaviour* towards us. In the early days of research on attraction, psychologists tried to find out whether it was similarity or complementarity in personality traits and needs that was more important for relationships. Is it more likely for both members of a couple to be, say, dominant, or for one to be dominant and the other submissive? The evidence showed that in fact, similarity of personality and needs is preferred to complementarity, but the evidence is less strong and consistent than it is for similarity of attitudes.[21] Some qualities – such as being kind and sensitive[22] – are valued by most people anyway, regardless of degree of similarity. What is probably more important for a relationship is not a precise breakdown and matching of two people's personality attributes, but the way the two personalities work together 'as a team' and whether their actual behaviour is rewarding for each other.[23]

I've been talking so far about what people are on the lookout for as they're just entering a relationship. As they stick a toe in the romantic waters in the late-twentieth century, the issue that raises its head a lot faster these days is sex. Here, too, trip-wires are at the ready.

Sexual attitudes

With the dramatic changes there have been in sexual mores in the last few decades, you might think that women's and men's attitudes to sex were becoming more similar. Once women had access to reliable contraception and could feel confident about having sex and not getting pregnant, the need to 'hold off' until marriage pretty well vanished (leaving, of course, the influence of religion or strict upbringing still operating for some).

Certainly women did start having more sexual partners than before,[24] and any notion that men have 'a stronger sex drive' was increasingly pooh-poohed. Evolutionary arguments that men are somehow programmed to want loads of partners and women not (because that way men could have lots of offspring, and women could preserve what offspring they had by ensuring that they and their children were cared for by a specific male) remain controversial. However, as I have already argued, such biological reasons for any differences in sexual attitudes do seem to me to be redundant nowadays. This is not to say that those biological reasons might not affect modern-day attitudes; they could have been transmitted from generation to generation through increasingly unthinking social mores and pressures. But to cite them as truly meaningful in the late twentieth century is absurd. Pigeons and rattlesnakes may be creatures of instinct, but humans have developed powerful and complex brains. Attitudes and behaviour in humankind cannot be adequately explained, in my view, by citing evolutionary or biological reasons as primary causes. Using 'men are just made like that' to explain, say, deliberately hurtful behaviour (by men) or why women should feel depressed and resigned about the male sex is, to say the least, a touch unconvincing. This is not to say that there aren't any sex differences, but to point out that they are not rigid and unalterable as is implied by biological perspectives.

Once sex could be separated from procreation, it would be reasonable to expect changes in sexual attitudes over time. And, indeed, there is no denying that both sexual behaviour and attitudes have changed, particularly for women. As it has become increasingly possible for women to have jobs and careers and not to have babies until they want them, for example, they are getting married later. This increases the time in which they can have relationships with different men, some of which are likely to be sexual. The days are long gone of women having little choice of partner because they didn't meet many men and had to marry fast for social and financial reasons.

But even though both men and women nowadays usually have a number of sexual partners in their lifetimes, and women can now have sex without fear of pregnancy (or not much, anyway), I'm afraid we would be indulging in false hopes if we believed that men and women now think alike and everything's okey-dokey.

No such luck.

Research in the 1980s by American psychologists Susan Hendrick and Clyde Hendrick and their colleagues reveals what differences between men and women in attitudes to sex still remain.

In one study, they gave a long questionnaire on sexual attitudes to about 800 students at the University of Miami.[25] Of the 102 individual items on the questionnaire, men and women differed significantly on 73. Men were more 'permissive' and 'instrumental' than women (a finding supported by other studies too[26]).

To understand what the researchers mean by these terms, I'll give you some examples of the questionnaire items they used to measure each concept. For each item, the participants had to rate their responses on a five-point scale, from 'strongly agree' or 'moderately agree' through 'neutral' to 'moderately disagree' or 'strongly disagree'. The responses for each sex were then averaged.

Of the 29 items used to measure 'permissiveness', the sexes differed significantly in their responses to every single one. The starkest contrasts were those where the men and women clustered on opposing sides of the 'neutral' point.[27] The men agreed but the women disagreed with statements such as: 'I do not need to be committed to a person to have sex with him/her'; 'Casual sex is acceptable'; 'I would like to have sex with many partners'; 'One-night-stands are sometimes very enjoyable'; 'Sex as a simple exchange of favours is OK if both people agree to it'.

The men were fairly neutral, while the women disagreed, with items such as: 'It is okay to have ongoing sexual relationships with more than one person at a time'; 'It is possible to enjoy sex with a person and not like that person very much'; 'Sex is best when people approach it as good physical release'.

The men were again fairly neutral, while the women agreed, that 'To have good sex, two people have to know each other pretty well' and 'Sex without love is meaningless'.

Sometimes the sexes did have similar views, but just differed in the intensity of their responses. Men disagreed, for example, that 'It is okay to manipulate someone into having sex as long as no future promises are made' – but women disagreed even more strongly. And while men did agree that 'People should at least be friends before they have sex together' and 'In order for sex to be good, it must also be meaningful', the women agreed even more strongly with these sentiments.

Men were more 'instrumental' than women in that, while they were pretty neutral about 'Sex is primarily physical' and 'Sex is mostly a game between males and females', the women disagreed. And although men disagreed (just) that 'Sex is primarily a bodily function, like eating', the women disagreed significantly more.

The idea that differences between men and women in attitudes to sex are still with us is supported by quite another line of research, on sexual fantasies. In one study, for example, two American psychologists shamelessly probed the fantasies of over 300 Californian students.[28] Bruce Ellis and Donald Symons thought that in fantasy, it would be possible to see what men's and women's 'sexual psychologies' were really like, as heterosexual behaviour in real life 'must inevitably compromise' male and female desires.

Their anonymous questionnaires revealed large sex differences. Twice as many women as men said they usually fantasized about someone with whom they were – or had been – romantically/sexually involved (59 percent vs. 28 percent). More men (38 percent) than women (25 percent) said they fantasized about someone – even if he or she wasn't a real person – whom they would like to become romantically involved with. And in the entirely emotion-free category, 'someone (even if he or she is made up) who you would simply like to have sex with', 29 percent of the men said this was their typical fantasy, but only 9 percent of the women did.

Men focused more on visual images, the sexual act itself and the physical characteristics of the fantasized partner, whereas women concentrated more on feelings and the personal or emotional characteristics of the partner. For 72 percent of the women, but only 50 percent of the men, 'the situation unfolds slowly and unhurriedly, so that a good deal of time passes before explicitly sexual activity occurs'. For 48 percent of the men, but only 17 percent of the women, 'the situation quickly includes explicitly sexual activity'. Men were significantly more likely than women actually to switch their imagined partner in mid-fantasy.

The researchers conclude, on the basis of this and other evidence, that both sexes can experience both lust and the feeling of being in love. (Well, that's a relief, I must say.) But they suggest that in women's fantasies, lust is the 'servant' of love and is 'intimately bound up with mate choice'; whereas in men's fantasies, 'the goal is the satiation of lust' in its own right.

Whether sex differences in sexual fantasy (as well as attitudes and behaviour) are down to nature or nurture is still debatable. To attribute it all to the former is, I feel, excessive. But whatever the precise reasons turn out to be, the important issue is the fact that, despite the social changes of this century, there are still male–female differences in attitudes to sex. They may be less than they were, but they have certainly not disappeared.

This is not to say that most dating relationships aren't conducted with affection on both sides.[29] If sex and emotion are more likely to be entwined for a woman, and less so for a man, this naturally doesn't mean that sex and emotion aren't frequently combined for a man. Also, of course, average differences between groups can't be used to predict the behaviour of individuals. But what they do is point to one arena where a man and a woman might have a rather unfortunate misunderstanding early on. She might interpret his sexual intensity towards her as more emotionally meaningful than in fact it is; he might not realize that his sexual interest and passion is being taken more seriously than he means.

Some people may already be aware of this danger, but others may labour under the hopeful illusion that sex differences are narrower than they actually are. In fact, differences between men and women in sexual attitudes – men being consistently more permissive and instrumental – appear more pervasive than sex differences in attitudes to love.[30]

One way of avoiding tears and guilt (well, trying to, anyway) is simply to realize and confront the possible difficulty from the start. Women can then be cautious about over-interpreting a man's sexual interest in the beginning. Men, in turn, can be aware of how their behaviour might be seen and – to save hurt – could make the tentative nature of their feelings (if that is the case) clear to the woman. It may for some men be a temptation to overstate feelings in order to get the woman into bed; obviously that exacerbates the potential for misunderstanding and hurt from her point of view.

One of the changes of the post-contraception era is that the pressure is on women to have sex very quickly. One study published in the early 1980s found that, on average, men didn't 'expect' sex until roughly the fifth date.[31] (In days of yore, it would've been the wedding night!) Another study of courting couples found that most men claimed they first decided to have sex as a result of peer pressure – the 'what, haven't you managed it *yet*?' syndrome – whereas women felt they first had sex because they wanted to personally.[32] But the evidence is that men tend to want to start a full sexual relationship before women do, so – barring rape – it's the women's wishes (or acquiescence) which set the time when intercourse first takes place.[33] It seems likely that the earlier a sexual relationship starts, the more potential there is for misunderstanding of what the sex actually means to each partner.

Matters are made even more complicated and delicate by the need to take precautions against sexually transmitted diseases, particularly AIDS. As I am neither an AIDS expert nor a medical doctor, I don't propose to start listing preventative measures. Keeping track of precisely what are currently regarded as 'safer' sexual practices – via the media, public information leaflets and so on – is obviously vital for everyone who is sexually active.

But knowledge of how AIDS is transmitted is not enough – it has to be translated into action. Apart from obvious things like cutting down on the number of partners one has, one of the messages constantly dinned in by the media is always to use a condom. Using condoms as an example, I want to discuss some of the psychological factors that might intervene to prevent people from realistically confronting the frightening problem of AIDS.

Assuming that the topic of s-e-x has now raised its head and that one partner does (wisely) introduce the subject of condoms, trouble and strife might then hit the relationship if the man refuses to use one or makes a constant fuss about it, or if the woman says the man 'doesn't need to' even if he says he wants to. The unfortunate fact is that although everyone's heard of AIDS, and there are some signs of a shift towards greater conservatism in sexual matters,[34] this doesn't mean they're all changing their sexual activities to reduce their risk.[35] Many people feel personally immune – men in particular – regardless of their actual sexual behaviour.

To illustrate the point: some American researchers surveyed over 200 men and women, from 18 to 25 years of age, in Los Angeles County.[36] To get a wide range of people, they tramped round university and college campuses and 'various parks, beaches and boardwalks', clutching their rather explicit questionnaires.

The researchers divided the sample into three 'risk' categories, based on their reported use of condoms during any sexual intercourse they had had during the previous week, and the number of their sexual partners in the past year. 45 percent of the respondents were classified as 'low risk' (no partner or only one partner during the past year, plus, if they'd had a partner, always used condoms during any intercourse in the past seven days); 46 percent were 'medium risk' (either up to ten partners and always used condoms, or up to four partners using condoms occasionally); and 9 percent 'high risk' (more than five partners and no recent condom use or more than ten partners regardless of condom use).

The men in all three risk groups saw themselves as having a roughly equal, and very low, chance of becoming infected with HIV. They estimated the risk as about one in a million, as did the low and medium-risk women. Only high-risk women saw themselves as being vulnerable (risk around one in a hundred).

The fact that people can see themselves as personally immune regardless of their actual behaviour is extremely alarming. Men seemed especially oblivious to the riskiness of their own actions, and they also saw other people's risks of contracting HIV as lower than women did. Asked to assess the risk for 'a person their age who has sex with many different partners and does not use condoms', men put it at 1 in 900, whereas women estimated it at 1 in 150.

As men are the ones who have to wear the condoms, their stronger denial of the risks must make women's efforts to protect themselves – and any future partners and children – even harder.

Other psychological factors might intrude too. For instance, a man may say he hates condoms and 'can't feel anything' when he wears them; social anxiety or embarrassment might inhibit people from talking about the issue; they might think that if they insist on condoms the other person might be 'offended'; they might not wish to imply that *they* could possibly be infected; emotional blackmail of the 'but if you loved me, you'd trust me' variety might be attempted; people might feel the whole thing is out of their control, and they simply have to trust to luck; they might think you can 'tell' if someone has it or is likely to do so.[37]

The fact is that you can't 'tell' any such thing, and it's only sensible *always* to take precautions.[38] Getting infected isn't a matter of luck; people can act to protect themselves. (Correctly-used condoms are extremely useful, of course, in protecting against other sexually transmitted diseases too.) If the other person is seriously resistant, then either their so-called 'reasons' have to be tackled one by one, or this is one early-stage relationship that shouldn't proceed any further. Counterarguments to someone being difficult might include: condoms these days are made such that little or no sensation is lost, and believing otherwise is no reason not to give them a serious try; with practice, they become easy to use and needn't interrupt the flow of lovemaking as people fear; and this is about protecting *both* of us (to minimize 'offence' or 'if you loved me you'd . . .' – both immature reactions in any case).

To minimize any emotional heat, it may be best simply to bring up the question of condoms in a perfectly matter-of-fact way ('if you haven't got any I have' kind of approach), or start things off by talking about a recent newspaper article or television programme on AIDS. A woman may fear the man thinking she's 'loose' if she already has condoms in her possession; or else that the sex becomes 'premeditated and not spontaneous'.[39] These again are immature deductions, and worth discussing openly with a partner if necessary. (After all, it's contradictory and sexist to expect women to have sex and yet not be prepared for it; and in any trade-off between notions of 'romantic spontaneity' and realistic protection it seems pretty obvious which should be the winner . . .)

Essentially, all such psychological inhibitions about dealing with the threat of AIDS are simply to be recognized for what they are – insufficient reasons for not taking proper care of oneself. If the reactions of the other person, male or female, to anyone's desire to take appropriate precautions and to discuss AIDS and the issues involved are negative (immature, inconsiderate, selfish, blackmailing, irresponsible, bullying, whatever), this can be very revealing of what they are like as a person. As a way into discussing intimate issues, sorting out the AIDS question between you is an interesting test – and one that may make the decision about whether or not to carry on with this person pretty damn clear. Women in particular appear to be becoming more assertive in the sexual arena, and so – let's hope – increasingly less likely to succumb to pressure from the man to act irresponsibly 'otherwise he'll leave me'.

Finally, if it's anxiety or embarrassment that is the difficulty, then the issue becomes, 'If I can't talk to this person about an intimate topic, should I be thinking of having sex with him or her?' The strange notion that physical sex can be less intimate than talking is interesting, to say the least, and I'll be returning to the role of difficulties with talking in male–female relationships later.

The essential point is that everybody has to decide – in an informed way – what they do and don't want to do in a sexual relationship, and *talk* to their prospective partner about it. Many people, both men and women, have great difficulty talking about sexual matters with their partners. Not only is it now absolutely vital to do so, but – looking on the bright side – it can bring an extra bonus. Discussing what to do about sex can improve generally the quality of the communication between two people. More broadly, every potential partner who agrees to, *and takes*, proper precautions contributes towards a society where more honest and responsible relationships are the rule for us all.

OK, assuming that two people have negotiated the sexual hurdle successfully and responsibly and haven't come unstuck at this point, let's move on to what other factors might be operating during the early stages of a relationship. Specifically, factors that can bring with them a risk of the whole thing slipping painfully down the drain.

FOUR

Uncertain Days

The early stages of a relationship often contain the seeds of its later demise. In the excitement of it all, potential problems are only too easy to overlook. These problems then simply lurk, clutching a psychological sock full of wet sand; and the time will come when they emerge to biff the relationship right in the mazzard.

Risk factors

Psychological research on factors that put relationships at risk has tended to concentrate on marital dissatisfaction and divorce. But a number of such factors are present at the early stages of a relationship, and so I think them worth discussing at this point.

Some of the findings will confirm most people's suspicions. Teenage marriages are particularly likely to break down, partly because they are often precipitated by an unwanted pregnancy. Marrying because the woman is pregnant – at any age – is a risk factor.[1] In a British survey of over 1,000 divorced and married interviewees, among the divorced couples 32 percent of the wives were pregnant at marriage, but of those still married, the figure was 19 percent.[2]

Sizeable age gaps are risky too. The older-woman/younger-man combination is the one people are more likely to comment on because it is against the 'norms' of society. When female film stars marry 'toyboys' we never hear the last of it, whereas men who marry much younger women are an all-too-frequent sight.

However, what evidence there is (and there isn't much) indicates that large age gaps are risky whether it's the man *or* the woman who is older.[3] Theoretically, difficulties are most likely to happen because of differences in interests and values. The younger wants to dance like crazy down the disco until 4 a.m.; the older wants to watch *News at Ten* and go to bed with a Wilkie Collins (the author, not a cocktail).

In the same way, differences in race, class or religion bring extra pressures.[4] Such differences often bring with them different attitudes and values that may strain the relationship in the long term. Classic love stories often delight in prince/beggar-maid or rich man/prostitute-with-heart-of-gold couplings that poke two fingers at generalizations about 'the right – or wrong – match'. And, of course, they are generalizations (and I must re-emphasize that as such they can't be used to make predictions about any specific couple). But they do indicate possible difficulties to watch out for.

There are also factors within the individuals involved that may bring trouble. As we have seen, lovers who are 'avoidant' in their attitudes to love and commitment, for example, may bring the edifice of a relationship crashing down.[5] Or a partner may be – or may become – mentally ill,[5] violent, or secretly (at first, anyway) homosexual or bisexual,[6] all hardly conducive to a stable and happy heterosexual partnership.

Even though it is obvious that some factors are highly risky for stable long-term relationships, there is no doubt that people find themselves in such situations in large numbers. Sometimes, really difficult strains might appear only quite some way down the line – a partner becoming alcoholic, or clinically depressed, or 'coming out', or whatever, some years into the relationship. But in the early stages, some risk factors in the other's personality might be visible. If a partner is violent during courtship, for example, he (or, more rarely, she) is likely to continue to be so into marriage.[7] Neuroticism[8] and ill-temper[9] (surprise, surprise) have been found to be risk factors for divorce.

Research looking specifically at premarital relationships finds that they are more likely to collapse if one partner (or both) is unwilling to disclose about personal matters,[10] has a 'ludic' love style (the 'game-playing' approach described in Chapter 2)[11] or has an 'unrestricted' (casual) attitude to sexual relationships.[12] Again, hardly surprising. But the fact that something seems unsurprising when set down in black and white doesn't mean that people don't enter relationships over-optimistically and shield themselves for as long as possible from warning signs. After all, people are marrying chronically ill-tempered partners, otherwise that wouldn't be showing up in divorce statistics as a risk factor. Perhaps qualities in the relationship or in the partner outweighed this for a time; perhaps they didn't face the truth for quite a while; perhaps they married for the wrong reasons in the first place; perhaps they didn't think they deserved better; perhaps they believed the partner would change for love of them. (Not something to bet on . . .) Again, people may submit to ill-treatment from game-playing and faithless lovers because they hope that true love will triumph.

As well as the dangers of individuals' own abilities to hide the truth from themselves, there may be personality traits that are not obvious risk factors. One that's been receiving increasing attention in recent years is a characteristic called 'self-monitoring'.[13] 'High self-monitors' are very concerned with how they appear to others, and are rather chameleon-like in adapting themselves to whatever social situation they happen to be in. 'Low self-monitors' are much less concerned with their public persona, and behave in accordance with their own character and attitudes when interacting with others. The evidence is that low self-monitors are more likely to commit themselves to a relationship, whereas high self-monitors prefer 'less close and rather non-exclusive romantic relationships'.[14] Falling in love with a high self-monitor, then, appears a more risky enterprise.

But on the whole, research into personality factors linked with successful relationships is thin on the ground.[15] It makes more sense to see relationships as a function of how two personalities work together, not how they are in isolation. As there are no perfect individuals, what people desire in a partner are good qualities they personally want, need and value, and faults they can tolerate.

As an example, some researchers have looked at 'Type A' and 'Type B' personalities in marriage. Type As are 'coronary-prone', and are usually defined as hard-driving, competitive, aggressive strivers who constantly feel under pressure of time and are easily made angry and irritable. Type Bs, in contrast, are laid-back. They don't suffer from a sense of urgency, or harbour hostility, they can play for fun rather than competition, and they can relax without guilt.

The researchers looked at about a hundred married couples, and found that of the four possible pairings of Type A and B husbands and wives, the combination with the worst marital adjustment was Type A husband/Type B wife.[16] It wasn't the presence of a Type A person in the marriage that was the problem. A/A matchings had on average the highest score, and B husband/A wife pairings weren't too far behind (and were very similar to the B/B couples). It was the *combination* that mattered, not the individuals' personalities as such.

It could be, the researchers speculate, that 'The poor adjustment of this pairing [A husband/B wife] may reflect the work (rather than home and marriage) orientedness of the A husband, a negative force in the marriage which may be contrasted with the wife's traditional commitment to the successful functioning of the home.'[17] (Type B women, the study found, were at a lower level of occupational achievement than Type A women.) However, it may be that Type A women are committed to success at home *and* work, and this is sufficient to offset the Type A husband's negative effect. The researchers' implication is that the Type A women's commitment to the home is more active and effective than that of the Type B women. This is possible, but it also seems reasonable to suppose that Type A women understand their husband's commitment to work because they share it, whereas Type B women do not.

Perhaps the Type B woman who marries a Type A man either doesn't realize the extent of her husband's focus on his work, or thinks that once married, she will become more of a priority for him. Instead of staying late to finish the report for Mr Perkins on Kittyfood publicity, he'll be rushing home to coo at her over the spaghetti bolognese.

It can be seriously risky if someone thinks another 'will change' in some significant way for the better. If aspects of the other person's personality are difficult to deal with during courtship, there is no solid reason to suppose that those faults will be banished by a marriage ceremony and one's continuing devotion. Unfortunately.

But 'difficult to deal with' for person X can be 'divine sugar lambkin' (mysteriously) for person Y. This implies that one way of reducing any risk factors inherent in the partner's personality – and in how it meshes with yours – might simply be to check him or her out properly first.

Even though it seems obvious that people should get to know each other as well as they can (accepting the fact, of course, that your partner – or yourself – might change in unpredictable ways later), very often this simply does not happen. Perhaps they commit themselves while still 'blinded' by passion. Perhaps they think they know the other person a lot better than they actually do. Perhaps they use purely their feelings as the gauge of the 'rightness' of the other person for them (oh risky, risky).

But commit themselves prematurely they do. And 'prematurely' can be further into a relationship than you might think. In one study of couples who had lived together before marriage, for example, those who were now divorced had dated each other for an average of 7.5 months and then lived together for 14 months before marrying. But those who were still married had dated for about 20 months and then lived together for another 16 months before marrying.[18] In another study, researchers found that the longer the courtship (up to two years, anyway), the more likely it was that a couple would stay together.[19]

Surprisingly, although the length of the courtship appears important, whether or not you live together before marriage doesn't appear to make a lot of difference. Quite a number of studies have found that cohabiting beforehand didn't make any difference to how happy the later marriage was.[20] Other studies have actually found that those who lived together first were rather *more* likely to have less satisfying marriages and to get divorced.[21] The reasons for this are unclear, and suggestions are numerous. For example, cohabitors tend to have more liberal attitudes, and perhaps they are therefore more relaxed about getting divorced.[22] Perhaps some cohabitors get married thinking that marriage will *per se* sort out their problems, only to discover their mistake.[23] Perhaps the act of taking on the role of 'husband' or 'wife', for some people, changes their behaviour and/or expectations of the partner in ways that didn't occur while the couple were just living together.[24]

However, measuring who stays married and who doesn't is rather a superficial indicator. If couples who get married without living together first are more conservative, then they might hang grimly on to their marriages longer than those with a more liberal outlook. So you could speculate that cohabitors may be wisely getting out of failed relationships more quickly.

The ambiguity of the findings about cohabitation do not imply that knowledge doesn't reduce risk. Getting to know the other person – *and* how you function as a couple – pretty thoroughly must reduce risk long-term, even if in the process you decide your early-stage relationship should be relegated to the psychological equivalent of Highgate Cemetery. Indeed, the exception to the findings about cohabitation just described occurs when partners are older. Cohabitation appears to have positive effects for *re*marriages, in terms of increased marital satisfaction and adjustment. 'It appears,' as some researchers put it, 'as if the remarrieds have the life experience to fully take advantage of the opportunities cohabitation provides.'[25]

Psychologists have been enjoying themselves in recent years devising questionnaires that will actually predict which relationships *are* likely to break up. It's all very well to say that good relationships have a better chance of surviving than not-so-good ones. The question is, what are the characteristics of a 'good' relationship?

REWARDS AND COSTS, INVESTMENTS AND ALTERNATIVES

An American social psychologist called Caryl Rusbult didn't believe that you could predict whether a relationship was going to survive or not simply on the basis of how satisfied individuals said they were with their partner/relationship. She theorized that how satisfied someone was was a function of how many rewards versus costs they got from the relationship; yet how committed they were to maintaining it was related not only to how satisfied they were, but also to how much they had invested in the relationship and whether they felt attractive alternatives (such as another partner, solitude, 'dating around' or spending time with friends and relatives) might be available.[26]

This is not to say that love and feelings don't matter, of course; psychological measures of love and liking are certainly related to relationship success.[27] Interestingly, there is some evidence that, looking at dating relationships, women's love for their boyfriends is a better predictor of whether or not the couple stay together than is men's love for their girlfriends.[28] The researchers involved guess that, 'the woman's feelings toward her dating partner may have a more powerful effect on a relationship and/or provide a more sensitive barometer of its viability than do the man's.'[29] But given that love is important, it is possible to specify other factors that matter too. Research on Rusbult's 'investment model' does find support for it.

In one study, for example, students dating for up to seven

months were given questionnaires at frequent intervals.[30] They were asked about rewards and costs such as: the partner's personality, attitudinal similarity to oneself, intelligence, physical appearance, similarity of values, satisfying of one's needs, sense of humour, shared interests, similarity of habits or pastimes and sexual relationship; the individual's loss of personal freedom; monetary and time costs of the relationship; and partner's embarrassing habits, unattractive personal qualities, unattractive attitudes about relationships and reliability.

It emerged that satisfaction with their relationship was related to how rewarding they judged it to be, and that, interestingly, the impact of costs on satisfaction was far less significant. The costs had a bit more effect in months three to seven than earlier on in the relationship, probably, Rusbult says, because the costs aren't terribly apparent in the early stages. 'At the beginning of a relationship, individuals may try hard to display their best selves, and their partners may be generous in overlooking any faults (or problems) that do become apparent. However, at later stages of involvement, persons may relax more, allow their true, flawed selves to emerge, and their partners may adopt a more realistic view of the relationship.'[31]

Nevertheless, later research by Rusbult and her colleagues supports the idea that, overall, rewards are more important in determining satisfaction than are costs.[32] Faults seem to be less troublesome for a relationship as long as the partner is getting plenty of rewards.

As Rusbult suggests, how committed you are to a relationship appears not to be solely a function of how satisfied you are with it. She also asked about the students' investment in the relationship, both 'intrinsic' and 'extrinsic'. 'Intrinsic investments are those resources that are put directly into the relationship, such as time, emotional effort, or self-disclosures. Extrinsic investment occurs when initially extraneous resources become inextricably connected to the relationship (e.g., mutual friends, shared memories or material possessions, activities/persons/objects/events uniquely associated with the relationship).'[33] Investments may also be rewarding (such as shared pleasant memories) or costly (such as monetary investments). What distinguishes them from rewards and costs, Rusbult says, is that investments are strongly tied *to that particular relationship* and will be lost – or dramatically decline in value – if it ends. (A reward such as reliability, for example, could be obtained from another partner.) These investments help to 'lock the individual into his or her relationship'[34] by increasing the costs of finishing it.

Another factor which Rusbult says serves as a 'locking' mechanism is a lack of good alternatives. What she finds is that commitment to a relationship is a function of satisfaction, investments and alternatives. Looking at the development of relationships over the seven months, those whose relationship was still operating at the end of that time reported increasing rewards, slightly increasing costs, increasing satisfaction, increasing commitment, increasing investments and a decline in the quality of alternatives. (Perceiving fewer alternative partners may come about because there actually are fewer, in that people see you're involved and stay away. But it may also be because there is evidence that people in dating relationships do see potential alternative partners as less attractive than they otherwise might. Being in a dating relationship at all seems to trigger a pervasive tendency to derogate the physical attractiveness and sex-appeal of members of the opposite sex other than the partner.[35] And the more committed someone is to their partner, the more they downgrade the personal qualities of tempting alternative partners, on dimensions such as intelligence, sense of humour, similarity of attitudes, dependability and faithfulness.[36])

Relationships that broke up were marked – for the person who left – by barely increasing rewards, noticeably rising costs, decreasing satisfaction, commitment and investments, and increasingly attractive alternatives. For the person who was left, Rusbult found a pattern of 'entrapment'. 'These persons showed fewer increases in rewards, greater increases in costs, and lower increases in level of satisfaction than did stayers (i.e., they were not tremendously happy with their involvements). However, their alternatives declined in quality and they continued to invest heavily in their relationships (this group invested at as great a rate, or greater, than did stayers).'[37] They remained involved, but trapped, until their partner ended it. This sounds to me like a description of people flogging a dead horse, but still hoping. She didn't ask in this study about levels of self-esteem. But to carry on even though unhappy, and see little alternative, I'd guess would be the choice of someone who – however sadly and mistakenly – didn't think they'd ever get (or deserve) better.

This investment model might sound a bit like an accountant's view of romance. But feelings alone are not enough, and what we need to look for is a clearer understanding of what else might be going on. Rusbult's research illustrates the point that calculations, no matter how subconscious, are taking place. What's more, they're measurable, are operating and developing noticeably within the first few months of a relationship, and distinguish those that fall apart in the early stages from those that don't.

JOINT ACTIVITIES

One of the noticeable elements in Rusbult's 'rewards' and 'investments' is that of *doing* things together: similar interests and pastimes, activities uniquely linked with the relationship and so on. Indeed, there is evidence that measures of 'interdependence' are more powerful predictors of a relationship's success than are simple questions about how close you *feel* to the other person.

Social psychologist Ellen Berscheid and her colleagues have developed what they call the 'Relationship Closeness Inventory'

(RCI).[38] This is designed to tap how interconnected the activities of two people are (and can, of course, be used for relationships other than romantic ones) as a way of measuring the rather nebulous concept of 'closeness'.

Respondents have to choose the person they regard as closest to them, and answer the questionnaire with that person in mind. In the study I am going to discuss, nearly 50 percent of the students given the questionnaire nominated their romantic partner, and these are the ones of interest here.

The questionnaire is in three sections.

First, respondents are asked about how much time they typically spend alone with this person.

Second, they are presented with a list of 38 diverse activities. These range from fun ones ('went dancing', 'visited friends', 'went to a play') through leisure interests ('outdoor recreation, e.g. sailing', 'went to a museum/art show', 'attended a sporting event'), work ('attended class', 'worked on homework') and intimacy ('discussed things of a personal nature', 'engaged in sexual relations') to practical activities ('did laundry', 'prepared a meal', 'went to a grocery store'). Respondents had to tick which of the 38 activities they had taken part in alone with their partner in the past week.

Third, the students were asked about their partner's impact on them, in terms of how much he or she influenced them in many areas of life. For example, 'which parties and other social events I attend', 'everyday things in my life', 'my moods', 'when I see, and the amount of time I spend with, my family', 'my vacation plans' and so on.

The researchers followed up the students three and nine months later. They found that scores on the questionnaire significantly predicted whether or not their relationships broke up. On average, those with high scores on the RCI (which was only filled in by one partner) were in relationships that still endured nine months after they were initially contacted. Those with middle scores had broken up between three and nine months, and those with low scores by three months. 'Being chosen as the closest relationship', the researchers say, 'did not guarantee that a current romantic relationship would survive even less than 1 year later, as 49 percent of these relationships had been dissolved by the last of our follow-ups.'[39] With what joy and optimism do we launch ourselves upon these things . . .

What's more, the RCI was a better predictor of which couples would last than were various measures of feelings. A 'Subjective Closeness Index' (SCI) consisted of responses to two questions: 'Relative to *all* your other relationships (both same and opposite sex), how would you characterize your relationship with this person?' and 'Relative to what you know about *other people's* close relationships, how would you characterize your relationship with this person?' Respondents had to estimate the closeness of their relationships on a rating scale for each question, and the scores were added together to form the SCI. The students were also asked how often they experienced each of 27 emotions in their relationship (e.g., anger and contentment), to measure its 'emotional tone'.

But while the measure of the intertwining of their activities (the RCI) could significantly predict relationship break-up, subjects' 'subjective closeness' and the 'emotional tone' of the relationship could not.

Obviously the interdependence of two people (the RCI) is significantly related to how they feel about each other. Nevertheless, the link between responses to questions about love and liking for the partner and the Relationship Closeness Inventory was less than between love and liking and the Subjective Closeness Index. But whereas the RCI predicted break-up, the SCI did not. Scores on the 'diversity of activities' sub-scale (high scores meaning the couple does a wide range of activities together) and the 'strength of influence' subscale (high scores meaning greater perceived influence from the partner) were each independently able to predict which relationships endured. (The measure of 'time together' was slightly mis-worded and so didn't predict break-up as the researchers had expected.)

It may be, of course, that the couples in this study were all at least fairly close, making feelings of closeness, as such, less of a predictor. As I have already pointed out, feelings can predict break-up. Degree of closeness and love can distinguish couples who stay together from those who don't (in the sense that 'low love' increases the chances of break-up compared with 'high love', but remembering that many 'high love' couples will break up too), as can equality of emotional involvement. In one study of dating couples, for instance, of the couples where both members reported at the beginning of the study that they were equally involved, only 23 percent had broken up two years later.[40] But 54 percent of the couples in which at least one partner reported that they were unequally involved later broke up. There was, however, a significant link between high intimacy (in terms of things such as feelings of closeness and love, and dating the partner exclusively) and reporting equal involvement.

But it is clear from, for instance, the work with the RCI, that what you *do* together matters in a relationship, not just what you feel.[41] Mixing romantic dinners with ferreting in supermarket freezers together appears to have a better prognosis than endless eye-contact in flickering restaurant candlelight.

Binding yourselves together with joint activities is one way relationships progress. How else do courtships develop?

Courtship development

When we use the word 'courtship', it brings to mind images of a smooth development. It needs two people who are not unreceptive to the idea of a long-term commitment if the relationship 'works out' (distinguishing it from 'one-night-stands' and 'flings'). It implies a process whereby two people meet, get to know each other, fall in love at some point, eventually decide that this is the one for them, and commit themselves (usually, but not always, by marriage). We expect this to happen within a reasonable time-frame. We regard both two-week courtships and seven-year courtships with considerable suspicion.

There is a loose, overall pattern that probably most people would agree on. At the very beginning, the man and woman probably see themselves as casually dating. They may even be seeing other people at this point, and don't yet see themselves as a couple. Gradually the time spent together increases, as does their range of shared activities and the amount of information they disclose about themselves and their feelings. They begin not only to regard themselves as a couple, but to be treated as such by their social networks. 'Darlings, you and Jane *must* come to brunch on Sunday . . .' In one study, over a period of about four months, the two individuals started to see their intermediate friends and acquaintances less frequently and for shorter periods of time (close friends were still seen as much as ever).[42] In the long term, the partners' social networks are likely to shift: they may shrink and blend to some extent, and new friends may be made by the couple as a couple.

The relationship may, of course, be knocked off the rails at any point, as we know. The gradual acquiring of knowledge of the other and monitoring of the partner's behaviour and apparent feelings for us might lead to us deciding to end it; or he or she might do the job for us. Perhaps the courtship is not progressing as one of the participants expected or desired; thus phrases like 'it doesn't seem to be going anywhere' (too slow) or 'it got too intense too quickly' (too fast). Courtships are particularly prone to break-up at about 15 to 18 months, as there appear to be expectations from the couple and friends and relatives that a judgement must now be made about whether or not it's going to end in marriage.[43] But about 90 percent of young adults will marry at some time in their lives,[44] so one courtship will eventually reach its societally approved climax. Wine, toasts, and mothers' tears.

Psychologists have found that among the courtships that lead to marriage, there is not one but four distinct patterns or pathways. In a major study, psychologists asked 50 couples who had been married 10 months or less to think about their premarital courtship.[45] With the researchers' help, they had to say at what points in their courtship the probability of marriage had risen or lowered. This made it possible to plot the progress of the courtship on a graph. The horizontal axis was time in months, and the vertical axis 'probability of marriage'.

The four patterns of courtship were:

Accelerated: moving rapidly towards near certainty of marriage (over 90 percent certain) within five months, and certainty by ten months.

Accelerated-arrested: showed a rapid start, with the probability of marriage rising sharply within two to three months. It then slowed up until about 15 months, when it moved to certainty of marriage.

Intermediate: moving smoothly to certainty at about 20 months.

Prolonged: a slow and rocky progression, with lots of ups and downs, towards certainty at about 40 months.

Obviously these are average trajectories, but the researchers say that the patterns are distinguishable. Other research supports these general pathways, but with some variation. Another study found the accelerated path moved to certainty in about 14 months, the intermediate path not quite so smooth and to take closer to 28 months, and the prolonged courtship to take more like 64 than 40 months.[46]

But what causes these differences in the approach to marriage, and what implications do the different pathways have for the satisfactoriness of the marriage that follows?

Obviously the various pathways could be caused by many factors. According to the research, it appears to be the amount of conflict that is a main factor distinguishing between the various routes to marriage, not, interestingly, the amount of love. Another study found very similar pathways to the ones described above – with the addition that sometimes there is initial cautiousness before a smooth rise (linked with being involved elsewhere at the time of meeting the future spouse, and having had a greater number of prior relationships), and that after a relatively smooth rise to a high level there may then be some ups and downs before the final commitment.[47] These researchers found that the love expressed by the participants *bore no relation* to the type of pathway they followed to marriage. For example, the particular feature of the prolonged courtship was increased conflict, not decreased love. The studies of courtship pathways have not followed the resulting marriages over time to see which ones come to a sticky end. However, we do know that too much conflict can be a bad sign.

This is not to say that conflict is always bad. It is, in fact, inevitable, once the first flushes of emotion and desperately trying to please the other – and not seeing the other clearly – begin to pass.

Some conflict may be of a practical kind, which should not be problematic as long as it is properly resolved. As two people's lives become increasingly interlinked – perhaps to the point of living together – disagreements will arise over lots of things, from which way round to hang the loo roll to what sort of holiday to have and how much time to spend with friends without the other person. What becomes important is how well the two partners deal with conflict. Is it negotiated well? Is it talked through and are satisfactory agreements and compromises reached? Because if this cannot be done during courtship, the prognosis is not so hot. Conflict, arguing and expressing negative feelings (such as anger and resentment) in courtship are significantly related to dissatisfaction in marriage.[48] Don't believe all you read about a good screaming match and a heap of broken crockery 'clearing the air'.

It may be that the conflicts are about more core matters, such as values and significant attitudes. Here, too, may lie danger. There is evidence that couples become more similar in attitudes and values over time,[49] but if there is a deep-rooted difference of opinion on serious matters that affect a couple's lives, then this may not be so open to shift or negotiation. Although people can tolerate differences to an extent, they will expect enough support and validation from the other person of the way they view the world to make the relationship seem important and valuable to them.

So although the 'courtship patterns' research doesn't address the question of later marital satisfaction directly, it may be deduced that a long and rocky courtship should make the participants very conscious of the need to examine exactly why they wish to marry. People sometimes decide to tie the knot more because of external forces (pressure to wed from family and friends, changing occupational circumstances) than from feeling strongly that they fit well together.[50] Any notion that marriage will sort things out is, as I have said, not madly realistic. Feelings of heavy investment – 'I've been in this for five years, surely it's not been a mistake all this time' – are certainly important for commitment. But as we have seen, another factor in commitment is satisfaction with the relationship. If you're spending your life storming out of the house in a huff or disappearing to the spare room in a sulk, scores on a satisfaction questionnaire aren't likely to be too stupendous.

There is some other relevant evidence on the question of rocky courtship/later marriage links. Comparing divorced and still-married couples who had had at least one premarital breakup, 50 percent of the divorced couples had split up two or more times during courtship, while only 29 percent of the couples who were still together had done so.[51]

Prolonged courtships, interestingly, seemed to be associated with partners who were relatively young when they met their future spouse.[52] The more rapid courtships were the realm of the older couples. The precise reasons for this aren't certain. But it may be that the older someone is, the more clear they are about what they want and need, and the more confident they feel (whether this turns out to be justified or not) about their ability to check the other person out faster. I'd say this should be even more the case with significantly older people – the couples in this particular study were on average in their early twenties. Second marriages, for example, are usually preceded by a shorter courtship than are first marriages.[53] It could also be that less experienced people put up with long and rocky courtships because they simply haven't experienced anything better, and think this is either 'how it is' or, if they have low self-esteem, all they deserve.

The causal factors distinguishing the more rapid courtship patterns from each other have not yet been fully teased out by the research so far, but certainly it would be naive to think that numerous factors were not involved. Feeling ready for commitment, for example, may be one element predisposing people to the fastest pathway (and lack of readiness to the slowest). Parental pressure to wed, too, can increase individuals' propensity to marry.

Partners in the two 'accelerated' clusters, compared with the prolonged and intermediate ones, withdraw more from their social networks, are more interdependent, in terms of doing things together (both leisure activities and domestic chores), and are more emotionally bonded.[54] As Steve Duck, a British social psychologist specializing in relationships, puts it, it seems that in terms of leisure 'there is an important integration between the development of feeling and the creation of joint patterns of activity for the spending of leisure time together'.[55] Having fun matters . . . In the swifter courtships, too, it appears that partners' expectations about how relationships *should* progress are well satisfied by its actual progress. 'Things are as they should be,' Duck says, 'so progress results.'[56] This is not so true, however, of the slower paths.

One distinction between the two accelerated pathways is that the accelerated courtships which are later arrested may encounter opposition from the social networks or situational constraints (such as occupational circumstances).[57] The role of social networks in all courtships, in fact, should not be underestimated. In research looking at 'turning points' in dating relationships that ended in marriage, where there were noticeable changes in commitment (either up or down), 20 percent of these were classified as being to do with outsiders — kin, friends, neighbours, co-workers, other dating partners.[58] As two American social psychologists prominent in this area, Catherine Surra and Ted Huston, have found: 'Examples of social network reasons are: "I met his parents"; "I knew my sorority sisters would think he was beneath me, so I didn't tell anyone about him for a long time"; and "He started hanging around with a wild crowd of friends."'[59]

Tsk.

The network tends to be implicated in negative more than positive shifts in commitment. Love can be battered by your friends' sneers . . .

Looking finally at the 'intermediate' pathway, it seems these may involve partners who are somewhat unsure about compatibility; and/or perhaps one partner who has a more positive attitude to marriage, and manipulates the relationship in that direction.[60]

What is becoming clear as the research in this area develops is the delicacy and subtlety of the processes involved in courtship. One feature of courtship is uncertainty about how the other person feels about you, which can go on for quite some time.[61] Rather than risk asking directly (discussing 'the state of the relationship' is the top taboo subject in developing relationships, in case people discover things they don't want to hear[62]), people may put the other person through 'secret tests'.[63] There is evidence of a variety of such strategies, which appear to be used more by women than men. Examples of secret tests of a partner's feelings are:

* setting up a situation whereby the partner must choose between the relationship and something else he or she wants
* the classic 'let's create a fictitious rival and see if he/she gets jealous' tactic
* monitoring how the partner behaves with an attractive member of the opposite sex at a party
* temporary withdrawal to ascertain how much the other person minds
* asking third parties for information about the partner's feelings
* presenting yourselves publicly as 'a couple' to check the partner's reaction to this
* 'testing the water' through hints and jokes

A person might feel tempted to use secret tests because evidence of commitment is extremely important to a developing relationship, and is involved in many of the significant turning points that people identify as their relationships grow.[64]

But some of these secret tests appear, paradoxically, to be quite risky strategies with considerable potential to backfire. Two partners' feelings of love and commitment to a relationship may not be of equal intensity at a given point in a courtship, even in cases where they later marry.[65] So even if the test itself doesn't do damage by lowering the other's rewards, its results may be misleading. What's more, it is important in a relationship to build up trust, and one can't help feeling that some of those secret tests may rock the boat a bit.

Two psychologists especially interested in the issue of trust, John Holmes and John Rempel, have described how trust is built up when two people make sacrifices or take risks for each other.[66] Trust, here, 'reflects confident expectations of positive outcomes from an intimate partner'.[67] One of the prime risks they take is to make themselves vulnerable to one other. A person may want a relationship badly, but there are factors in many people that also pull them back from it. Six in particular have been suggested: fear of hurt and rejection, fear of losing one's individuality or of being engulfed, fear of having one's faults exposed, fear of one's destructive impulses if one were to 'unleash' one's feelings, fear that information disclosed now will later be used as ammunition, and fear of losing control.[68]

Given people's fears and anxieties, the more they are drawn into a relationship and come to love the other, the more power that other person has over their lives. To say something that makes you vulnerable is, therefore, a big thing: for example, saying something more intimate and loving than has been said before. This gives a sense of movement and progress, assuming that the other reciprocates. But mere reciprocation on the spot – the 'I love you', 'I love you too' syndrome – is not enough. The first speaker may not be terribly reassured, as the second speaker may simply be adhering to the strong social rule about reciprocity. But if *over time* there is reciprocity – sometimes he says 'I love you' first, and sometimes she does – then that does feel more reassuring and as though progress is being made.

Another aspect of vulnerability shows up in what partners talk about. It is very important to understand what the other person is like, and how well you fit together. Love, in my view, is not terribly helpful in this department. First, it may lead an individual to ignore or play down faults in the other that, in fact, need most seriously to be confronted. 'Well, she's always putting me down in public, when we're out with friends. But it's just joking, you know. She doesn't mean it. Really she doesn't.'

Second, it may lead to hiding things about yourself that are bound to emerge sooner or later. Of course, in the early days of a relationship, everyone tries desperately hard to make a good impression. Tendencies to forget to wash or be rude to waiters are temporarily squashed. Such efforts may, indeed, serve a function. As one social psychologist puts it in a slightly different context (discussing how it may be useful to avoid direct talk about the relationship itself too soon): 'Early on, the two parties lack a stockpile of relational investments and rewards necessary to cope effectively with difference and conflict.'[69]

But with a relationship that's developing well, both members of a couple should gradually feel able to reveal their faults, weaknesses and disagreements. Again, that means exposing oneself to the danger of rejection, but it is an essential part of building a strong relationship base. We also should feel increasingly able to reveal our secrets — which also increases our vulnerability in case the partner ever turns against us.[70] But making ourselves more vulnerable is part of a developing relationship. We can't expect it to progress if we surround ourselves with psychological armour-plating. In fact, one study found that the total amount of self-disclosure given and received predicted very well which couples remained together over a four-year period.[71] Indeed, as Steve Duck writes, 'It is clear from a number of studies that the intimacy level of a relationship is often advanced by one of the partners' strategically releasing more intimate information than is usual in the relationship and the other partner responding with equally (increased) intimate responses.'[72]

However, a sizeable minority of people, out of fear of rocking the boat, avoid discussing matters that would be better aired. One American study looked at whether there were 'taboo topics' in relationships.[73] The researchers analysed in-depth interviews with 90 students. Questions focused on a current (or recently finished) relationship with a member of the opposite sex that was either platonic, or oozing with 'romantic potential', or definitely romantic.

The relationships were, on average, 21 months long. Yet among the taboo topics were: any explicit discussion of how they were to treat each other, either because it would lead to an argument or, in the case of sexual matters, because it was embarrassing (25 percent of the respondents); any topics that showed how different the two of them really were (22 percent); and the disclosure of things about themselves that might damage their image (17 percent).

It may be perfectly possible for relationships to progress to full commitment, then, with the forbidden zones still unexplored. Love combined with fear of disaster may, by leaving vital areas untouched, simply postpone the evil time when all is revealed and the relationship cracks open. Remember Sternberg's triangles from Chapter 1? It is possible to experience love and commitment without true intimacy.

As we have seen, love does not guarantee that a courtship will culminate in marriage – nor does it guarantee that the marriage will last. In the next three chapters I shall look at what psychologists have discovered so far about nurturing a relationship once it appears to be up and running.

FIVE

Maintenance Strategies

OK, let's assume a relationship has survived the potential pitfalls of the early stages. It's running on rails. Can it be left to chug on, fuelled by love?

Sadly, no.

The concept of 'working at relationships' is slowly gaining ground. There is little discussion, however, of precisely what this means or how best it can be done. But nurturing one's relationship really is vital to its long-term success. With the current premium placed on psychological and emotional gratification, people can no longer 'get' their partner, relax with a huge sigh of relief and spend the next forty years down the pub.

It is noticeable that most divorces take place after only a few years of marriage.[1] Perhaps this is because the serious dissimilarities have become clear; perhaps the marriage was driven more by outside pressures than genuine love and intimacy. Perhaps when passionate sexual attraction to an extent diminished (as we saw in Chapter 1, this may well happen), other problems in the relationship began to shriek for attention. In the case of avoidant and anxious/ambivalent partners, for instance, their relationships tend to last only a few years on average, and this may be largely because their difficulties in giving the other proper care become more obvious over time.[2]

Getting over the first few years, of course, renders no one 'safe'. A fifth of American divorces are of couples in midlife or older.[3] And marriages that survive over 50 years can still be miserable.

It is worth emphasizing at this point that, to be brutal, not all relationships are worth nurturing. Relationships that make people miserable, damage their self-esteem, injure them psychologically or physically, should clearly not be maintained; such cost to the individuals involved is not worth it.

As we all know, however, people do very often stay in unsatisfactory relationships. It could be that their self-esteem is so low they don't hope for anything better. It could be, in the case of women who don't work or earn much but have children, that practical reasons alone hold them locked into a relationship they would otherwise leave like a shot. It could be that no alternative partners are in sight, and security is preferable to the void. It could be that their expectations of relationships have sunk so low that they can't even imagine what a satisfactory relationship must be like. It could be habit or convention. It could be that they have put so many 'irretrievable investments'[4] into the relationship – including time – that it's hard to let that go. It could be that the children are the only thing keeping them hanging on. It could be that they don't ever face the unsatisfactoriness of their relationship.

The idea that lack of love isn't actually a good enough justification for breaking up a marriage appears quite wide-spread. In a survey in 1984, American university students were asked to respond to the statement, 'In my opinion, the disappearance of love is not a sufficient reason for ending a marriage, and should not be viewed as such'. Although 43 percent of the men and 45 percent of the women disagreed with this, a sizeable 31 percent of both sexes did agree with it (the rest were neutral).[5] The same sample had nearly all agreed that romantic love was an essential prerequisite for getting married in the first place; and 45 percent agreed that 'If love has completely disappeared from a marriage, I think it is probably best for the couple to make a clean break and start new lives.' (More women than men disagreed with this: 33 percent versus 27 percent; the remainder were neutral about it. Perhaps the women were more conscious of the likelihood that it would be they who ended up as single parents . . .)

However, there could be quite a gap between what students think a loveless marriage is in the abstract and what it might be like in reality. Also, such views are definitely subject to changes in the *Zeitgeist*. Students' responses to the same questions in 1976 showed a much higher proportion (roughly 60 percent) thinking that the end of love was sufficient reason to end a marriage. Perhaps an increase in conservatism has been responsible for the shift. But whatever the cause of overall opinion change, I don't think anyone would disagree with the proposition that a marriage in which love remains is a more attractive notion than one in which love has gone belly-up, where the partners are remaining in it for other reasons.

The latter is a more frequent event than one might imagine. On one famous occasion, the American columnist Ann Landers asked her readers, 'If you had to do it all over again, would you marry the same person?'[6] She was deluged with replies from all over the country. A staggering 52 percent said they wouldn't marry the same person again. This is a self-selected sample, of course, but it makes the point that there are large numbers of people who are less than thrilled with their marital set-up.

What I am interested in here is how to fend off such declines into misery. If two people love each other, what can they do to make it stay that way?

Once one accepts the harsh truth that love between adults is not unconditional, then the logical conclusion is that it can wither and die without due care. I think Western myths about the power of love have done us all a disservice, by seriously glossing over this uncomfortable truth.

None of this means that love cannot last. Naturally it can, and some people do manage the whole business successfully. As one American social psychologist, Robert Baron, puts it: 'Many couples remain happily married for several decades and report that although their love has changed (from passionate to companionate), it is as strong as or stronger than ever . . . Such happy endings do not occur by chance, however. Rather, they are the result of strenuous efforts by two deeply committed persons who actively choose to keep their love alive.'[7]

For many people, the outcome is very different. I want now to take a look at the incidence of problems and the speed with which they can arise – and at strategies for keeping the relationship on course.

Incidence of relationship misery

The high incidence of divorce is now well known. What started off – in the main, at least – with love, collapses in pain. To rely on love to see you through as the romantic myths decree is probably life's least reliable strategy. But as I have said, even for those who do recognize this and talk happily about 'working at their relationship', that doesn't mean they're clear about what actually to *do*. This bewilderment is borne out by the divorce statistics, and by the fact that at the time of publication of any such statistics, even more couples are separating, and still more are together but not terribly happy. Add to this the huge number of premarital relationships where the love that has developed tumbles into the abyss before getting to marriage, and the result is an unquantified mass of relationship misery. Divorce statistics are just the bit that shows.

Research on marriages finds that problems often begin within the first three years. A British survey of divorced men and women found that 37 percent claimed that serious marital problems were already manifest within a year of marriage; another 15 percent said within two years, and a further 9 percent within three years – a total of 61 percent.[8] But there was usually a lengthy interval between the onset of trouble and separation, and between separation and divorce. Some of these may have been marriages that were of dubious viability from the outset, and were relatively quickly terminated by divorce. However, any lessening of happiness in longer-lasting relationships may have been counteracted by other factors that serve to keep people in their marriages: children, finances, day-to-day lives being very closely intertwined, lowered expectations, pessimism over what life might have to offer if one left, getting satisfaction from other sources (such as friends, work, interests).[9] In fact, the same British survey found that, of couples who divorced after more than 20 years, as many as 30 percent said their problems had actually started by the time of their first anniversary.[10] (For some this may have been a way of justifying the divorce; for others it may have been quite true.)

Difficulties can, needless to say, rear their unpleasant heads at any time. The survey showed the average period before the start of the problems, according to how many years the couple were together before separating.

Separation in:	Average time before problems:
less than 5 years	1.4 years
5-9 years	3.3 years
10-14 years	5.2 years
15-19 years	5.8 years
20+ years	7.9 years[11]

Something has gone seriously amiss here. To at least begin to understand what is going wrong with people's relationships, let's start with the most obvious factors which might be at work. That is, those aspects of a partner's behaviour that seriously cheese off their other half.

Behaviours that disturb a partner

Well, the two mega-factors here – most upsetting for both sexes – are unfaithfulness and abuse, both physical and verbal. Not too much of a surprise. This was a finding in one of a series of studies by an American psychologist, David Buss.[12] He was interested in what he calls 'upset elicitors' for men and women in heterosexual relationships.

His first move was to survey two samples: undergraduates who had been involved in a relationship in the last 12 months, and couples who had been married no longer than a year. They were given a list of nearly 150 actions, and asked to put a cross by those things which their partner had done in the last year that had irritated, annoyed, angered or upset them.

Actions such as infidelity and abuse were reported as upsetting equally by both sexes. But there were also sex differences. Men more than women said they had been distressed or angered by sexual withholding and rejecting, and being 'moody'. Another irritant for men was the partner being 'physically self-absorbed', measured by items such as 'fussed too much with her appearance' and 'focused too much on her face and hair'. (Given the fact that the physical attractiveness of a partner is more important to men than women, this seems rather unfair! It sounds as though men want their woman to look maximally divine, as long as she does all that concentrated business in front of the bathroom mirror *discreetly* . . .)

Women more than men reported being upset because their partner had been neglecting or rejecting, condescending, inconsiderate, 'emotionally constricted' and drinking too much.

Buss moved on to concentrate on the newlywed sample only, and asked them how satisfied they were with their marriage. He then looked at links between how satisfied each respondent was and what upsetting actions they had reported their partner as doing in the last year.

Of the total list of actions, responses to many of them tended to cluster together in groups. So as to make clear what exactly words like 'moody' and 'emotionally constricted' cover, I'll give examples of the items that made up those clusters.

For both men and women, reporting that they'd been upset by the following actions was linked – strongly enough to reach statistical significance – with being less satisfied with their marriage. (Over time, you'd expect the list to be larger, since within the first year few people had been unfaithful – well, 'only' about 2 percent – or abusive, and upsetting factors you might be able to tolerate in the first year might have a cumulative effect by the fifth.)

'Sexually withholding-rejecting'. Things such as: 'refused to have sex with me', 'told me that he/she was not interested in my sexual advances', 'led me on, then turned me off'. (Surprising as it may seem, this can happen even in the first flush of marriage – and, as we have seen, is reported more often by men.)

'Moody'. This was rather a complex cluster. It covered not only 'moody' and 'acted "bitchy"', but 'planned everything for me', 'flirted with another woman/man', 'took too long to get ready'. This, you will remember, was more often reported by men as an upsetting set of actions. 'This factor appears to capture the negative elements of a stereotypically feminine behaviour style,' Buss says.[13] But when such actions occur in a partner, they are related to lower satisfaction for both men and women.

'Possessive-jealous-dependent'. Items were: 'too possessive of me', 'acted too dependent on me', 'demanded too much attention', 'demanded too much of my time', 'acted jealous'.

Neglecting-rejecting-unreliable'. Items: 'was unreliable', 'would not spend enough time with me', 'did not tell me that he/she loved me', 'ignored my feelings', 'did not call me when he/she said he/she would'.

'Sexualizes others'. Items: 'talked about how good-looking another woman/man was', 'idolized a member of the opposite sex who appeared on TV', 'talked about women/men as if they were sex objects'. (Clearly women should keep their feelings about Mel Gibson, and men theirs about Kim Basinger, to themselves . . .) Not surprisingly, these newlyweds reported indulging in these behaviours infrequently. But when they did, the marriage itself wasn't too blooming . . .

Referring back to what men and women identified initially

as upsetting them in the past year, it's clear that the sexual withholding and moodiness reported more by men is significantly linked with being less satisfied with their marriage. And, though reported less by women, it's bad news if it occurs for them too. The other factor reported as a pain more often by men, the physical self-absorption, wasn't significantly linked with them being dissatisfied in marriage. Perhaps the end result compensates . . .

The women originally reported that their partner was upsettingly 'neglecting-rejecting-unreliable' more than the men did. This was linked with less marital happiness for them and, when it occurred in a woman's behaviour, this was true for men too.

However, the other three factors reported more often by women as disturbing were significantly associated with feeling less satisfied with their marriage *only* for women. These were:

'Condescending'. Items measuring this (to use the third-person pronouns given on the women's version of the questionnaire) were: 'placed more value on his opinions because he was a man', 'tried to act like he was better than me', 'treated me like I was stupid or inferior', 'made me feel inferior', 'acted condescending towards me'.

'Inconsiderate'. Items were: 'left the toilet seat up', 'did not help clean up', 'burped or belched loudly', 'yelled at me', 'teased me about how long it took me to get dressed'.

'Abuses alcohol-emotionally constricted'. This referred to drinking and smoking too much, and 'hid all his emotions to act tough'.

Women were also less happy if they reported any sexual aggression (such as 'tried to force sex acts on me') on the part of their spouse.

So it looks as though these charming sets of activities, if indulged in by husbands, won't do much for their marriage. This doesn't necessarily mean that it wouldn't matter to men if their wives did them. In another study, Buss asked a different sample of students how much they thought all the actions would upset men and women.[14] They thought that being condescending, inconsiderate, drinking too much and acting tough would be equally upsetting for both men and women if their partner acted like that. (The exception was sexual aggression, which they thought would be more upsetting if a man did it than a woman.)

So the finding that these three factors are linked with dissatisfaction for women but not men can't be because men don't mind being treated like that. It may simply be that women are far less likely to behave in such ways (which fits with the results of the original study) and that the link with men's dissatisfaction that one might expect just hasn't reached statistical significance.

I think the value of Buss's series of studies lies in pointing out clearly exactly how both sexes can hurt their marriages. Merely accepting that love isn't enough doesn't give any clue as to what the hell else might matter. These studies address that question very directly. Certain 'upset elicitors' are linked with marital dissatisfaction. That is, they are more likely to occur in unhappy marriages than in happy ones.

However, I must point out that this finding *in itself* does not say what's causing what. It doesn't say whether upset elicitors cause unhappiness, unhappiness causes upset elicitors, or whether some unknown third factor – such as an aspect of the individual's personality – is responsible both for being dissatisfied and for being on the receiving end of upsetting actions by the partner. But what one *can* say from such findings is that certain things are more characteristic of unhappy than of happy marriages, and deduce that these things are, at the very least, not going to help matters. In Buss's research, we can be very sure of this, as the factors he looks at are already identified as actions that annoy or upset the respondents. It seems perfectly reasonable, therefore, to deduce that such behaviour can cause trouble in their marriage. It may also be the case that the reverse is true too: if you're feeling unhappy with the relationship, you might start acting in a way that causes the other to behave badly towards you. Perhaps sometimes each causes each – the behaviour causes dissatisfaction, say, dissatisfaction increases the behaviour, and so on, round and round . . . But what does seem clear is that if you want to piss off your spouse, Buss's findings show you the ways to go about it.

Other researchers, too, have looked at factors linked with being less satisfied with marriage. Being criticized is one of them. The Marital Transgression Scale consists of 'anger-arousing marital situations', and includes items such as 'Your spouse criticizes you in public' and 'In private, your spouse ridicules an idea that you have expressed'. For both husbands and wives, high ratings of the frequency of such behaviour were related to feeling dissatisfied with the marriage.[15] It does seem justifiable to conclude, as Buss's findings implied too, that provocative behaviour by a spouse isn't somehow negated by love – it can put stress on the relationship.

You don't have to be married not to like people attacking your ego with a meataxe. In another study, undergraduates were asked to report on hassles they'd experienced in the last week with their romantic partner (or roommate).[16] One of the two most frequently reported hassles was that the partner 'was critical of me' (55 percent of the sample). (The other, notably, was that the partner 'was stubborn and wouldn't compromise' – 58 percent.)

You could argue that being unhappy in a relationship might lead you to behave in ways that trigger the other's criticism. However, it is also likely that criticism does cause dissatisfaction too. After all, criticism can be undermining, damaging to one's self-esteem, and might make people worry about their partner's affections. This doesn't mean, of course, that couples shouldn't let each other know what upsets or angers them. But there are various ways of doing this, and 'I do get anxious/find it difficult to plan when you don't let me know you're going to be late' is obviously a tad better than 'you thoughtless, inconsiderate, selfish bastard, why didn't you call?' I'm going to discuss communication strategies and ways of dealing with conflict in more detail later.

Dangerous expectations

If you have embarked upon a relationship with love, it is not only a partner's behaviour that can whittle away at those feelings; you can damage them yourself. There is evidence that people can enter a relationship with what psychologists call 'dysfunctional beliefs' – beliefs and expectations about relationships that are going to serve to undermine rather than support them.

Two American psychologists, Roy Eidelson and Norman Epstein, have devised a scale to measure such beliefs. The Relationship Belief Inventory assesses five unrealistic notions that people may bring to bear on their relationship:

1. *Disagreement is destructive.* 'Spouses may believe that disagreements regarding values, attitudes, goals, or preferences are threats to a secure, loving relationship. Although interpersonal differences can produce conflict in any relationship, an individual's belief that disagreements represent a lack of love or even a sign of imminent divorce is likely to create additional difficulties . . . The person holding this belief tends to attempt conflict resolution by coercion or avoidance of direct communication.' This is not productive.

2. *Mind-reading is expected.* 'Also viewed as dysfunctional is the belief that partners who truly care about and really know one another should be able to sense each other's needs and preferences without overt communication. This expectation generally results in disappointment, misperception, and escalation of conflict . . . The person who believes in "mind-reading" may put less effort into clear communication and then experience dissatisfaction when his or her partner fails to respond as desired.'

3. *Partners cannot change.* Believing that partners cannot change either themselves or the quality of their relationship

is thought to be damaging because it holds out no hope that problems can be solved. Someone who feels like this 'is likely to experience diminished satisfaction with a relationship, feel less committed to it, and make fewer active attempts to constructively resolve conflicts'.

4. *Sexual perfectionism.* 'Believing that one must be a "perfect" sexual partner is also likely to produce relationship distress because it acts as an impediment to sexual arousal and performance.' Seeing sex as a task to be performed can produce negative feelings, such as anxiety, which can inhibit sexual responsiveness and reduce pleasure.'

5. *The sexes are different.* 'The belief that men and women differ dramatically in their personalities and relationship needs is likely to encourage stereotyped perceptions of one's partner and diminish sensitivity to his or her idiosyncratic desires and characteristics.' What's more, putting conflict with the partner down to such stable factors may lead to increased blaming of the other person, to low expectations of being able to solve relationship problems, and to other feelings of helplessness about the relationship.[17]

These five beliefs tend to cluster together: if you strongly believe in one of them, you're likely to believe in the rest. Collapsing them together into one score to measure dangerously misleading beliefs, one study of married couples found that for both husbands and wives, being less satisfied with their marriage was related to greater endorsement of unrealistic relationship beliefs.[18] Other research has found the same thing.[19]

Let's run over those five beliefs again.

1. It's not disagreement itself that's destructive, it's failing to resolve it in a way satisfactory to both of you without treading heavily on each other's egos on the way.

2. Love partners are not telepaths. Getting whipped up about their words or behaviour when they don't know they're doing wrong, and expecting them just to work it out somehow, is asking too much.

3. Of course partners can change in ways that benefit the relationship. Treating you with more consideration, for example, and setting aside time to be together.

4. Expecting to be the perfect lover is a bit of a killer. One who wants to make your partner happy, yes. Perfect and knows the Kamasutra off by heart, no.

5. If you really believe the sexes are fundamentally different, you erect a barrier in your own head to prevent true understanding and communication.

This research on unrealistic beliefs is rather chastening. People can wear away at their own feelings without the poor lamb they're with doing anything wrong at all . . .

Spending time together

Another way to nibble away at the foundations of a love relationship is not to *do* things together. Fun, pleasurable things. (I mean activities other than sex, which I'll get on to in a later chapter!) When a couple live together, they need to negotiate an intertwining of their lives. This has to occur on every level, from how much time to allocate to work and to personal life, down to the cleaning of the oven and who uses the bathroom first in the morning. On top of co-ordinating the practicalities of everyday life, there is the question of how to spend leisure time. Some people may be so knackered at the end of the day that watching TV exhausts their remaining feeble energies. Others may spend time with friends – which may be mutual, or one of the partners may be putting up with them for their other half's sake. 'But darling, Sheila was at school with me, we simply *must* go.'

How leisure time is spent is, again, an area where negotiation is important. 'OK, I'll come to Sheila's sherry party – but can we go to the cinema tomorrow, my choice of film?' Ideally, the majority of joint leisure pursuits shouldn't be those where one partner is there on sufferance. To start to associate being with the partner with feeling miserable, bored or irritated doesn't seem madly prudent.

The evidence is that how partners spend their leisure time *is* related to their satisfaction with the relationship. At the most basic level, one study of married individuals found that doing leisure activities alone, or with others but not the spouse, was linked both with feeling dissatisfied with the quality and quantity of time spent with their partner and with a measure of global marital distress.[20] One can picture the scene. 'Oh well, go to your sequin collage class then. See if I care. I'll just eat some spaghetti hoops and go and spot a train or something.' 'Fine, good idea, I'm going.' The link between spending leisure time with people other than the spouse and feeling maritally miserable was true especially for wives, more so than for husbands.

Being with others including the spouse, or the spouse alone, involved feeling happier with both time spent together and the marriage itself. But the strongest association this study found was between not spending leisure time with the partner *on his or her own*, and being particularly dissatisfied with the time spent together.

Of course, links and associations between two factors don't tell us which is affecting which, as I said earlier. It's likely that you would spend more time doing things without your partner if your relationship wasn't going too well. But it is also likely that if you spend too much leisure time not doing things with your partner, particularly not being with him or her alone, this could – over time – dilute the relationship. If an individual avoids interacting with his or her spouse, while this may cut down the chances of any disagreements or bickering, it also reduces opportunities for positive exchanges which can support or boost the relationship. There are some studies of marital therapy which have generally found positive effects of getting couples to do more leisure activities together.[21]

There are, however, different ways of doing things together.

It's possible to go for a walk together and not talk. Or to play tennis together and not to talk except to shout the score. Or to go to an art gallery together, and stroll round in silence. Researchers who have looked at communication and leisure find that joint leisure time bears no relation to marital satisfaction – or indeed is related to *dis*satisfaction – when communication is low to moderate.[22] Only when the time together is accompanied by high communication is it linked positively with marital satisfaction. 'Ooh, look at the ducks.' 'Yes, aren't they cute – what on earth are those two doing? Is it *legal*?' is much better than 'Ducks.' 'Mhumph.'

It might help to choose activities which of themselves provide things to talk about. These researchers found that of their sample of mostly married couples, 38 percent saw their communication as 'high' when visiting a museum, 42 percent as 'moderate' and only 6 percent as 'low'.

So although it's likely that happiness will affect time spent together, it does seem plausible to suggest that doing pleasant things together *and talking about it* can improve satisfaction. First, it's a way of associating pleasant feelings with the presence of your partner; linking him or her with nothing but thoughts of washing the dishes, the loo-cleaning rota and silent TV-watching smacks of danger. Second, talking – about work and the events of the day, no matter how apparently trivial, as well as things done together – is a way of maintaining and developing intimacy. It enables couples to keep in touch with the way the other is looking at the world, and how they're feeling and thinking. It helps them develop 'shared meanings', by which they intertwine their views of the world and maintain and elaborate their understanding of each other.[23]

Sharing activities is a part of this process, and a part of the way couples organize (or fail to organize) their lives together. But structuring their daily lives together can contain a hidden monster, one ready and waiting to drag a love relationship down. That is, boredom.

The need for novelty

Little research has been done on the role of boredom in undermining a love relationship, but psychologists believe that emotions can become deadened by absolute predictability and routine.[24] Early in relationships, the theory goes, when everything's unpredictable and uncertain, emotions are swishing around like nobody's business. As certainty increases, there are fewer interruptions or eddies in the relationship, and this is where the danger of deadening emotions lies. They may be aroused by an event that breaks the routine – such as discovering the other is having an extramarital affair – but the effects of such events won't always be good for the relationship.

What relationships need, the argument goes, is a mix of predictability and novelty. Predictability is needed to keep the relationship stable, novelty to prevent deadening of the emotions. It has been suggested that the best combination is to have predictability in elements that are central to the functioning of the relationship (in knowing that the other is not going suddenly to disappear, will look after you in times of serious illness, will remain faithful, that sort of thing) and novelty in the more peripheral elements of life.[25]

So, as social psychologists Robert Baron and Donn Byrne suggest: 'When boredom does occur, it might be overcome by a husband and wife who together seek new stimulation in the form of vacations, joint educational efforts, unfamiliar dining experiences, new hobbies that are enjoyed by both, new sexual techniques, and so on. Different couples might find quite different solutions.'[26] (I think the 'sex' suggestion is the one here that doesn't count as peripheral, by the way, but I'll be looking at that in a later chapter.)

Novel and unexpected expressions of love can also serve to reduce the chances of a partner's emotions going into a sort of coma.[27] Coming home one Friday night, expecting a really hot weekend – Saturday morning down the hypermarket, afternoon doing the washing, you know the scene – and finding your partner waiting with the car engine revving and two tickets for a romantic break in Paris . . . Well, that'd keep your emotions awake all right. If you can't afford Paris, even calling the other unexpectedly in the day to say hello works on the same principle.

I know it sounds like the stuff of the slushiest romantic fiction, but the bottom line is that there are sound psychological reasons for making the effort to make life more interesting and exciting for a partner – and oneself.

Expressions of love

Let's examine more closely the question of expressing one's love. It is perfectly possible to feel love for a partner, and yet not to express it. But expression is crucial.

In Chapter 1 I described Robert Sternberg's 'triangle' conception of love, involving intimacy, commitment and passion. Sternberg himself emphasizes what he calls the 'action triangle' – the need to translate emotions and thoughts into action. 'The actions that convey the three components of love differ. For example, intimacy might be expressed through communication or doing concrete things to support the other person. Passion might be expressed through hugging or making love. Commitment might be expressed through fidelity or some tangible symbol, such as a ring. However the three components are expressed, the actions will have tangible effects on the relationship, because just as the levels at which the three components are experienced will affect the actions that are generated from them, so will the actions affect the components. Feelings of intimacy, for example, lead to intimacy-based actions, which lead in turn to more intimacy. But if the feelings are not expressed in action, then often destruction of the feelings will follow, especially if lack of follow-through leads to lack of trust on the part of one of the partners . . . It is necessary to take into account the ways in which individuals express their love. Without expression, even the greatest of loves can die.'[28]

The evidence is that Sternberg is right – being able to express feelings is associated with being satisfied with one's relationship for both men and women.[29] Again, for both sexes, describing oneself as being higher on stereotypically 'feminine' traits – such as being affectionate and warm – is related to the marital happiness ratings of both oneself *and* one's partner.[30]

Not only do our feelings affect our actions, but our actions feed back to affect our feelings. If you express your love, you remind yourself that you feel it, and give it a boost. Also, of course, that expression affects the partner positively. Who could resist 'Darling, I love you so, and you still make my spine turn to custard . . .' (Unless, of course, the relationship is already dead in the water and it's too late.) The feedback you get from him or her reinforces and encourages both your love and your willingness to express it.

Without expression, love can become a weaker creature, and one's partner may become distressed, which may lead them to behave in ways damaging to the relationship. The importance of a partner's misunderstanding of one's feelings should not be underestimated. Sternberg finds that the best single predictor of relationship happiness is the difference between how you want the other person to feel about you and how you think he or she *actually* feels.[31]

One problem is that men tend to be less expressive than women (I shall be looking at this in the next chapter). Women want to be hugged without that always being a prelude to sex, to have their hand held in public, to be told they're loved without them having to say it first.

Men may feel that their mere presence in the relationship is 'enough proof'. If more were needed, they can point to, say, their financial contribution and faithfulness.

One tiny study touches on this very issue of how men and women express love.[32] Only seven couples were examined, which in social scientific terms doesn't make it possible to place much weight on the findings. I am going to mention it because I found the results intriguing, and intuitively very plausible.

The researchers asked the couples to record their interactions for several days. This included how pleasant the interaction was, how often the spouse did something like cook a good meal or mend a tap (labelled by the researchers 'instrumental behaviour'), and how often the spouse expressed acceptance or affection.

What transpired was that the wives enjoyed their marital interaction when their husbands expressed affection; the husbands when the wives did something positive in the instrumental department. The husbands apparently saw instrumental actions as affection. When the researchers told one of the husbands to be more affectionate, he decided to wash his wife's car. He was then surprised that neither she nor the researchers regarded that as an 'affectionate' act.

The point is brought vividly home by another researcher's description of a husband talking about his wife's complaints about lack of communication. 'What does she want? Proof? She's got it, hasn't she? Would I be knocking myself out to get things for her – like to keep up this house – if I didn't love her? Why does a man do things like that if not because he loves his wife and kids? I swear, I can't figure what she wants.' (In cases where the husband actually has a job that he personally gets a lot out of, this kind of line may not sound terribly convincing . . .)

His wife's view was very different. 'It is not enough that he supports us and takes care of us. I appreciate that, but I want him to share things with me. I need for him to tell me his feelings.'[33]

What does seem crucial is for each partner to understand the ways the other expresses his or her love, the way their partner wants to have love expressed to them, and also to make clear their own needs in terms of how they would *like* the other to express their feelings. It might help to know that, say, cooking a special meal for a husband can be disproportionately appreciated; and telling a wife how much she's loved may be valued more than the speaker might guess. To discover any differences in perspective, talk is required. Relying on telepathy, as I have had occasion to remark earlier, just won't do.

Taking the other's perspective

Finding out what the other's views are on expressing love is just one aspect of a broader issue – that of exploring the other's perspective as a general strategy.

Psychologists have studied the impact of 'perspective taking' – defined as the tendency to put oneself in the other person's place – on relationship satisfaction. In one study of married couples, for instance, participants were given two sets of questions to explore perspective taking in their marriages.[34] One set asked people to report on their own behaviour, such as 'Before criticizing my partner I try to imagine how I would feel in his/her place', and 'I sometimes try to understand my partner better by imagining how things look from his/her perspective'. The other set examined how they saw their partner's behaviour, asking them how true were statements such as 'My partner is able to accurately compare his/her point of view with mine', and 'When my partner is upset with me he/she tries to put him/herself in my shoes for a while'.

Looking at each scale separately, taking one's partner's perspective was positively related to that partner's marital adjustment, for both husbands and wives; and believing that the partner puts him or herself in one's shoes was positively linked with one's own satisfaction. Both sexes agreed that the wives were better at perspective taking than were their husbands. Yet wives' perceptions of their husbands' abilities in this direction were more strongly related to wives' marital satisfaction than were the husbands' perceptions of their wives' abilities linked with husbands' happiness. A man showing competence in this area appears to be especially appreciated by his spouse.

The ability to take another's perspective is not something laid down in stone in the genes – it can be learned with, it seems, positive benefits for the relationship. In the study just described, the couples had been married on average for about 24 years. Other evidence has suggested that as time goes on, a couple may make fewer and fewer efforts to keep tabs on their partner's feelings and state of mind because they are overconfident – they feel they know nearly all there is to know.[35] But as this study shows, trying to put yourself in your partner's shoes is a strategy related to happiness even after more than two decades.

Believing you know all there is to know is clearly a risky strategy. What's more, there is some evidence, consistent with these sex differences in perspective taking, that wives understand their husbands better than husbands understand their wives. (Thus boring a hole in the classic married man's sympathy-inducer, 'My wife doesn't understand me'.)

A Canadian researcher got nearly 90 married couples to fill in a questionnaire individually about their attitudes towards family size, physical discipline of children, leisure time and work; plus the questions of economic contribution to the marriage, chores, who gives more in the relationship and women's rights.[36] (Both husbands and wives saw the first four issues as being more important to their marriage than the last four.) They also had to say what they thought their spouses' attitudes to each issue were. Over half the couples had been married more than ten years.

The results indicated that the wives scored higher in the 'understanding of spouse' stakes. The women were consistently more accurate in predicting their husbands' responses to the questions than the men were in predicting their wives' reactions. This was particularly true for the issues most salient to the marriage. The researcher's chastening interpretation was: 'It has always been more important for those of lesser power to understand those with greater power and control over their lives.' (A situation that's changing, of course, but slowly.)

Perspective taking and understanding are facets of 'communication', and there is some evidence that feeling there is good communication between you has a stronger effect on women's satisfaction with a relationship than men's, even relatively early on. This, at least, is the implication of a study of mostly dating (rather than engaged or married) student couples.[37]

For men in relationships of over a year's duration, their satisfaction was significantly predicted by their partner's warmth, 'positive outlook' (in terms of being 'confident, friendly/outgoing, positive/optimistic, ambitious, honest/dependable, and intelligent'), trustworthiness and lack of possessiveness. For women in relationships longer than a year, the significant predictors were their partner's warmth and positive outlook (not trustworthiness, surprisingly – perhaps it was too early days; and possessiveness only seemed to bother them in relationships of 12 months or less). Plus, for women only, the feeling that their partner 'opens up' and 'readily listens' to them affected how happy they were with the relationship, whether they'd been dating less than or more than a year.

Women's apparently greater emphasis on the importance of communication is not misplaced. I want now to examine sex differences in intimacy and expression of feelings, and look in a bit more detail at communication – both good and bad.

SIX

Intimacy, Communication and Conflict

Intimacy is crucial to the maintenance of a good relationship (remember Sternberg's triangles?). And yet, just to make life a little perilous, it is not embraced with quite equal enthusiasm by men and women.

Intimacy

The first question is: what is intimacy anyway? It has been defined in lots of different ways, but one I like is 'a process in which one person expresses important self-relevant feelings and information to another, and as a result of the other's response comes to feel known, validated (i.e. obtains confirmation of his or her world view and personal worth), and cared for'.[1]

I think that sums it up rather well, and makes explicit an element that psychologists regard as vital to intimacy – self-disclosure. Disclosing facts about oneself – one's adoration of avocado bathroom suites, early years at Lower Muddleford Comprehensive, deep loathing of the current prime minister – may be more prevalent in the early stages of a relationship, when the two people are finding out about each other. Disclosing feelings, however – about oneself, the partner, the relationship – can go on indefinitely. There is some evidence that in marriages, disclosure of feelings, more than of facts, affects marital satisfaction (positively or negatively, depending on what those feelings are and how the couple deal with them).[2] This may be because the couple already know a lot of facts about one other.

The general image of the sexes includes the idea that men disclose their feelings less than women do. Psychological research supports this on the whole, but matters are a bit more complicated than they might at first appear.[3]

The general thrust of findings from studies of sex differences in intimacy is that 'females are likely to express greater interpersonal intimacy than males do'.[4] But some studies find no sex differences, and others that men disclose more than women. The latter, however, tends to occur when a specific goal is in sight – such as a prospective romantic encounter.[5] One possible explanation is that at that point, the man may be disclosing in an attempt to create a favourable impression and perhaps to lure the woman into a more intimate relationship.

Under what other circumstances do sex differences appear? Research hasn't teased out all the complexities, but so far it looks as though sex differences in intimacy are stronger in same-sex friendships than in opposite-sex relationships. That is, it looks as though women have significantly more intimate relationships with their women friends than men do with their men friends. But the differences between men's and women's expressions of intimacy – including self-disclosure – with an opposite-sex partner may not be so great. It may be that society's 'expectations' of men – that masculinity means not showing your feelings too much – are stronger in male-male friendships than in heterosexual relationships or, indeed, opposite-sex friendships. For women, such constraints do not apply.

In one study of friendship the researchers asked about 200 students to think of one close same-sex friend, and one close opposite-sex friend (who was not a current romantic partner).[6] Then the students had to imagine vividly each of four problems happening to them, and to say which friend they'd rather go to for help and how they thought that friend would react. They had to consider two relationship problems – 'a fight with a roommate and a break-up with a romantic partner', and two 'task' problems – how to handle being passed over for a promotion and 'receiving a third speeding ticket'.

The researchers thought that both men and women would rush to women (theoretically the human race's 'emotional experts') with their relationship problems, and to men with their work and practical problems, in true stereotypic manner. To their surprise, both the men and the women preferred to talk to friends of their own sex about both relationship *and* task problems. Although the men reported that they strongly preferred to talk about task rather than relationship issues with their male friends, whom they expected to be relatively dismissive of relationship difficulties, they still, it appeared, would rather talk to other men than to women.

It seems peculiar that men apparently choose to discuss their relationships with the friends least likely to be helpful. 'Perhaps avoidance was the males' preferred mode of coping with problems',[7] the researchers speculate, and they wanted to talk to someone with a similar world view. Women, in contrast, expect emotional support and problem-tackling from their female friends over mystery questions like why their beloved Dick's run off with a traffic warden.

But if women are more able to bare their soul over delicate matters to each other than men are, one has to be careful about saying that therefore men are less disclosing than women in their relationships with lovers. The sex differences here do appear to be less strong. Presumably as well as society's rules about disclosure being weaker in such circumstances, one's lover might actually influence one's own level of disclosure. If you spend three years revealing your angst about your legs and your eldest child and your joy every time your boss gets your name right, and all the while get no more than a grunt from your partner, you're probably going to give up and confine your conversation to whether or not it's time to change the upholstery. Or, if your partner expresses his or her feelings on a regular basis, you might begin to think that your own continual grunting seems tedious or is being badly received, and start letting the occasional revelation emerge tentatively from your lips. But there is evidence that individuals tend to be in relationships with partners who are roughly similar in how comfortable (or otherwise) they are with closeness and intimacy,[8] as well as that husbands and wives are similar in how much they disclose.[9]

There is some evidence, too, that men and women don't differ that much in disclosing positive emotions to spouses and lovers: feeling happy or delighted about something, for instance. However, men do report being less likely to reveal certain negative emotions – depression, anxiety, anger and fear – to their partner than women do.[10]

If one assumes that intimacy – including self-disclosure – is a good thing for a relationship, then men's greater inhibitions in this area could be dangerous. Psychologists do believe, on the whole, that open communication between members of a couple is beneficial for a relationship. This essentially assumes that the communication is positive – about the partner and the relationship, at least – or, if negative, properly dealt with. Feelings of love, as we have seen, are not the only factor that affect how satisfied two people are with their relationship: intimacy is another. Increased self-disclosure is linked with higher satisfaction with the relationship.[11] Those who are highly motivated to form intimate relationships, too, tend to have happier ones.[12]

But some psychologists have argued that in certain circumstances intimate disclosures might not be so beneficial: in very 'traditional' marriages, for instance, where men and women play out the classic roles of husband (dominant and work-oriented) and wife (nurturant, concerned with the relationship). In these marriages, there is some evidence that self-disclosure about the partner and the relationship is limited to positive feelings and thoughts.[13] This leads, argues Mary Anne Fitzpatrick, the researcher in question, to a satisfying marriage. For such couples, total openness – of the 'I'm feeling utterly miserable at the prospect of spending Christmas with your mother yet again' variety – might not be so good. Then again, Fitzpatrick says, perhaps traditional couples, where both partners know what's 'expected' of them, have less to argue and negotiate about anyway. However, the notion that traditional marriages in the more liberated climate of the late-twentieth century are going to be relatively conflict-free seems most unlikely.

I feel myself that *apparent* satisfaction, which involves saying what the other wants to hear and keeping quiet about the rest, is risky. Yes, the other person might be happy if you never mentioned that you were sick to death of his/her too-frequent outings to the pub/pottery classes/bird-watching without you. You might be, well, *quite* happy because there are no arguments.

Thin ice.

If you disclose something that gives the other person a bit of a turn, it might lower satisfaction temporarily. But matters unaired remain unresolved. As such, they always have the potential to rear up and bite the relationship severely in the seat of its pants.

If men have a bit more difficulty in talking about feelings – negative ones in particular – this could remove a strong source of support and help from them, and by definition lowers the level of intimacy of their relationship with their partner. It is noticeable that men's abilities to be intimate have a stronger impact on relationship satisfaction than do women's. In one study of dating couples, for example, the extent to which their partner was comfortable with closeness was, for women, the best predictor of relationship quality.[14] But for men, this was not so.

It may be that women expect greater expression of emotion and intimacy nowadays than they used to. Men's problems with coming clean over their feelings have been much discussed in society at large, and the pressure is on to change this. Therefore, it's reasonable to suppose that how their lover rates in this department has become very important for women. Men, on the other hand, expect women to behave in a reasonably intimate fashion, and on the whole they get that. As a result, women's behaviour in this area has less impact on the men's satisfaction than does men's on their female partner.

Intimate disclosures of feelings do matter to relationships. Sometimes, of course, they may be negative and focused on the relationship, which is what tends to happen when the relationship is in the process of breaking up.[15] Of course self-disclosure can have negative effects, depending upon what feelings are revealed and how the couple copes with them.[16] But taking intimacy as it is defined at the beginning of this section, it's clear not only that it matters but, as one researcher sums it up, that 'There does seem to be some evidence . . . that women feel slightly more comfortable with intense intimacy in their love relationships than do men'.[17] Obviously this is a generalization; all research findings are. There are undoubtedly plenty of men around who will be better at exposing their inner feelings than are some women. But images of masculine restraint in this department aren't dead yet, and the fact that women discuss feelings and relationships with their friends more than men do must, I feel, have some impact. Women get more practice at doing it, and at developing concepts for dealing with relationships. Wine bars throb with in-depth analyses of why Jim didn't phone yesterday and why Phil's been a bit funny lately and what's Sue going to do about the fact that she thinks Pete's the eel's pyjamas . . .

In extreme cases, a big difference between a man and a woman in expressions of intimacy could bring a relationship to its knees. In one survey of 400 therapists, they reported that the largest single reason why marriages fail was the husband's inability to communicate his feelings.[18]

Given that there seem, overall, to be some sex differences in expressions of intimacy, this does not mean that nothing can be done about it. Self-disclosure is something that is under one's own control. Furthermore, it is only part of what intimacy means – the definition I gave earlier includes the other person responding appropriately. The whole realm of how couples communicate is one where strategies for improving matters are abundant. And often they need improving if the relationship is to be maintained.

Communication skills

The essence of communication is that A expresses what he or she wants to say and that B understands it. This is not so jolly simple as it sounds. A may fail to say their piece clearly, concretely and specifically enough. This has been found to occur more in distressed than in nondistressed marriages.[19] For instance, there is a big difference between 'Your friends don't half talk/drink too much' and 'It would be terrific if we could have a bit more time to ourselves. How do you feel about agreeing on a rough number of nights per week when we see friends?' If the former is code for the latter, it simply won't have the desired effect. It doesn't make the person's real wishes clear nor does it contain a specific point to be tackled. All it sounds like is an insult.

Even assuming A has said his or her piece openly and clearly, B may not have fully taken it in. A crucial part of good communication is to be a good listener. This involves first, concentrating on what the other person is saying (rather than, say, thinking more about what *you* want to say), and second, being what psychologists call an 'active listener'. This means asking questions and, if the issue is complex or difficult in any way, perhaps restating what he or she is saying in your own words.[20] 'So you feel that . . .' This makes certain that you have actually got it right, and also serves to reassure the other that you do understand (and demonstrates how hard you are listening).

Of course, what A wants to say may be entirely negative. 'You're never here when I want you, your mother drives me wild, you know I can't stand wallpaper with blasted pink roses all over it,' that kind of thing. Not much doubt about the speaker's meaning here. But this raises two issues. First, if A feels badly about the partner always coming home late, inviting mother to Sunday lunch every week and making domestic decisions without consultation, there are better ways of saying so. 'I feel X about Y' is less critical and blaming, where X are the true emotions (hurt, lonely, left out, whatever) and Y is a specific action or statement of the other. It's OK to say how you react to something specific someone has done, without implying that he or she is awful as a person for having done it. 'I feel upset that we're not spending enough time together' is better than 'you think more of your work than you do of me, you're so *selfish*'.

Such a negative outburst is more likely to occur, not surprisingly, when the marriage is already in trouble. Researchers have found distinct communication styles when comparing distressed and nondistressed marriages.

In happy marriages, there tends to be: more talk; more self-disclosure (in both depth and breadth); clear, direct messages without hidden meanings; active listening skills; more agreement; more expressions of love, approval, affection, encouragement, respect and esteem; more emotional support; more positive statements and fewer negative ones (including criticism); a greater likelihood of interpreting the partner's behaviour as positive; greater ability to express feelings about a marital problem in a neutral manner; more sensitivity to each other's feelings; more use of idiosyncratic codes; more laughter; and more positive 'non-verbal communication' (warm tone of voice, touches, etc.). Most matters – including intimate ones – are discussed, and happy couples convey to each other the feeling that each understands what the other says to them.

In unhappy marriages there is, unsurprisingly, more negative behaviour – both verbal and non-verbal – and fewer positive actions (such as being affectionate and supportive). But it doesn't stop there. There are fewer attempts to solve problems and exchange information; a greater likelihood that negative behaviour will be reciprocated; a lower ratio of agreements to disagreements; more conflict and longer-lasting 'scenes'; more coercion; one spouse is often significantly more dominant than the other in conversation; statements by the spouse are interpreted as being more negative than the speaker intended. Discussions are more likely to start out with complaints which then trigger an escalating cycle of negative exchanges – 'you're a beast', 'you're a nag' – with each partner repeating their position again and again.[21]

Strewth.

Looking at these two patterns (if you can bear it), it might be tempting to conclude that people who love each other communicate fine until they get fed up with each other, in which case the whole thing starts to go down the pan. In other words, that satisfaction affects communication, not the other way round. But this would be a mistake. Communication and satisfaction are a two-way street.

Concluding one review of the 'firmly established' connection between communication and satisfaction in marriage, the writers point out: 'While good communication skills are not expected to be a panacea for marital distress and divorce, the strong support for a relationship between satisfaction and communication cannot be ignored. Whereas good communication could just serve to elucidate wide and seemingly irreparable differences in values and perspectives, it seems more likely that good communication may increase intimacy and reduce misunderstandings and conflicts.'[22]

It does indeed seem more likely. There is some evidence that training in communication can actually help to prevent distress. In a long-term study of 42 couples who were planning marriage, half were assigned to a 'cognitive-behavioural marital distress prevention programme', and the remainder acted as controls (and didn't do the programme).[23]

The programme consisted of training in four areas:

Communication skill training: Couples were shown 'active listening and expressive speaking skills'.

Problem-solving training: 'Couples were taught how to monitor their own and their partners' behaviours and how to make specific requests for behavioural change in addition to skills such as brainstorming and contracting as problem-solving techniques.' Brainstorming involves thinking up as many ideas for solving the problem as possible (no matter how odd-sounding) *before* making judgements about the worth of each idea. It encourages creativity. Contracting means that sometimes it might help to draw up a contract between you: 'I'll clean the loo every other Thursday and we'll always go out, just the two of us, at least once a week', that kind of thing.

Clarification of marital expectations: We've come across this little bugaboo before, have we not. In this programme, couples were encouraged to discuss with each other their expectations about themselves, their partners and their marital relationship.

Sensual/sexual education and relationship enhancement: Here the focus was on sexual functioning and problems, and ways to prevent problems and 'make a good relationship better'.

There were then three follow-up sessions. At the first follow-up, eight to ten weeks after the couples were first assessed (during which time they either did the programme or acted as controls), there were no differences between the intervention and the control groups in their reports of their relationship quality. However, at the second follow-up, one and a half years later, the intervention couples reported higher satisfaction with their relationship. And at three years after the programme, the couples who'd gone through it showed higher levels of both relationship and sexual satisfaction than did the control couples, as well as less intense problems.

What was happening was not that the intervention couples were getting better and better. The researchers conclude: 'The results suggest that premarital intervention prevents the declines in marital quality that occur in most relationships over time . . . The intervention couples generally maintained high levels of relationship quality, whereas the control couples showed the predictable declines found in other longitudinal samples.'[24] Hard as it is to face, research evidence implies that, far from being able to run on love, relationships tend to decline in quality without due care and attention.

Obviously the programme packed in a lot of things, and the couples who agreed to take part were motivated to do it, it must be said, and so were perhaps more likely to function better in the first place, and certainly to try to make use of what they were taught; but the majority of these activities were to do with *talk*. The social psychologist Steve Duck refers to relationships in terms of permanently 'unfinished business', which is dealt with and negotiated through talk.[25]

One of the most vital functions of talk should be to resolve conflicts. This can be one of the trickiest areas in a love relationship. Just as generally poor communication can undermine love, so too can poor methods of resolving conflict.

Conflict resolution styles

When you have a disagreement with your partner, what do you do? Do you subscribe to the 'Let's hurl his mother's hideous floral vase out of the window' school of conflict resolution, or the 'If I don't say anything it'll all blow over' theory?

Some Dutch psychologists have analysed five 'typical conflict styles' in intimate relationships.[26] These are:

Aggression-pushing: 'Being extremely assertive, but neglecting the interests of the relationship.'

Avoidance: 'Physically and emotionally retreating from the situation', and ignoring both your and the relationship's interests.

Soothing: 'Trying to prevent an open conflict', and making co-operation a priority over defending your own interests.

Compromise: 'Trying to find a fair solution', involving concessions on both sides.

Problem solving: Being both assertive and co-operative, by 'the open and direct discussion of feelings, the exploration of the causes of the conflict, and the search for a mutually satisfactory solution'.

The researchers compared men's and women's uses of these styles. Students were asked to assess both their own and their romantic partner's approaches to dealing with conflict, focusing on what had happened during a recent serious disagreement.

The men thought they were similar to their partner in aggression-pushing and problem solving, but reported themselves as using more avoidance, soothing and compromise.

The women agreed that their male partners were more avoidant and soothing than they were, yet they felt they were equally willing to compromise. However, the women reported using more aggression *and* more problem solving than their partner.

The researchers didn't comment on *why* the sexes saw each other's use of three of the styles rather differently. As aggression is less 'acceptable' for women, being 'unfeminine', they may exaggerate their use of it in their own minds and report using more than their partner might perceive.

Nor did the researchers comment on which strategies are likely to be most effective. But avoiding emotional discussion, soothing and aggression don't sound to me like terrific tactics for getting at the root of the difficulty. Compromise sounds good, problem solving even better. Interestingly, the men seemed to feel they used those two styles more than the women thought they did. Perhaps men are more satisfied with lower levels of problem-tackling than women are. Women reckoned they definitely got to grips with problems more directly; and men didn't disagree that they avoided emotional discussions or tried to skate over them more than their female partner did. Taken together, these findings imply that men may be less prone than women to confronting difficulties in relationships – perhaps because this involves actually talking about *feelings*. This can only make the tricky process of resolving conflict between men and women that much harder.

Other studies, of both dating and married couples, have also suggested that women are more likely than men to confront disagreements in their love relationship.[27] Researchers have also been investigating which approaches to dealing with conflict are likely to have the best results in terms of feeling satisfied with the relationship. In one study, for example, American psychologists John Gottman and Lowell Krokoff asked married couples to discuss a problem which had been causing them a lot of conflict.[28] They were also asked to complete questionnaires measuring their marital satisfaction. Three years later, the couples were recontacted and the majority filled in the questionnaires again. The researchers then calculated whether there had been any change in satisfaction, either up or down.

Observers had coded in detail what the couples did while discussing the high-conflict issue. They divided the couples' actions into eight categories, the first four labelled 'positive' and the second four 'negative':

Positive problem solving: Accepting responsibility, compromise, paraphrasing or reflecting back what the other has said, and suggesting positive solutions.

Positive verbal: 'Agreement, approval and humour.'

Positive nonverbal: Assenting and looking attentive, smiling and laughing, any positive physical actions such as touching.

Compliance: A combination of actions appearing under other categories too – agreement, assent and approval.

Defensive: making excuses, denying responsibility, suggesting negative solutions ('What I'd like to do to my mother-in-law involves chains, quick-setting concrete and earplugs').

Conflict engagement: Disagreement and criticism. Criticism is defined here as 'a hostile statement expressing unambiguous dislike or disapproval of a specific behaviour of the other', said in an 'irritated or hostile tone of voice'. Any expression of anger would be included here.

Stubbornness: Refusing to comply with what the other may suggest; putting the partner down; commanding the other to do (or not do) something; and complaining. Complaining includes statements of 'being frequently deprived, wronged, or inconvenienced either through the partner's action or non-action or because of external circumstances', which may involve 'whining'.

Withdrawal from interaction: Not responding, turning off, and 'incoherent talk'.

What Gottman and Krokoff found, in common with other research, was that 'in the resolution of marital conflict, there is a stronger relation between concurrent marital satisfaction and negative interaction than positive interaction'.[29] In other words, negative actions engaged in while trying to resolve conflict are more strongly linked to feeling unhappy with the relationship at the time than positive ones are linked to happiness. It looks, then, as though avoiding the negatives may be even more important than actively using the positives – although the latter matters too.

However, these findings also showed that what may seem to be good or bad currently may not be good or bad long-term. Specifically, wives being positive verbally was linked with the couple feeling more satisfied at the time, but decreasingly satisfied over the period of three years. (Wives' positive non-verbal behaviour followed a similar pattern, without reaching statistical significance.) Wives' compliance, while not strongly linked with satisfaction originally, was again related to a significant deterioration in the couple's happiness over time. And most surprising – at first sight, at least – were the findings for 'conflict engagement'.

For both wives and husbands, disagreement with and criticism of their spouse were strongly related to feeling dissatisfied with the marriage at the time of the original discussion. But three years later, such apparently negative actions were associated with having become *more* satisfied.

What turned out to be linked for both husbands and wives with distress at the original point and/or with deterioration of marital satisfaction over three years was defensiveness, stubbornness and withdrawal. Not all the findings quite reached significance, but they were not far off. When husbands were defensive, both husbands and wives were cheesed off and satisfaction deteriorated over time. The same pattern held true, but less strongly, when wives were defensive. When husbands were stubborn, satisfaction was lower for both husbands and wives, both originally and over time. When wives were stubborn, the satisfaction of both parties was significantly lower at the original point, but that was not related to any change in satisfaction on either side over time. When husbands were withdrawn, while it seemed to have little relation to current satisfaction, it was linked with feeling increasingly dissatisfied for both husbands and wives over the three-year period. When wives were withdrawn, it was very strongly linked with both sides feeling dissatisfied originally, but not to any change over time, either up or down.

The tactic I would have put my money on was positive problem solving, but while such behaviour on the part of the husbands was positively associated with satisfaction for them and their wives originally, and with improving satisfaction over the three years, it did not reach statistical significance; and wives' problem solving seemed unrelated to satisfaction.

I have gone into these findings in detail because, in my view, how conflict is resolved is one of the most important and tricky issues in any long-term relationship. And there is going to be conflict, whether it's confronted or not, where two individuals live together long-term, no question. There is more conflict between an individual and his or her spouse – or equivalent – than with anyone else in the social network (friends, siblings, parents, work colleagues).[30] So only a look at the real nitty-gritty will do.

What does this complex pattern of results really boil down to? I think the key to understanding the effects of different conflict resolution styles is to analyse which of them involve *a true tackling of the core of the difficulty* and which do not.

It is noteworthy that defensiveness, stubbornness and withdrawal are prime ways of avoiding the issue. It is important to be able to discuss with a partner what he or she is criticizing you for without becoming defensive/obstinate/refusing to listen, hard as this may sometimes be. Other research supports the idea that trying to skirt matters won't work. Another study of married men and women found that for both husbands and wives, seeing the partner as 'critical/defensive' is related to marital distress.[31] In this study, 'critical/defensive' was measured by respondents rating how frequently his or her partner did things such as: 'refuses to acknowledge when wrong'; 'refuses to accept criticism'; 'inappropriately blames you for problems'; 'fails to compliment you or say positive things to you'; 'inaccurately attributes feelings and motives to you'; 'refuses to discuss a topic'; and 'criticizes you in an unhelpful manner'.

Not only should criticism not be destructive, but it should also be selective. As two American researchers specializing in marriage put it: 'Constructive criticism – that is, pointing out significant ways to improve another's behaviour – can be a meaningful part of developing a close relationship. But it is a waste of time to complain continually about trivial matters. Criticism must be discriminate, taking into account the fact that nobody is perfect and that there are many matters that are so unimportant that they should be ignored. Indiscriminate criticism, or faultfinding, usually leads to very destructive consequences.'[32] Criticizing a loved one's gamboge-check underpants on a regular basis gets the thumbs-down; remarking on his miserable habit of spending every Sunday under his car with an oily rag is OK.

Reserving criticism for what matters is wise advice. After all, human beings want to feel validated by their partners – accepted and appreciated as they 'really' are – not made to feel a mass of miserable faults and have their self-esteem reduced to the size of a walnut.

But superficial niceness isn't going to do the trick either. Those wives in Gottman and Krokoff's study who were positive verbally at the original session were less happy bunnies three years later – and so were their husbands. Being nice and agreeing might be fine after the problem has been properly explored and an agreement satisfactory to both parties has been reached. Agreeing and appeasing before that point only keeps the home sweet temporarily; the problem has not been solved, and agreeing to what you don't want – or what isn't a real solution – is not going to have good knock-on effects.

If confronting the true source of the problem is the real issue here, then this makes sense of that apparently puzzling finding about 'conflict engagement', which is associated with marital unhappiness at the time, but increasing happiness thereafter. As the researchers describe it, it is the only tactic where the real point of contention is specifically stated. Sometimes this involves irritation and anger, which at first sight look like bad moves. But it may be that, as Gottman and Krokoff say, to 'vent' anger may sometimes be helpful. Perhaps the bottom line is that it is worse to feel that you mustn't ever get angry with your spouse for fear of the consequences than it is to do it if you really need to.

But whether expressing anger is a good move or not will depend on how it is done. Psychologists think it important that anger be expressed without unfairly putting the other down, or attacking or blaming. It is possible to remain reasonable while feeling angry, to focus on the specific issue (not get into global statements of the 'you're so selfish' type) in a search for a solution. It's better to report one's anger in a calm, nonaggressive way: 'I feel X' is better than 'You're a . . .'

Getting angry and not taking the other's feelings into account, no matter how tempting this may sometimes be, is not going to be an effective way to resolve problems. There is evidence that rage and yelling make people feel worse, not better 'because they've let it out'. What's more, verbal aggression is linked with physical aggression, the worst possible way of behaving in a so-called 'love' relationship.

If anger isn't dissipating during a discussion – and it may be better to wait until it *has* dissipated before beginning any sorting-out talk – then it's better to stop and wait until you're calm. Equally, if a partner attacks you verbally, it's more effective to respond in a calm and concerned manner, 'I'm sorry you feel like this, let's talk about it', rather than shooting back a psychological poisoned dart. The calm, caring and constructive response is a sign of strength, not weakness.[33]

It is also worth noting that disagreement without anger, according to the Gottman and Krokoff study, showed a similar pattern of results to 'conflict engagement'. Using a different coding system, the researchers found that disagreement expressed with neutral emotion was also linked with dissatisfaction currently but with an increase in marital happiness over time. 'The confrontation of disagreement by itself,' they say, 'is functional for marriage in a longitudinal sense.'[34]

Conflicts truly faced now, it seems, can result in increased happiness later. If that is so, then why didn't 'positive problem solving' have a stronger effect? Certainly, other studies have found such behaviour occurs more in happy couples than in miserable ones.[35] My suspicion is that as it was coded here, it didn't necessarily involve a proper exploration of the issue in question. It might be possible to rephrase the other's statements, say, when the other's statement is not particularly positive or germane to the problem. 'So, you feel the extermination of my mother is the best solution, is that right?' If the researchers had added, say, the 'disagreement' element of 'conflict engagement', then I think 'positive problem solving' would have shown a much more positive link with marital satisfaction. To problem solve after a clear, even if painful, exploration of what the hell the difficulty really is would in my view be the most effective overall strategy.

Further clues that this is correct come from even more recent studies. One looked at whether there are signs in a couple's relationship before they marry that might prove to be risk factors for their later happiness.

Some American psychologists got young couples (on average 25 years old), six weeks before their wedding, to discuss a relationship issue about which they disagreed.[36] The researchers audiotaped their problem-solving attempts, and then rated how much positive (e.g. friendly, kind, relaxed) and negative (e.g. dissatisfied, upset, annoyed) emotion was expressed. They also rated the amount of 'disengagement' − 'silence and quietness'.

The next step was to measure the couples' satisfaction with their relationship 6, 18 and 30 months after the marriage. The results show that the amount of positive and negative emotion washing around in the discussion before the wedding bore no relation to how happy the couple was after it. What turned out to be important was not expressing emotion as such, but whether the couple engaged fully in talking about the issue at hand. Those who were disengaged in the pre-wedding discussion were more likely to be dissatisfied with their marriage 18 and 30 months later. (Interestingly, disengagement was not related to how satisfied the couples were *before* the wedding, or at 6 months, only to how they felt later on.)

It's hard to say from this finding whether being disengaged is a factor leading to increased dissatisfaction, or whether some third influence − such as the partners' personalities − is responsible both for their failing to engage actively in conflict discussions and for a lack of marital oomph. But it looks as though a particular way of relating to the other person is, at the very least, not going to enhance marital joy. As the researchers put it, 'The more satisfied couples at 18- and 30-month follow-ups were those who at premarriage [communicated] about problems in a nonquiet, nonsluggish, nonsilent, energetic, and excited manner.'[37]

In other words, they got to grips with their problems. This fits with the findings of another study showing that using a particular set of 'power strategies' – techniques for getting your own way – is linked with marital misery.[38] These psychologists call them 'indirect' strategies. They are:

Positive affect: 'I become extremely pleasant, cheerful and smile a lot.'

Hinting: 'I drop hints about what I want.'

Negative affect: 'I sulk, refuse to talk to him/her, or act cold towards my spouse.'

Withdrawal: 'I ignore my spouse or won't listen to his/her side.'

Laissez-faire: 'I go ahead and do what I want without telling my spouse.'

What these strategies have in common, whether they involve being nice or not, is a failure openly to discuss and confront whatever the issue is.

These two studies imply not only that a certain style of dealing with each other is associated with being unhappier in the relationship, but also that it can be spotted before the marriage, and predicts unhappiness two and a half years later.

But if getting to grips with the issue at hand is essential, and if this has to involve some negative emotion, the pain quotient should still, I feel, be kept to the minimum necessary for getting whatever it is off one's chest. Other studies have found, as we've seen, that distressed couples do criticize each other and escalate conflicts more than happy ones do. It is noteworthy that a number of studies find that men avoid confronting marital conflict more than women do. Why this is so is not yet clear although it may, as I suggested earlier, be because probing the roots of a conflict will involve expressing feelings. Marital researchers, interestingly, note that a very common pattern in unhappy marriages is a withdrawn husband and an aggressively conflict-engaging wife.[39] Presumably he can't stand the aggro and can't bring himself to confront the issue, and she is beside herself with frustration that he won't talk things through. So they've got into a seriously bad cycle of increasing attack and retreat.

If one partner doesn't want to face up to and resolve conflict, this is an issue which in itself needs to be resolved. As this research illustrates, the harvest otherwise could be that a relationship begun in love and high hopes deteriorates and deteriorates.

VIOLENCE

When I talk about dealing with conflicts and communication skills, these are not likely to be a lot of help in a violent marriage. Just as love won't teach you how to resolve disagreements in the most effective way, nor will it act as a magic shield if your partner takes it into his or her head to beat you to a pulp, physically and/or emotionally.

The majority of physical violence is male to female; although the reverse does occur, most research has concentrated on 'wife batterers'.[40] I regard a violent relationship as the greatest exception to what I have been saying – and will continue to say – about the power of talking things through in a marriage.

Men who abuse their wives are often real experts at psychological manipulation. Because they have periods of being remorseful, kind and loving, the woman thinks that there's hope for them. 'One day,' she says to herself, 'he could be lovely to me all the time.'

Women in this position may keep reminding themselves of his 'good points' – exhibited during his 'nice' phases – which are what they fell in love with in the first place. But in the 'nasty' phases the husband may beat them up and subject them to emotional abuse such as humiliating them in public, a typical tactic of this kind of man.

What is very hard to accept is that there is a deep-rooted nice/nasty cycle here which is desperately hard to break – and only the man can do it.

Men who batter their wives are trying to exert control over them. They think this is what 'being a man' is all about. Their self-esteem is probably low, and being abusive is the only way they feel able to 'keep the wife in line'. They have very likely come from a family background where the father abused the mother – and perhaps them too. This then gave them the sick idea that this was how a man could control members of his family. Because they are often insecure and regard their wives as their possession, they are frequently uncontrollably jealous.

Heavy drinking is also a common feature of wife abusers, and wives may sometimes attribute their husbands' behaviour to this. However, the evidence is that alcohol is not the *cause* of wife abuse, through breaking down inhibitions and leading to 'out of character' behaviour. Rather, it's now thought that such men often drink to *provide an excuse* for becoming violent. They know that when drunk, people are supposed to be 'not responsible for their actions'. So when they want to attack, they get drunk. This accounts for the fact that such men are also perfectly capable of going for their wives when sober.

Women who remain in such relationships frequently do so because they are at home with children and feel economically dependent and trapped.[41] They may also often feel some emotional ambivalence, because they have not realized the true depths of the problem. They think they keep having tantalizing glimpses – during his 'good' periods – of the 'real man', and that the violence and temper are unfortunate aberrations. They believe that 'If only he can stop drinking/I cooked better dinners/the children could learn not to speak when the football's on, then everything would be all right.' But what lies behind the 'nasty' behaviour is the real man too. Failing to realize this is a serious psychological trap. The romantic notion that love can redeem someone – the 'rescue fantasy' – is a dangerous myth. The causes of his behaviour are extremely hard to alter, and impossible unless the man recognizes and takes full responsibility for his physical and emotional abuse of his wife, and goes for professional help with a real desire for change.

If there are no signs of this, it would be naive to suggest that talk will do the trick in circumstances like these, and ending the relationship is the wisest alternative for both the woman and her children. Men who abuse their wives often do the same to their offspring.

Women who are abused are often very isolated, and to reveal what has been happening to family, remaining friends and professional agencies – and thus get outside support and practical help – can be a very effective first step in breaking away and gradually regaining self-esteem and independence. Being abused wears away at a person's self-esteem, which may not have been terribly high in the first place. Such erosion is likely to make women feel vulnerable and inadequate, encourage them to think that they can't manage on their own, that no one is ever going to love them in the future – all sorts of pessimistic things that are quite wrong. What these thoughts serve to do is help to keep the women in relationships which violate all that a human being has a right to expect of a so-called 'love partner'.

Even where there is no violence, there *is* going to be conflict. As I hope I have demonstrated, how it is confronted is crucial to a healthy relationship. One major aspect of relationships that can cause conflict is imbalances between the two partners – to which we now turn.

SEVEN

Negotiating Imbalances

One of the major challenges in long-term relationships is to face up to and cope with imbalances. A general sense that the relationship isn't fair or equitable can, like moles under a lawn, undermine it over time. One element that can make equity a serious issue is the arrival of children, particularly if both partners go out to work. This chapter explores the need to negotiate over imbalances – if you don't, the whole loving enterprise may come apart at the seams.

Equity

It might seem a bit unromantic to suggest that a couple's feelings for each other might be affected by whether or not they feel they're getting an equally fair deal. However, there are some indications that, calculating as it might sound, equity can be an issue in relationships.

But what exactly does 'equity' mean here? A study by two Dutch psychologists provides some interesting pointers.[1] They recruited hundreds of men and women who were married or cohabiting – among them about 260 couples – through an announcement in a local newspaper. They then asked the respondents to rate the overall equity of their relationship. They had to think, 'Considering what you put into your relationship, compared to what you get out of it and what your partner puts in compared to what (s)he gets out of it, how does your relationship "stack up"?' Their answers could shade from 'I am getting a much better deal than my partner' through to 'My partner is getting a much better deal than I am'. They were also asked to make a similar judgement about all sorts of specific 'exchange elements' such as being nice to be with, sexual needs, domestic chores and so on.

What became clear was that when people are asked to make a global assessment of how fair their relationship is, they do not do a fine-grained calculation involving large numbers of elements. Rather, they focus on a few. In this study, most men as well as women took three factors consistently into account: commitment to the relationship, being sociable and pleasant to be with, and being attentive and thoughtful. (One of the additional factors for women who felt deprived, surprise surprise, was 'spending more time accomplishing housekeeping tasks'. Reach for the loo cleaner, guys.)

But although both sexes regarded equity in these three areas as especially crucial, there is a tiny problem here. They are, the researchers say, 'all socioemotional services, traditionally within the realm of women'. This could partly account for their disturbing finding that 25 percent of the women felt they were getting a worse deal out of the relationship than their partner was, while only 13 percent of the men felt similarly short-changed.

You could argue that perhaps people only say they're getting a worse deal because in fact they're not at all satisfied with their relationship for quite separate reasons. But the results indicated that among women (the picture for men was not so clear), inequity does seem to produce dissatisfaction with the relationship, and not vice versa.

The danger is that one partner might not realize how the other feels. In only 60 percent of the couples did both partners agree on who was deprived, overbenefited, or equitably treated. This potential danger zone in a relationship can't be rectified if it isn't spotted in the first place.

Other researchers, too, have found evidence that equity is related to satisfaction in intimate relationships.[2] Feeling underbenefited is obviously the worst; second worst is being very overbenefited. This might seem strange, but the theory is that equity is what's important, and overbenefiting is inequitable. So it is thought to affect satisfaction because the overbenefited party feels guilty (this is particularly true of women[3]). Feeling slightly overbenefited, or equitably treated, does seem to be the best alternative. Within the equity category, it's likely that 'strictly perceived equality of both partners' inputs and outcomes is preferred to a proportional balance where one partner's gains and contributions are perceived as greater than the other's.'[4]

However, as the Dutch researchers themselves point out, equity appears to be more important for some people than others.[5] What's more, other evidence finds that the absolute level of rewards a partner feels he or she is receiving affects satisfaction more than equity does, in both premarital and marital relationships.[6] Perhaps if someone feels a relationship has many rewarding aspects, they're less likely to start looking at it in terms of each partner's relative inputs and outcomes. But if a person does look at it in those terms and it's 'stacking up' badly, it can be undermining to the relationship.

To know what partners find rewarding requires talk, trying things out to see how much they're appreciated, and increasing knowledge of who they are and how they feel. To discover if they feel the relationship is unfairly balanced requires talk too, and not turning a blind eye to hints of the 'It's 9.30 p.m., your dinner's in the hamster and I'm going on strike' variety. This may sound obvious – but if it were that jolly obvious then why do researchers find two out of five couples disagreeing over the equity of their relationship despite the risks that poses? And why are inequity and lack of rewardingness allowed to build up and weaken the relationship?

I rest my case.

The time has now come to touch upon the topic of children. The arrival of a child is a major event in many couples' lives, and one that can eat into a relationship's reward levels and equity like a starving tiger cub getting its first taste of meat.

The effects of children

The popular image of children is that they 'bring couples closer together'. That tiny, mewling, puking bundle, which will gradually grow through toddlerhood, school days and the joys of adolescence, will bind its parents' souls together with hoops of steel.

Unfortunately the evidence is that, on average, marital satisfaction is lower when there are children living in the home. Looking at graphs of changes in marital happiness over time, they tend to start out high, dropping during the children-at-home stage (particularly when they're teenagers). Then there is disagreement among researchers over whether (for those couples who are still together) satisfaction rises again to what it was before the children arrived, or never makes it back to that level.[7]

Obviously, these are averages. For some couples their marriages may improve, for some the quality of the relationship will be unaffected, for others it will decline.

One British study looked at marriages a year after the birth of a first baby.[8] On average, the initially high marital satisfaction fell for both parents. But the fall wasn't uniform across couples. Comparing satisfaction when the baby was a year old with satisfaction scores in early pregnancy, about 60 percent of each sex showed little or no damage or even a bit of an improvement: around 28 percent showed a slight increase in score, and about 34 percent no change or only a very small decrease. But around a quarter had a moderate fall and just over one in ten a substantial fall in marital satisfaction. (About 40 percent reported a damaging impact on their sex life.)

However, the researchers say they think that 'the proportion of marriages severely affected by the transition to parenthood is probably substantially greater than our study would suggest.'[9] This is because the sample under-represented or excluded 'at risk' groups such as very young couples, or lower-social-class couples, who already have a lot of difficulties to cope with – poverty, bad housing and so on. What's more, 'there is evidence that marital satisfaction declines as children get older'.[10]

So although couples vary in their reactions to the arrival of a child, what this finding – that there can be quite a drop in satisfaction – does do is point to a potential difficulty. There is evidence that, in general, the arrival of a child won't make a good marriage bad, or a bad marriage good.[11] So having a baby as a strategy to mend a marriage is not a madly wise move. Yes, it may mean it lasts longer than it otherwise would, but if the marriage itself is not working a child is unlikely to make it work, and it'll probably all collapse in the end.[12]

Children do have this apparently paradoxical effect on marriages: they may lower marital happiness, but they also lower the risk of marital break-up, for a while at least.[13] Having children raises greatly the costs of ending a marriage, and acts as a strong barrier against doing so. For instance, there is evidence that 'unsatisfied spouses report that their children are the greatest or only source of marital satisfaction; satisfied couples report many sources of satisfaction'.[14] However, we only have to look about us to know that children's mere presence is not always sufficient to hold things together. Indeed, a survey back in the 1970s found that 'nearly two-thirds of Americans rejected the idea that parents should stay together for the children's sake, even if the partners were unhappy with each other'.[15]

One American study found, rather peculiarly, that 'sons reduce the risk of marital disruption by 9 percent more than do daughters'. The researchers explain this in terms of 'a father's greater role in raising sons than daughters and his consequently greater involvement in the family. Children provide a new basis for marital cohesion, one that rests on attachments and obligations to children. For fathers, the obligations and attachments are greater if they have sons.'[16]

Be that as it may, I don't regard marital 'stability' coupled with marital dissatisfaction to be good enough, not by a long chalk. So it is the relationship between the presence of children and satisfaction that I shall concentrate on here.

Having a child can strain a good marriage, so it doesn't take a lot of imagination to guess what it might do to a weak one. It requires adjustment to increased demands for both parents, obviously. For men, who nearly always carry on working, it means (initially) broken nights, change in routines, going out less, a threesome (or more) in the home, a shift in his wife's attention away from him, tiny wails and demands – and delights too, of course. Perhaps that shift in attention, mind you, need not always be as great as it is. When new parents are observed at home, they seem less involved with one another, and show less affection, than during the pregnancy.[17] Yet the idea that a couple can just shove their relationship on the back burner when children are young is, in my view, a little risky.

For women, the adjustment required is much more far-reaching.[18] The mother may give up work, a major shift no matter how much she liked her job. If she loved it, it's a serious loss; if she didn't, it still means a loss of adult companionship, a degree of independence, a life outside the home and so on. Matters may be complicated by postnatal depression. This occurs in about 10 to 15 percent of mothers, and milder depression may be reported by a further 16 to 20 percent.[19] Arguments still rage about the role of hormones and psychological and social factors in these negative feelings. If there is already marital disharmony before the child arrives, however, this is related to an increased risk of depression.

The evidence is that many parents do not realize fully how much the new arrival is going to alter their lives.[20] For women in particular, the inequity which is going to enter their day-to-day existence is usually of serious dimensions. They are going to find themselves doing significantly more housework than their husbands, and take on the majority of the responsibility for childcare, whether they go back to their outside employment after the baby is born or not.[21] Even in couples that are pretty egalitarian before the birth, afterwards there is often a shift towards a more 'traditional' division of labour in the home.[22]

Women do not expect this to happen. In one study carried out in America and Canada, relatively few of the pregnant women in their samples expected to be doing much more of the childcare than their husbands.[23] Indeed, a third or more expected an equal division of both housework and childcare. Perhaps they still live in hope of the New Man; perhaps because most women get increased support from their husbands during pregnancy, they think their relationship is 'different' from other women's; perhaps they have been lulled into a false sense of security because men often take on a greater share of 'traditionally feminine' household chores when women are in the late stages of pregnancy.[24]

That doesn't last.

According to an in-depth British study of 25 new mothers by social psychologists Rosaleen Croghan and Dorothy Miell, women have what sounds like a rather exhausting internal struggle to make sense of what is happening.[25] They see marriage (and cohabitation) as a relationship which is mutually beneficial and supportive. But they have to deal with the 'lack of fit' between this and their experience of the serious inequity which they face on a day-to-day basis.

At some level, many of these women didn't seem to feel they had the right to demand equity or equality. 'For mothers who accept that the responsibility for parenthood lies with them,' the researchers write, 'to blame the father for not contributing equally would necessitate a major ideological shift. For this reason, they cast around for other explanations which do not call the relationship into question.' The researchers emphasize that what is important to the women is that the male and female role in a marriage is equivalent, not equal. So the issue becomes not the inequality in the division of labour, but how well the man fulfils the role that's expected of him. 'It therefore becomes illegitimate to ask the male to increase his participation in childcare, since to do this would be to expect him to exceed male gender norms.'

So the women talk about how busy their husband is, how it is important financially that he works as hard as he does, how his work is more important than theirs, childcare isn't 'real' work like paid work is. The women are trying to locate the explanation for what is happening in external factors, not within the power structure of the relationship itself, the researchers say. 'The division of labour is seen as a constant, fixed by an external order, and dictated by economic necessity.'

The women really do fight hard to maintain these types of explanations. 'Even when experiencing acute stress,' Croghan and Miell say, 'mothers resisted locating the responsibility in their marital partner, opting for explanations which stressed social-structural factors like bad housing or low income factors, or naturally arising personality differences, rather than active choice and responsibility.' The women would say, for example, that their husband was much slower to notice things wrong with the baby than they were, or that they were much more organized than he was and he would do what he was told but couldn't initiate, or that the husband was simply incapable.

The trouble, as the researchers point out, is that 'If the man's contribution is optional, and his "help" with childcare and domestic work is evidence of his goodness, then the mother's anger becomes illegitimate.' The women were very uncertain about what it *was* fair to expect, and so 'often felt guilty about raising questions of work sharing and were easily defeated if their partners were unwilling to co-operate'.

New motherhood is a tremendous shock to the system: deeply exhausting, often suddenly isolating, and involving unremitting work. Over half of this sample of women reported that their partner had difficulties in coming to terms with fatherhood, too.

Women who give up full-time work, then, may often not negotiate a fairer deal because, at some level, they don't feel they have the right to, thanks to 'the powerful ideological apparatus surrounding motherhood'. Also, they 'must negotiate from a newly allocated position of weakness at a time when their social and economic autonomy is depleted'. In this particular sample only two women were working full-time, so no conclusions can be drawn from this study about dual-earner families. (But it was interesting that these two women were more likely to try to resolve imbalances because they defined their roles in the relationship in a more equal fashion: 'I work too . . .' They were not very successful at it, however, and did their paid work 'without relinquishing any of the responsibilities of the maternal role'.)

So if fathers are doing very little in the way of practical help, what are they doing? 'The payoff from the sexual relationship,' Croghan and Miell say, 'comes from emotional rather than practical support, and mothers will go to great lengths to preserve their vision of the companionate marriage striving to maintain harmony and to avoid overt conflict . . . Women put a high premium on affection and communication in their sexual relationships, and as long as these are present they are willing to accept a marked degree of inequality.'

However, if such psychological benefits are not present, the women seem more likely not to take it all lying down, and may begin to put self-interest above preserving the relationship at any cost. Some of them had already suffered violence in their relationship, and others' relationships were already quite conflictful. 'Mothers in violent or unstable relationships were jolted out of their belief in a mutuality of interest between partners and began to take steps to preserve their financial and emotional independence.' (I have said my piece about violent relationships, but will re-emphasize that what I am going to say shortly about negotiations with spouses is more applicable to relationships where conflict is not dealt with by the fist.)

The researchers conclude that the balance of power in the relationships of all the mothers they interviewed was weighted in favour of the man. In a few relationships it was reinforced by violence or the threat of it, and 'in many it was underlined by mothers' economic dependence'. But for most mothers, they argued, the limits of what they were prepared to ask for were set by their unwillingness to put pressure on the relationship which they saw as their main source of emotional support at a time when they felt very vulnerable.

But relationships are capable of being truly beneficial and rewarding, not just pretend-beneficial and rewarding because you are resolutely closing your eyes to what is making you unhappy. This is true of both women and men, and of single-earner and dual-earner couples. The idea that men and women are 'supposed' to behave in certain ways is the most dreadful straitjacket for *both* sexes. Charlie Lewis, a British psychologist who has made a major study of fathers, says: 'Perhaps the most important reason for the clear division of labour is that nobody really expects fathers to play a major role in childcare as long as their wives are capable of coping themselves. They simply accept the cultural prescription that the mother should take primary responsibility for the baby.'[26] Women aren't 'allowed' to feel a sense of grievance at what has happened to their lives after the advent of children. Not all women will have such feelings, but the point is that they should be able to have them and not be condemned for them – and that they should be accommodated.

Men may be very unsure what is expected of them these days. Most men probably did not have a participant-father/chore-sharer role model in their own childhood homes which they could now copy; and notions of what it is to 'be a man' are in any case even more rigid than those of what it is to 'be a woman'. While women are increasingly (slowly) able to be assertive, to carry on working after childbirth and so on, many men may still feel their masculinity to be compromised by nappy-changing and getting those nasty stains off tiny Jane's jumper. (In Croghan and Miell's study, for example, the men played with their offspring rather than tackling those smelly little *practical* childcare tasks . . .) Part of the problem may be that many men are scared of handling a small baby (whereas women get guidance and practice in hospital),[27] which gets matters off to an unequal start. To make things worse, often women may not trust men to do the business of childcare 'properly'. Keeping the main responsibility for childcare – *if* that is what is wanted – whilst also demanding fairness in the relationship is possible, but it may be that women don't fully realize to what extent they are hanging grimly on to the reins. As Charlie Lewis puts it, 'It is the case not only that men exploit their wives by "dodging" their responsibilities in the home. Both mothers and fathers actively strive to perpetuate the differences between parental sex roles.'[28]

Some unusual Australian research by psychologist Graeme Russell illustrates the point. He studied couples where, for various reasons, the man played a large part in looking after the children.[29] The results were rather revealing. He describes his results like this: 'Shared caregiving couples reported that their relationships were affected in quite diverse ways. Some reported greater equality in terms of power and responsibilities, whereas others reported conflict and tension associated with the process of renegotiating family tasks and responsibilities. Fathers expressed discontentment with: the lack of quality couple time and reduced affect [emotion] resulting from mothers being physically and emotionally exhausted; difficulties encountered in sharing responsibilities; their partners not letting them make decisions about the children and being critical of their approaches to childrearing; and their partners not being genuinely supportive of them when they experienced problems as caregivers.

'In contrast, discontentment for mothers focused on: frustrations involved in feeling tired and rushed; resentment of fathers taking over family responsibilities, and developing closer relationships with the children; being irritated by their spouse's standards of childcare and approaches to childrearing; their partner's failure to share domestic work; and feeling resentful of the status that other people gave their spouses because of their involvement and perceived competence in childcare.'[30]

Dearie me.

In this research Russell found that the shared caregiving couples were less satisfied with their relationships than were more 'traditional' couples. But some of them were under the extra strain of the situation not being of their choosing, the fathers' greater participation being because, say, they'd lost their job.

However, in a later study, Russell examined couples where the woman worked and the man had the main responsibility for looking after the children for a minimum of 15 hours a week (the average was 26), and where the couples had chosen this course of action.[31] They were not forced into it by external circumstances. Again, however, 'Mothers were less satisfied when fathers took over more responsibility for children and when they perceived themselves to be more competent as parents. This supports the hypothesis that mothers feel threatened by, and resent fathers moving into, their traditional domain.'[32]

In this study, the couples were not less satisfied with their relationship than a matched sample of more traditional couples. However, as Russell points out, this proves nothing about the effect of shared caregiving on satisfaction (either up or down) as no data were collected before the change to that lifestyle was made. It seems unlikely, though, that continual and unresolved sources of upset, grievance and resentment will leave marital satisfaction undamaged.

The research I have discussed here makes clear that there can be barriers to confronting the difficult issues that arise after the arrival of children: feeling that one 'ought not' to have negative feelings, that one doesn't 'have the right' to negotiate inequities, not being sure exactly what's fair, feeling economically vulnerable, not wanting to lose control over the childrearing process, being uncertain as to what one is supposed to do anyway.

The first step to overcoming barriers, in my view, is to recognize that they are there in the first place. Some men and women may be in the early stages of facing them; others may not have done so yet. There is no question that either way there is still a long way to go.

We have seen how there can still be difficulties even in couples where a man does do a fair bit of housework and childcare. Other research supports this. In one American study of middle-class married couples, for example, the more husbands did their house-and-child bit, the more they felt resentful and the more wives felt guilty.[33] This was despite the fact that the wives were still doing far more than the husbands, whether the wives worked or not.

The notion that children are women's responsibility more than men's is still, even as we approach the 21st century, doing its deadly work.

So, indeed, is inequity in carrying out household chores. A British study published in 1989 found that far fewer teenage boys than teenage girls reported doing their stuff with the dustpan and mop.[34] So the new generation is being trained in the old ways.

The dashing of women's expectations about chore and child-care sharing will, of course, be even greater if they return to work themselves. To have to manage the day-to-day practicalities of life with both adults working and one or more children to be coped with as well strains the system, and it is women who are experiencing the greater pressure.[35] Love, sad to say, doesn't get the carrots peeled or Jemima off to her ballet class.

It would help a great deal if society provided better assistance with childcare and flexibility in working arrangements for both men and women, but those days are not yet here. Having money to pay for help can make life a great deal easier – but many people, of course, are not so lucky.

Nevertheless, there are ways of negotiating imbalances between the sexes. Life does not have to be a series of increasingly bitter cries of 'And when did you last clean the loo?' and 'Well, you couldn't change a plug without incinerating yourself'. To deal with this situation appropriately requires the communication and conflict skills discussed earlier. For example, if one spouse is having a particularly busy time at work and feels the other needs to do more chores/childcare, this needs to be stated calmly, clearly and explicitly. 'I'm going to be desperately busy on the new "road bridges for hedgehogs" campaign for the next two weeks. Do you think we could discuss how to organize the housework and take James to tap dancing and Joanna to her martial-arts-for-tots class?'

This is an 'assertive' approach to the problem, which involves making one's feelings known without attacking the other.[36] It has a greater chance of success than a 'passive' stance, where people don't express their feelings for fear of offending or disturbing the other. 'Gosh, I've got such a lot to do. Erm . . . oh well. Better go and put on the chicken supreme and read James a story and staunch Joanna's blood flow where she put her hand through the kitchen window and get that stain off the floor.' (Sigh.)

The assertive style is far more likely to bring home the psychological bacon than the 'aggressive' tactic. 'You know I've got a hell of a lot to do, checking the maximum length of hedgehog prickles to calculate the width of the bridges, how high above the ground hedgehogs can walk without getting vertigo and tumbling off, fighting off nature-hating motorists, the works. You never do any bloody work in the house and you've got to do it now.'

Attack and unconstructive criticism are big no-nos for effective negotiation.

Without negotiation, serious resentments may develop underground that may then burst out in destructive ways. Division of housework and childcare are classic areas of conflict. Couples may also seriously disagree over methods of childrearing, and this has been associated with likelihood of divorce.[37] Sometimes disagreements may be so fundamental that no amount of talking will solve them – but undoubtedly many more trouble-causing issues can be thoroughly explored and resolved between couples than are done at the moment.

Psychologist Cary Cooper, who specializes in stress, suggests that sometimes negotiation could actually be semi-formal. He outlines a strategy that may come in useful for dual-earner couples with children in particular:

Step 1. Prepare balance sheet of work and home commitments (listing details of hours spent, tasks undertaken, etc.).

Step 2. Call formal family meeting to share concerns and detailed balance sheet.

Step 3. Renegotiate various family commitments.

Step 4. Create mutual action plans for the next three months, which are agreed by all family members.

Step 5. Review success or otherwise of action plans at the end of three-month period.

Step 6. Develop new action plans based on experience of previous one. Continue process until all parties are more or less satisfied with arrangements.[38]

Negotiations are crucial even where there are no children. Women in full-time employment still retain major domestic responsibilities, and could still therefore benefit from negotiation about chore sharing, whether they are parents or not.[39]

The practicalities of life are very important, but another

facet of the dual-earner lifestyle[40] that matters is how each spouse feels about the other's work. Research has found that in 'high quality' dual-earner marriages, the couples 'had similar perceptions of the importance of careers and of the wife's stress level'; 'husbands *listen* and are *sensitive* to their wives' work-related problems, activities, and achievements'; the couples maintain a reasonably satisfying social life despite time constraints; and husbands approve of their wives' employment.[41] As two American sociologists describe it: 'The majority of husbands in dual-career marriages are initially very supportive of their wives' career goals. In many instances, however, this level of support diminishes over the years. Researchers found that for wives in happy marriages the support had often increased, while in unhappy marriages it decreased or was a mixture of support and sabotage ... Intimacy is most likely to be enhanced when the dual-career partners perceive themselves as having equal support for each other's work.'[42]

In 'low quality' dual-earner marriages, not only is there less acceptance and approval of the wife's work, but also husbands underestimate their wives' stress levels, don't listen or are insensitive to their wives' work difficulties and successes, and there's a lack of social activities.

These features which distinguish low from high quality marriages are ones which can be worked on and talked over by the couple involved. 'Tell me all about how Scoggins pinched your best idea, darling, then let's ring Bill and Jane and go to the cinema. The popcorn's on me.' Not too impossible, surely?

There is obviously a difference between a 'career' where the nature of the work really matters to the individual, and work where it's done for other purposes – primarily to make money. I am using the phrase 'dual-earner' to cover both types of situation. Even though the meaning of the work itself differs in the two set-ups, this does not alter the need to negotiate conflicts, and to understand the other's work problems and stresses and so on.

The point is that any aspect of one's spouse's – and one's own – behaviour and attitudes can be discussed and negotiated. As the British psychologist David Fontana puts it, 'Often even well-established partners . . . are unaware of how deeply their behaviour is troubling other family members, and of how it is often possible to change this behaviour, especially where there is the promise that other people will respond by changing in equally helpful ways.'[43]

It is not the dual-earner lifestyle *in itself* that is the problem. Research finds that whether or not wives are employed as such is not related to the reported marital satisfaction of husbands or wives.[44] Although it can bring conflict, having both husbands and wives working can also be beneficial. Apart from any personal and financial satisfactions, it can provide them with similar experiences and concerns.[45] What is important is how the couple *deals* with the situation. It can be difficult, and many couples are clearly not yet coping – the increasing number of dual-earner families has, indeed, even been blamed as the main culprit of the rising divorce rate.[46]

I have had cause to write about the problems of dual-earner couples before, and I stand by what I said then:

'It seems to me vital, in the course of your negotiations, to build in time for pleasure, fun, friends and interests. Sleep, work and domestic drudgery isn't exactly a high-quality mixture. Building in some time to *talk* to each other – about work problems, gossip, whatever – isn't a bad idea either . . .

'For women, the currently overburdened ones, the benefits of sharing responsibilities are obvious. For men, though it might mean more domestic work and childcare, it could also bring a more rounded, involved and happy lifestyle, with a less stressed and perhaps happier marriage, and the chance to develop – through sharing the messy and difficult as well as the delightful bits of child-rearing – as a responsible human being.

'And women must not feel guilty when men do what is, after all, only their fair share. You have just as much right to a satisfying and successful career as your partner; and, more than likely, you both need the money, too. As for male resentment, probably the best way to deal with it is to drag it out into the open. It should eventually wither away under the harsh light of scrutiny.

'There is no way that family life is ever going to revert to the "traditional" pattern. With time, perhaps men and women will stop expecting things of themselves and each other that are unrealistic, and start taking *joint* responsibility for their lives together.'[47]

Even though marital satisfaction can drop when there are children in the home, in either dual or single-earner families, this is not inevitable. Two of the biggest ways children can strain a relationship are by decreasing couples' time together and leading to feelings of dissatisfaction with how the household labour is divided.[48] Couples can take action by coming clean about feelings, talking through difficulties and resolving inequities, by allocating time for themselves to be together alone, and by giving themselves space to have fun – and to make love. Only by facing up to the fact that children can place strains on a relationship do couples have the best chance of minimizing them.

So far I have talked a lot about talk. Now I'm going to focus for a while on making love. The possible effects of having children on parents' lovemaking is obviously only a small part of the story, but the physical expression of love in long-term relationships is a topic of all-consuming interest. I used often to find that when I told person A that I was writing a book about the psychology of male–female relationships, they'd turn to person B and say '*Hey*, she's writing a book about sex!' This was then followed by giggles or guffaws, according to taste.

Sigh.

But of course sex does matter. And now its turn has come.

EIGHT

Sex

Love does not, sadly, guarantee a good time in bed. Nor will love alone remove any sexual difficulties.

Harsh, but true.

Sex is an area which can cause great anxiety. Men in particular feel pressure to 'perform'. People worry about whether they're making love 'enough'. They fear that sexual excitement with a partner can't possibly last, that he/she will get increasingly bored with them – and they with their partner – as the years pass, until having sex has the rarity value of a singing lizard.

However, looking at what we know about frequency of intercourse, pessimism about the inevitable collapse of one's love life in a long-term relationship is not justified. It does seem to be the case that frequency declines to an extent, but this does not mean that it disappears.

One study, for example, looked at frequency of intercourse per month after marriage. This showed a lot of lovemaking for newlyweds, which then dropped a bit and plateaued out for about fifteen years before falling again:

Time after marriage	Frequency per month
1–2 mths	17.2
3–6 mths	13.4
7–12 mths	11.6
2 yrs	9.5
6–15 yrs	9.4
16–20 yrs	6.8
21–25 yrs	5.6
26+ yrs	4.8[1]

Of course, sex surveys are notoriously difficult to do. Are people telling the truth? Is it really a random sample?[2] Nevertheless, the finding of some fall in frequency of sex over time seems to be a consistent one.[3]

There could be several factors operating here. One researcher concluded that the reasons for a decline after the first year of marriage fell into four major categories: 'birth-control and pregnancy-related reasons; children; work; and familiarity (including settling into a routine)'.[4] External stresses, such as exhaustion from overwork and lack of privacy, can depress lovemaking.

At older ages, the physiological changes of the female menopause and of later aging have been cited as possible reasons for the decline in sexual activity. However, there is some evidence that it may be more psychological (for instance, mistakenly believing that the menopause means the end of sex) than physiological. Even if there are physiological changes, they may not be that bad. The much-discussed and fretted-over 'vaginal dryness', for instance, in fact troubles less than 10 percent of women; and while a greater number report some loss of vaginal lubrication, lubricants to compensate are available. Some of the changes of the later years, such as shrinkage of the vagina, are actually lessened if intercourse still takes place regularly.[5]

For men, too, physiological changes take place at older ages. For example, erections tend to develop more slowly and hold for less time.[6]

However, there is not necessarily any reason at all for the elderly not to have an enjoyable sex life. As an American psychologist specializing in human sexuality, Janet Shibley Hyde, puts it: 'While sexual behaviour and sexual interest do decline somewhat with age, there are still substantial numbers of elderly men and women who have active sex lives, even when in their eighties.'[7] Other researchers agree: 'If a couple has had a satisfactory sexual relationship through years of marriage, the chances are that they will be able to continue to experience mutually rewarding sexual activity in their retirement years also. The physiological changes that occur with aging need not hinder sexual enjoyment.'[8]

As the British expert John Bancroft points out, a simple catalogue of the physiological changes which can occur due to aging – less marked vaginal lubrication, slower erections and so on – might sound gloomy. But, 'It is important to realize that for most this process is extremely gradual, allowing a couple to adjust to a less intense, less frantic but not necessarily less enjoyable form of sexual activity.'[9] Concern about declining performance (and such concern would be much less if everyone realized this was a typical part of the aging process) can do more damage to the sexual relationship than aging itself, Bancroft says.[10]

I think this is a terribly important point. As the years pass, there may be a bit less of the 'can't wait to get to the bedroom what are kitchen tables for' routine. But this doesn't mean sex cannot still be most pleasurable, and one should certainly not start *worrying* that sexuality may change a bit over the years.

What's more, it must be stressed that any findings about, say, frequency of intercourse, are averages only. There is enormous variability among couples. Another study, a major American survey of happily married couples done in the 1980s, illustrates the point.[11]

Looking at a sample of couples who had been married for up to two years, for two to ten years, and for over ten years, frequency of sex was as follows:

	Married up to 2 years	Married 2–10 years	Married over 10 years
Once per month or less:	6%	6%	15%
Once a month to once a week:	11%	21%	22%
One to three times a week:	38%	46%	45%
Three times a week or more:	45%	27%	18%

As you can see, although there is a shift to less frequent lovemaking overall, there is huge variation and sex is still a frequent event for many couples even after at least a decade. And, as mentioned earlier, some couples are still making love in their eighties.

But, of course, frequency of intercourse is not a guide to how happy each couple is with that frequency or to how much both parties are really enjoying it when they do do it.

Although some people may worry about whether they have sex 'less than the average', averages – as we've seen – don't mean very much here and shouldn't be a source of concern. Not doing it five times a night? Don't worry about it . . . What is important is not frequency *per se*, but whether that frequency is more or less than either partner would like.[12] A serious mismatch in sex drive can lead to dissatisfaction on the part of one or both partners – but this doesn't mean the imbalance can't be accommodated.[13]

As we saw in the last chapter, lovemaking can drop after the birth of a child. There can be many reasons for this. For example: fatigue; vaginal bleeding or discharge; fears of wakening the infant; painful intercourse as a result of an episiotomy.[14] Frequency of intercourse – which tends to drop during pregnancy – rises slowly back to prepregnancy rates for many couples during the first year after the birth.[15] But a year after the birth, a British study found that as many as 40 percent of women and 38 percent of men still felt that having a child had adversely affected their sex lives.[16]

Taking it all in all, the evidence is that even if the frequency of lovemaking declines over the years, a couple with a good sex life are not doomed to lose it. Lots of reason for optimism there. However, it is important to face the facts that (a) it *can* run into trouble and (b) for some couples, it may not have been all that good in the first place.

Let's take a look at some of the sexual problems that can occur.

Sexual problems

It's very hard to know the extent of sexual problems in the general population. Researchers criticize each other's definitions of the various problems,[17] people may not always tell the truth, and samples are often not representative. What does seem agreed, however, is that sexual difficulties are quite common. More importantly for my theme – why love isn't enough – is that a couple can still have sexual problems even though they love each other.

Details of the types, causes and treatment of 'sexual dysfunction' are enormously complex and outside the scope of this book.[18] The most popular classification of sexual disorders is into the general categories of desire, arousal and orgasm. (Of course, people can have difficulties at more than one stage.)

Both men and women can experience problems with sexual desire (feeling uninterested in sex), women somewhat more often than men. At the arousal/excitement stage, women may have difficulty becoming aroused; men may suffer from impotence, now referred to as 'erectile dysfunction' in the trade because it has less negative connotations. It means being unable to get an erection or to keep it long enough for intercourse, or having difficulty in doing so. At the orgasmic stage, men may have no trouble getting an erection, but may have trouble with ejaculation – most often ejaculating prematurely. Some women, even if sexually aroused, are unable to reach – or have difficulty reaching – orgasm (this is termed 'orgasmic dysfunction' or 'anorgasmia'). Rarer occurrences are problems such as vaginismus, where the muscles of the vagina go into involuntary spasm and impede or prevent penetration; and retarded ejaculation. This means the man, though he has an erection, cannot ejaculate – or has difficulty ejaculating – during intercourse. (This may occur even when he is able to do so if stimulated by hand or mouth.) Some individuals may have a 'primary' dysfunction, i.e. they've always had this particular problem; others will have a 'secondary' one, where the person at one time did not have the problem, but does now.

It is worth saying that something is a problem only once people feel it is. Some people apparently have sexual difficulties and yet say they feel satisfied with their sex lives. In one study of 100 married couples who were not currently seeking therapy, some degree of sexual dysfunction was reported by nearly two-thirds of the women (mainly difficulties in getting excited and in reaching orgasm), yet only a fifth of them said they were sexually dissatisfied.[19] 40 percent of the men reported some sexual dysfunction – mainly premature ejaculation – but only a third of them were sexually dissatisfied.

Again, this study was not of a representative sample and the precise percentages shouldn't be taken too seriously, but it does make the point that sexual dysfunction as such doesn't always equal sexual dissatisfaction. The researchers themselves concluded that it wasn't the absolute level of sexual functioning but the 'affective tone' (emotional tone, that is) of the marriage that determined sexual satisfaction. Other research, too, supports the idea that there's a distinction between performance and satisfaction.[20]

Presumably some individuals with a specific difficulty are still getting a number of rewards – physical expressions of love and affection, cuddling, stroking, perhaps orgasm in ways other than by intercourse, tenderness after lovemaking, and so on. Equally, apparently, 'some men and women complain of sexual dissatisfaction despite the fact that motivation, arousal and climax are relatively unimpaired' – because, say, the person feels sex is boring or the partner isn't sufficiently attractive.[21]

A couple where each partner has a low sex drive is not going to be troubled by a low frequency of lovemaking as other couples might be. At the same time, overly high expectations might make people think that they have a problem when others might not see it as such. Most women, for instance, don't have an orgasm every single time they make love. Most men will on occasion fail to get an erection. What can turn these quite natural occurrences into a full-blown problem is anxiety about future performance, which then inhibits it – and lo, the person's fears have come true.

The causes of sexual difficulties are legion, and within each individual several factors may be operating. The problem may be partly or wholly organic (physical). Painful intercourse ('dyspareunia'), for example, for either men or women, quite often has some physical cause. Diabetes mellitus and certain drugs, amongst other things, can sometimes cause erectile dysfunction. Sometimes both physical and psychological factors may be involved, for instance where a physically-caused difficulty is greatly exacerbated by anxiety about it.

There might be psychological causes that lie back in the person's past. For example, a repressive home background where sex was regarded as 'dirty'; being sexually abused as a child; or sexual trauma as an adult, such as rape.

The causes may be to do with the individual's current circumstances, and be nothing to do with the partner. The person concerned might, say, be feeling stressed, depressed or exhausted because of external factors such as overwork, anxiety about money, or a recent bereavement. Or the occasional 'failure', as already mentioned, may make sex a source of anxiety. To illustrate the point, one British study found that, in their sample of men who agreed to fill in a questionnaire, 68 percent of those reporting untreated problems with erections said the difficulty had righted itself without help.[22] And the most common reason according to the men themselves, cited by just over half of them? 'Stopped worrying about not getting an erection.'

Both men and women may fear sexual 'failure' ('performance anxiety'). Men in particular seem at risk of holding overly high expectations of themselves. One British study compared a group of men referred for sex therapy with a matched group (matched for age, educational and cultural background, length of relationship and religion) of men who had a regular partner and had never sought help for any sexual problems.[23] The men seeking therapy believed more strongly in certain sex myths: that 'In sex, as elsewhere, it's performance that counts'; 'On the whole, the male must take charge of and initiate sex'; 'A man always wants and is always ready to have sex'; and 'Sex equals intercourse'. The men seeking help were also less likely to believe that 'An erection is not essential for a satisfying sexual experience' and 'Good sex need not necessarily include orgasm'.

A set of unrealistic internal pressures like that is certainly not going to help matters.

It may sometimes be that the cause lies in the current situation, and is to do with the partner – but not in an emotional sense. It may simply be that the person experiencing the problem is not receiving enough sexual stimulation. Many women, for example, complain of too little foreplay.[24] Men do not always know that women often take more arousing than men do, they don't know about the clitoris and its 'fantastic erotic potential'[25] (the clitoris has a larger number of sensitive nerve endings than the vagina), and they think physical penetration should automatically be enough to get any woman excited any time.

Wrong . . .

However, there is help available and it is a great shame that more people don't take advantage of it. Not only do book shops heave with helpful books on sex, but medical help and individual therapy are there if that is what's required, and sex therapy is available for those who would like it. Sex therapy won't always work,[26] but how sound the couple's relationship is in the first place is an important element in increasing the chances that it will. The British psychologist Maurice Yaffé, when talking about 'presenters' (those who seek help, which usually involves carrying out specific exercises at home as well as attending the therapy sessions themselves), put it like this: 'In general, positive outcome in sex therapy is directly related to high motivation for change, presence of a co-operative partner . . . good non-sexual relationship and commitment to the relationship, perceived physical attractiveness of presenter to partner and good exercise (homework) practice at home.'[27] What matters is not so much the occurrence of a sexual problem in itself, but how the couple cope with it.

Looking at the evidence so far, then, it is clear that lack of love is not necessarily the cause of sexual problems (nor can the presence of love always cure them). However, sometimes, of course, that is what's behind it all: the sexual problem may have occurred because the relationship itself is in difficulties. Sexual desire, for instance, might well suffer. It's pretty hard to make love to someone with a whoop and a holler if, say, you're boiling with anger and resentment. In recognition of this, couples who go for sex therapy may receive marital therapy as well.

I'd like now to look at the issue of sex the other way round. We've seen that lack of love need not be the cause of sexual problems, although it can be. But can sexual unhappiness damage love?

The role of sexual satisfaction in long-term relationships

Anyone who wants simple answers in the sphere of human relationships is doomed to disappointment. The answer to the question of whether sexual dissatisfaction can damage a relationship is: sometimes it does and sometimes it doesn't.

We know that 'Many studies have found an association between sexual satisfaction and marital happiness.'[28] Close, intimate marriages tend to have satisfactory sex. And indeed, as the social psychologist Steve Duck writes, 'Many married couples regard their sexual activity as prompted more by love than by pure sexual desire.' He adds, interestingly, that 'people kiss far more during sex if their overall relationship is working well.'[29]

Not such good marriages are more likely to have less pleasurable sex. But the fact that two things are linked says nothing about what is causing what, as we know. It is certainly the case that marital misery can affect sexual functioning. Psychologists also think that the reverse can occur, and sexual problems can damage the relationship.[30] Often the two may influence each other to such an extent that it's hard to say what was the original cause.

But couples can have sexual difficulties without necessarily being miserable with their marriage. In one study of British men, for example, 'The presence of erectile and/or ejaculatory difficulty was related to sexual dissatisfaction but not to ratings of relationship happiness.'[31] This does not mean it will be true for all men, of course. No research findings can be generalized to that extent, and also this was a sample of, on the whole, 'a remarkably happy and sexually satisfied group of men'. But the findings make the point that it *can* be true. 'Obviously,' the researchers say, 'relationships can still be rewarding in spite of sexual "performance" problems.'[32] Indeed, the British psychologist Maurice Yaffé wrote: 'Although the relationship between sexual dysfunction and marital conflict may be causal, a good sexual relationship is neither a necessary nor a sufficient component of a satisfactory marriage.'[33] So the sexual dysfunction may cause marital damage, but it won't always.

There is evidence from a couple of studies that marital distress and sexual dysfunction are more strongly related in men than in women, although the samples were small.[34] And again, this says nothing about causality. The researchers who carried out one study concluded, 'It seems likely that ... some marital problems result from sex problems, some sexual problems result from marital problems, and sometimes a common extraneous factor causes both.'[35] They believe a particularly common loop is that marital unhappiness leads to a lowering of male sexual desire for the partner, perhaps leading to erectile dysfunction, and this exacerbates the unhappiness. They found that 'For women, the level of marital discord is higher when their partner has a sexual problem than when they have a problem themselves.'[36]

Precisely why there is this sex difference in the strength of the link between marital and sexual misery is a matter of conjecture. It is not the case, as the stereotype has it, that the average man has a more powerful sex drive than the average woman.[37] One possibility is that 'Male sexual performance may be more susceptible to marital problems, and consequently aggravate the situation, while female sexual dysfunction may be less intrusive as far as the relationship is concerned.'[38] Or sexual satisfaction may, for some reason, be more important for marital satisfaction for men than women. As British social psychologists Michael Argyle and Monika Henderson put it: 'There is some evidence that for men sexual satisfaction leads to marital satisfaction, while for women the reverse is true.'[39] (This doesn't mean of course that sexual gratification is *all* that's necessary for men to be happy with their marriages! Just that it may play more of a role for them.)

It seems also unfortunately to be the case that physical attractiveness continues to matter more to men than women throughout the marriage. One study of married men and women found that those husbands who believed their spouse had declined in physical attractiveness – specifically, had put on weight and/or had somehow worsened in body shape – while they themselves had not (i.e. it was relative, not absolute, decline that mattered), were more likely to report sexual problems, particularly their own lack of interest in sex.[40] This was not true for wives. However, a man's appearance isn't completely irrelevant. Steve Duck writes: 'In a significant number of cases in which a couple has little sex, one or both partners attribute this to the fact that they do not find the other physically attractive.'[41]

It is possible that men unhappy with their spouse sexually are more likely to say that the other is declining in attractiveness, of course. But, as the researchers of the above study point out, 'This cannot . . . gainsay the conclusion that attractiveness and sexual relationships in marriage are more closely tied for men than women.'[42]

It looks, tentatively, as though women may put less weight on sex than do men in determining how happy they feel with the marriage – and that, perhaps, their partner's overlarge belly plays less of a role than it does for men. But this does not mean, of course, that sexual satisfaction and the partner's attractiveness *don't* matter to women.

We don't know precisely under what circumstances sexual trouble will make marital trouble, although not feeling able to talk about it and solve the problem constructively may well be a factor.[43] The tragedy of it is that if unhappiness in the sexual arena can sometimes hurt a loving relationship, very often this need never have happened. Early talk about the issue, for instance, could have stopped the rot. If the damage has already occurred, steps can still be taken: we saw in the last section that help is available for specific sexual difficulties. But even an OK sexual relationship may run down on passion power if boredom sets in; and an OK sexual relationship may well have the potential to be a great deal better.

Enhancing sexual pleasure

For some couples, sex can be routinized to extinction. The 'It's Saturday night, lights out and missionary position, dear?' syndrome.

Aaargh.

There's a difference between making sure one makes time for sex – which may be particularly important, say, with children around – and doing it only on certain days and in precisely the same way.

The two key issues in enhancing one's sort-of-OK (stifled yawn) sex life are communication and knowledge/imagination.

Psychologists have been known to say that the main reason they think sex therapy works – when it does – is because it has actually encouraged the couple to *talk* to each other.[44] In one British study of men with erectile difficulties, the top cause – according to the men themselves, mentioned by nearly half of them – was 'unable to talk to partner about sexual matters'.[45] But communicating about sex is just as important when there's no specific difficulty. We have already seen that communication is a vital part of a happy relationship.

The psychologist Janet Shibley Hyde has analysed communication techniques in the context of improving a sexual relationship.[46] The basic idea is that it's vital to understand what the partner enjoys, and for one to convey to him or her what one enjoys oneself. Often, too, people don't know what they really enjoy, and the other person can help them find out.

It is a strange and unfortunate truth that most people find it hard to talk about sex with their partners. As I pointed out earlier on, human beings seem to regard the physical act of sex as less intimate than talking about it.

Hyde's analysis of techniques applies to communication about any topic; I have already discussed the central ideas involved in effective communication. But the difficulties in communicating about sex can be so great that I think some tactics in particular are worth emphasizing and illustrating here.

Levelling and editing: The first – and often hardest – step is to 'tell your partner what you are feeling by stating your thoughts clearly, simply, and honestly'. Your partner needs to know what you want and need, what you like and don't like. However, levelling has also to be accompanied by a bit of editing out of things that would deliberately hurt your partner or are irrelevant. Being straight does not mean blurting everything out regardless of a partner's feelings. Sexual performance is an area where people are especially sensitive, and they don't want to be told they have the sexual expertise and sophistication of a dogfish.

Good messages: Using the word 'I' is less likely to put the partner on the defensive than using the word 'you'. 'I feel a bit unhappy because I don't often have orgasms' is better than 'You never give me orgasms'. And 'You're a hopeless lover, I never have orgasms' is – see above – a disastrous line to take.

Hyde points out that '"I" language' avoids mind-reading, which, you may remember, is also a good move. She gives as an example of mind-reading: 'I know you think women aren't much interested in sex, but I really wish I had more orgasms.' The poor man may not think that at all. Even worse, someone may be mind-reading and not even try to check it out with the partner, and have got things quite wrong.

Hyde also suggests that 'documenting' – giving a specific example of the problem – may help the other to understand, particularly if it's accompanied by a concrete suggestion about what the other could have done. She cites an instance of this technique: 'Last night when we made love, I enjoyed it, but I didn't have an orgasm, and then I felt disappointed. I think what I needed was for you to stimulate my clitoris with your hand a bit more. You did it for a while, but it seemed so brief. I think if you had kept doing it for two or three minutes more, I would have had an orgasm.'

Listening: As with all good communication, it's vital actually to attend to what the other is saying rather than concentrating on what you're going to say or wondering if you're going to get to the dry-cleaners in time. Restating what you think the other meant back to him or her, as I discussed earlier, will also clarify matters.

Validating: 'This means that you communicate to your partner that, given his or her point of view, you can see why he or she thinks a certain way. It doesn't mean that you agree with your partner or that you're giving in. It simply means that you recognize your partner's point of view as legitimate, given his or her set of assumptions, which may be different from yours.' Making clear that you understand even if you don't feel the same way makes it possible at least to discuss it and perhaps make some progress. Perhaps, say, the loved one has fantasies it would be interesting to hear about? After all, one's partner may have special feelings about hanging from chandeliers that one could at least consider.

Positive communication: As Hyde quite rightly points out, discussing difficulties isn't the only thing that matters. It's also important to give the other person some positive feedback. Occasionally saying 'That was simply wonderful, my toes tingle and I've think I've lost the use of my knees' gives a partner a terrific boost. Relying totally on gasps and groans to make one's feelings clear isn't really enough . . .

Other than good communication about sex, I regard the other crucial factor as the 'knowledge/imagination' axis. Making love, like most other human activities, is something one can learn about and acquire skills for. After all, we hardly burst into the world with a gene marked 'full sexual knowledge' nestling smugly in our interiors. Often couples could have a considerably better time in bed if they acquired greater knowledge. In fact, if you remember the training programme for premarital couples which I discussed in Chapter 6, parts of it involved 'sensual/sexual education' and communication skills.[47] The results showed that three years later, not only was marital satisfaction higher than in couples who hadn't been through the programme, but sexual satisfaction was higher too.

There are books galore on sex to be had, and in my view it's a pity sales aren't even higher than they are. In addition to the information they contain, Janet Hyde suggests that sex manuals can be used for 'breaking the ice'. If a couple read the book and discuss it together, it may help them to raise specific topics − such as oral sex − that they've been too shy to talk about. What's more, they may discover techniques they hadn't heard of. (How much a couple are in agreement over specific sexual preferences has been found to be related to marital satisfaction[48] – but couples may not know each other's preferences if they don't talk about or indicate what they are.) One's own imagination can help too. To suggest something to a partner and ask if he or she would like to try it could enhance sexual enjoyment a treat. The partner might never have known, say, that being licked behind the ear was quite so erotic if it had never been tried . . .

But it's also important not to go to the other extreme, and start building up huge expectations of oneself and the other person. Sex isn't going to be great every time, the earth will sometimes remain stationary, and the whole enterprise isn't supposed to become *work*, for goodness' sake.

Although it's possible to have a not-brilliant sex life and yet feel happily married, (a) sexual dissatisfaction *may* (though it won't necessarily) wreak some damage and (b) why in any case shouldn't one have a better time sexually if it can be managed? Good sex won't do one's love relationship any harm, that's for sure. This is not to say that good sex will guarantee a happy relationship – indeed, some couples may continue to have satisfactory sex until the day they separate.[49] Sex isn't the only thing in marriage that matters, as we have already seen. The British sex therapist Martin Cole rightly says, 'Sex does not necessarily lead to affection, nor its absence alienation.'[50] But it's reasonable to assume that sexual and marital happiness – and unhappiness – may often feed into each other. Sex is a part of a long-term relationship that matters to many people, and often steps can be taken to improve it. Don't spoil the ship for a ha'p'orth of sex talk.

Extramarital sex

It is not only sex that matters in committed relationships, but sexual exclusivity too. The breaking of the implicit (sometimes explicit) 'exclusivity clause' of the love/marriage contract – adultery, infidelity, whatever you want to call it – is a strand of human life guaranteed to have people agog. It is a major theme of novels, films, plays and gossip; and it's a big draw.

The reasons are that (a) there is a lot of it about, (b) it can happen to anyone, and (c) if it does, it can mean the loss of the primary relationship in which a person has invested a great deal. It intrigues people because they want to know why and how it can happen, different ways of dealing with it and what might be the result. It's frightening in its implications – and, if one is the person contemplating it, may be alluring in what it can offer.

There have been a number of surveys on the frequency of extramarital sex, but there are usually problems with them. In particular, the samples may not be representative of the population as a whole, and some people may be reluctant to confess to such behaviour. Perhaps the most famous surveys, those of Kinsey and colleagues in America in the late 1940s and early 1950s, found that about 50 percent of men and 26 percent of women admitted to extramarital intercourse by the age of 40.[51] However, these samples included a lot of divorced people, who are more likely than the still-married to have been unfaithful.

That research is also dated. More recent work implies that whatever the precise percentages (two British surveys in the 1980s, for example, found 26 percent of men and 30 percent of women admitted to extramarital sex[52]), the numbers of women who are unfaithful are catching up with the men.[53]

I don't personally think the precise percentages matter that much. The fact is, it can happen, and it's not that infrequent. A quick scan round one's own group of friends – or even closer to home? – will probably make that amply clear. This is despite the fact that if asked, the majority of people in Western cultures such as Britain and America will say that extramarital sex is wrong (although more Americans say this than do people from

Britain and some other Western European countries).[54]

There are signs that the old double standard – where extra-marital sex was deemed more 'acceptable' for men than for women – may be on the way out.[55] A couple of studies of American men and women, for example, found that infidelity is disapproved of for *both* sexes, and 'showed that marital dissatisfaction is generally regarded as the only justifiable reason for engaging in an extramarital affair . . . To do so more than once is, however, not as acceptable or justifiable.'[56] So the idea that it's, well, understandable – and therefore to be condoned – if a man 'just wants a bit of a sexual adventure' may be expiring in its tracks.

Yet even though infidelity is widely regarded as wrong, it is pretty widely indulged in. So what is going on here? Most crucially, what exactly does marital love, or lack of it, have to do with extramarital sex?

Yet again, there is no simple answer. The main causes of infidelity that people identify are:

> dissatisfaction with the marriage
> sexual dissatisfaction
> wanting variety/experimentation
> excitement
> revenge against the partner/anger/jealousy
> ego bolstering
> agreement between the couple that it's OK[57]

The stereotype that extramarital sex is just about sex is untrue. Although of course it can be,[58] the evidence is that, for men as well as for women, sexual dissatisfaction with one's spouse is not always the main cause of sexual straying. In a British study of just over 100 men who agreed to answer questions on close relationships and sex (who tended to be better-educated under-45 year olds), 18 percent admitted that they were currently having an affair outside their main relationship.[59] Compared with the men not having affairs, they were significantly less happy with their permanent relationship, regretted it more and found their permanent partner less sexually attractive. Of course, it's impossible from these findings to say whether the unhappiness caused the affairs or vice versa. Often both may occur and be difficult to untangle.[60] But what's interesting is that reporting that they were dissatisfied sexually with their main relationships was *not* related to the likelihood of these men having affairs. Again, in an Australian study looking at dating, cohabiting and married couples, 'lower love scores' were associated for both men and women with having had sex with someone other than the partner since the start of the relationship.[61]

However, one still can't tell what's causing what – whether lack of love leads to an affair or, as these Australian researchers say, 'liaisons outside the primary relationship seem to dilute that love'[62]. Undoubtedly both can happen. But the idea that unhappiness in the marriage, rather than urges for greater sexual gratification, can frequently lead to infidelity is supported by evidence that the unfaithful often emphasize other aspects of their extramarital relationship – such as feeling loved and wanted, self-discovery, talk.[63]

These are all generalizations, however. All one can say with any confidence is that lack of love may often be the main cause of an individual's infidelity, a fact which can be obscured by the common image of adultery as no more than a failure to control sexual lusts.

But if a failure of love can trigger infidelity, more central to my theme of why love isn't enough – and more alarming – is the fact that researchers agree that it *is* possible for a person to be unfaithful to his or her spouse while being happily married.[64] This is probably more the case for men: it seems that women are more likely than men to be unfaithful because of unhappiness with the marriage,[65] and men are more likely than women to have had extramarital sex without emotional involvement.[66] Women, compared with men, seem more influenced by the possible risks that infidelity will involve – for instance, to their main relationship, of pregnancy, of guilt – and they see those risks as more likely to occur.[67] Women who are unfaithful also tend to have fewer adulterous liaisons than do unfaithful men.[68] Women often have more to lose by adultery (such as a greater chance of relative poverty and the struggles of single parenthood if the husband finds out and decides to leave, never mind the risks of pregnancy). So for them, marital dissatisfaction is likely to be the prime motive for infidelity more often than it is for men. Any less important motive may simply not be worth the risk for many women.

But if a lack of love is not the cause of an individual man or woman's adultery, then what might be? It may be, as already mentioned, that the person wants some variety and excitement. It may be that the couple have an agreement that extramarital flings (but perhaps not love affairs[69]) are OK. It may be that the person who strays simply does not regard sexual exclusivity as essential to a marriage. He or she could be having a midlife crisis. Or going through a bit of a difficult patch in a basically good marriage (and, say, is feeling angry with the partner or needs a boost to the self-esteem). Or is feeling sexually dissatisfied. Or the unfaithful could have some internal difficulties which they choose to deal with by having affairs. Or . . .

One could go on. Adultery is an extremely complex phenomenon. The word itself covers a variety of activities, from a one-night-stand on a business trip to a prolonged and loving relationship. Although an opportunity presenting itself is a bit of an essential start, the reasons for taking it are probably multifarious.[70] Behaviour is usually, as one social psychologist puts it, 'multiply determined',[71] and simple answers probably simple-minded.

The fact that love isn't always enough to stop a partner – or oneself – being unfaithful is not a reason to throw in the towel, turn one's face to the wall and wonder why one bothers. If you look back at the sample of reasons I have given as to why love isn't always a protector, you will see that they are not all inevitable. If there is love but unsatisfactory sex that, as we have seen, is dealable with. If either partner is feeling rough – a mid-life crisis, a sticky patch – then communication and conflict skills can help to talk it through constructively. For more serious internal difficulties and unhappiness, professional help is available if necessary. If a partner feels life is passing him or her by and their wrinkle and eyebag quotient is increasing daily, then it's time for a bit of creative thinking: dragging them into bed more often, going for an exciting holiday, discussing job changes, taking up paragliding.

If a partner feels that extramarital sex isn't a threat to the marriage contract, this is something that should be discussed – and ideally, should have been made clear at the beginning. In a study of nearly 600 British women and men who agreed to take part in research on adultery, respondents were asked to recall 'agreements or pacts either implicit or explicit which sample members felt they had with their spouses when they married'.[72] The results showed less infidelity when both partners were clear that they were expected to be faithful than when the matter had not been discussed and was a bit ambiguous. This in turn was linked with less infidelity than when partners agreed that sexual fidelity was not essential and they could be 'free'.

There are, in other words, things to be done that could help to prevent unfaithfulness in the presence of love, if that is what is wanted. Equally, if it does occur, a good relationship to begin with might heighten the chances of dealing with what has happened in a constructive way. (This assumes that the infidelity is discovered or disclosed, of course. The British adultery study mentioned above found that a straying spouse is more likely to tell the partner than the partner is to discover evidence of the affair.[73] In some cases, a partner may never know.) To be constructive means exploring what has happened, not laying months' worth of blame and anger on the other person until they can't bear it any more. Understanding why it has happened in one's own unique case makes it possible to come up with solutions and agreements to stop it happening again.

This is not to deny the great pain, hurt and jealousy that the revelation of a loved partner's infidelity is likely to bring. But, if the betrayed partner decides the relationship is still worth fighting for, then accepting that the other is not perfect, understanding the reasons and taking steps to deal with them might help to restore a feeling of power and control as well as to minimize the chances of it recurring.

The destruction of trust in a partner is a major issue here. But again, if the reasons for the infidelity were other than lack of love and are dealable with, and particularly if the strayer makes strong attempts to be reassuring about his or her love, that should increase the chances of negotiating a way through the crisis. One study of styles of conflict resolution about a partner's infidelity found that being maritally satisfied was associated with a problem-solving approach. Other styles – avoiding the issue, being soothing, being aggressive, compromising – were all linked with dissatisfaction.[74] (Problem solving over infidelity does not mean, however, that the wounded party shouldn't initially make their feelings very clear before attempts are made to sort things out.[75] Being incredibly nice immediately may not be the way to probe and resolve the issue, and must be a hell of a strain, too, I should imagine . . .) But again, one doesn't know what's causing what. It may be that initially strong marriages are most likely to use the conflict-resolution technique that has the greatest chance of success; or that problem solving can help to restore the marriage. Probably both are true.

It may, however, turn out that the disruption to the marriage is too great. Or it may be that an extramarital relationship develops to such an extent that it damages the marital one, even if the marriage was not unloving.[76] Furthermore, no matter how much he or she professes love, if partners have internal difficulties that lead to them being persistently and incorrigibly unfaithful, then an individual who is suffering greatly over this has to decide whether to persuade their partner to seek some therapeutic assistance or start helping them to pack.

I have been talking mainly about a partner's unfaithfulness, but of course the same issues apply to one's own. It may often be that infidelity is a way of dealing with issues in the relationship that would be better dealt with through talking and problem solving. That would make sense of one Dutch study's finding that three quarters of a sample whose marriages or live-in relationships broke up after infidelity (80 percent unfaithful themselves, 86 percent had an unfaithful partner) didn't cite 'found alternative, more significant relationship' on their part as a reason for breaking up.[77] They were much more likely to refer to difficulties in the marriage. (American research, too, has found that fewer than 30 percent of those who'd been unfaithful and were divorcing said their infidelity had a major or even a moderate effect in causing their divorce. A partner's infidelity, on the other hand, was far more often rated as significantly influencing the break-up.[78]) Perhaps if these difficulties had been dealt with earlier, disaster might not have struck.

Indeed, the Dutch study compared 44 individuals in relationships where one partner – or both partners – had been unfaithful but the couple had stayed together, with 44 individuals who were in partnerships where there had been infidelity and they had broken up. The researcher, social psychologist Bram Buunk, looked at those who were either married or cohabiting (so he investigated what he calls 'extradyadic' – dyad means a pair – rather than just 'extramarital' relationships), and where partners knew about the other's infidelity. The two groups were matched on factors such as the number of children (the presence of offspring raises the psychological costs of a break-up), educational level, age, sex and length of relationship.

The main factor distinguishing the two groups was that those who split up reported being significantly more dissatisfied with their relationships. While it's possible that this was just a face-saving way of justifying what had happened, Buunk still believes the findings suggest that outside relationships have a relatively high chance of threatening the main one when it isn't that wonderful anyway, and that lack of wonderfulness may have motivated them to become sexually involved with other people in the first place. This fits with other research, as we have seen, and with another finding of this study. Namely, that those who split up after infidelity were more likely to be disapproving of long-term extradyadic relationships. So if such people are unfaithful, particularly if they become involved in a long-standing affair (as opposed to a brief fling), they are only likely to do so if extremely dissatisfied with the main relationship. The findings, Buunk says, 'do not support the assumption that extradyadic relationships alone pull a person away from the primary relationship,'[79] although with small and select samples it remains possible that 'The direct pulling impact of extradyadic relationships on primary relationships could be more powerful than is suggested by this study.'[80] Nevertheless, the point remains that, as one might expect, a weak relationship is more vulnerable than a strong one to the potential pull of a third person.

As British social psychologist Robin Goodwin describes it, there is 'a large body of data indicating that if an individual feels that he/she can obtain more satisfaction from leaving his/her present relationship (either to form a new relationship or to remain single) then he/she will do so, provided that the interpersonal *costs* involved are not prohibitive, and that the perceived future *benefits* are sufficiently attractive ... A number of writers have suggested that relationship alternatives are likely to be of greatest importance when commitment and satisfaction in a relationship is poor.'[81]

Ideally, those who contemplate infidelity might be better off examining exactly why they want to do it, and whether or not there is something that can be adjusted in their main relationship that would make them less likely to give in to the temptation.

However, it may sometimes be that it is the extramarital relationship itself that clarifies feelings about the main relationship, be they good or bad.

There is no doubt that infidelity can be a threat to the main relationship. But some unfaithful partners report that the extramarital relationship benefits – or has not harmed – their marriage. However, psychologists now think that such statements, while sometimes accurate, are likely often to be either a rationalization or a failure to see what is actually happening to the marriage.[82] Such a comforting view would probably be completely untenable if the infidelity were revealed. In studies where people were asked to rate various contributions to an intimate relationship, the most negative (apart from alcoholism) was unfaithfulness.[83] Another study found that infidelity was judged to be one of the most upsetting things for either sex to have to deal with in a relationship.[84]

Adultery may also place stresses on the third party, an interestingly under-researched phenomenon.[85] The stereotype of the third party is of the female bimbo, possibly with a dash of wicked cunning or a- (or im-) morality. However, we have no evidence that third party IQs are lower than the average, nor their morals lower and cunning higher than anyone else's. The third party will by definition very frequently be a man (thus making it excessively irritating that the language has no word for a male 'mistress'), may already be married him or herself, and have his or her own complicated reasons for entering a relationship (or having a fling) with a married person. Difficulties all round will be at a maximum if the extramarital affair develops into a love relationship.

There is no guarantee that any individual will never be unfaithful. However, the elements involved in nurturing a relationship which I discussed in earlier chapters may minimize the chances of it happening to oneself or a partner, and those chapters also offered techniques for dealing with it – or having a good go at doing so – if it does happen.

But it may be that the infidelity has occurred because the marriage or committed partnership is already headed seriously for the rocks. I want now to focus on this situation: where the relationship is in trouble and people may wonder what, if anything, can be done to mend matters.

NINE

Repairing Relationships

Two people can love each other and keep going for really quite a long time – but then find things start to go wrong. They are standing on either side of a crack in the rock – and as it creaks slowly open into a chasm, it seems unstoppable. Indeed, they may not notice the gap until it is perilously wide.

Rather than let go of the myth of the power of love, at this point people may often reconstruct history[1]: 'Well, maybe I/she/he never really loved him/her/me.' But they probably did.

So what is happening here? And what can be done?

The possible causes are legion; and each break-up will usually spring from a whole complex of reasons, not just one.[2] If the relationship is seriously in the doghouse quite early on, then it's very likely that the two people, in getting to know each other a lot better, have discovered that they're not as similar or as suitable as they thought they were. In which case, even if already married, they may decide to hop it and cut their losses rather than hang around trying to repair the relationship. Or they might have married not for love but for some other reason – a pregnancy, to get away from home, whatever – and may find their motivations to make the relationship a goer really rather weak.

In long-standing relationships, the causes could lie, crudely speaking, in the relationship itself and/or in one or both of the individuals involved and/or in external circumstances such as serious stress, a job move and long periods spent apart, something like that (although, of course, such events need not wreck the relationship; it depends how the couple cope).

It may be that the relationship has become less rewarding for one or both parties. In distressed couples, as we saw in Chapter 6, cycles of negative actions and reactions often seem to have been set up. Happy couples are more likely to be affectionate, supportive, positive, attentive, to try to understand the other's point of view and resolve issues, and to say potentially negative things themselves in a neutral or pleasant way: 'I do find it a bit of a shock when I find your used socks in the bath, darling' rather than 'Your habit of dropping your niffy socks in every conceivable container is disgusting, and while we're on the subject . . .' The happily-paired are also more likely to respond positively to negative statements or actions by the partner. This can be difficult for people, mind you, but responding constructively – and, especially, stopping themselves reacting destructively – is more likely to happen in satisfied and committed relationships.[3] In unhappy couples, neither partner manages to inhibit their destructive impulses and reactions. They carp, complain, criticize, and react to anything negative said or done by the other with the psychological equivalent of a sharp bite on the leg. Thus matters spiral downward.

While diminishing feelings of love for the partner can be the cause of that sort of cycle, as one would expect, the danger is that individuals may inadvertently set up such cycles even though they would say, if asked, 'of course' they love their partner.

It is illuminating that research finds married people to be more polite and considerate to strangers than they are to each other. In one study, married couples were observed talking to each other, and also each spouse was observed interacting with a stranger.[4] Married couples were more negative and less positive to each other than they were to strangers. They tended to agree and express approval to strangers, and were more likely to complain to and criticize spouses. The differences between behaviour to the spouse and to a stranger were more pronounced among the distressed couples. But what I find most interesting is that that pattern was present, in a milder form, even in happy couples.

Even taking into account the fact that people may be unnaturally polite to strangers, there is a big difference between feeling one doesn't have to watch every word with someone and making criticizing and complaining a permanent fixture of one's married life.

The trouble is that marital satisfaction is associated with expressing positive, rather than negative, feelings and information[5] . . .

One can imagine that a habit of treating one's spouse in rather unrewarding ways might develop without the person even realizing that he or she is doing it.

The danger is that once people feel 'Phew, I've got 'em', they think they can just completely relax about the whole thing. The other person 'must know I love them', and now I've got to get on with the rest of life. Paying the milkman, shampooing the dog, arguing with my mother, trying to make sure my boss doesn't give that promotion I want to Blenkinsop, the little toad.

A study making the point rather vividly looked at changes in the frequency of affectionate behaviour in the first year of marriage.

Are you ready for this? In the first year of 'wedded bliss':

Your partner	
approved or complimented you	30% less often
did or said something to make you laugh	34% less often
said 'I love you'	44% less often
initiated sex	39% less often
did something nice for you	28% less often

The two of you

had sexual intercourse	38% less often
shared physical affection (apart from sexual intercourse)	39% less often
shared emotions, feelings or problems	34% less often
talked about day's events	6% less often[6]

Now, one would expect a lot of these sorts of behaviours during the courting period, and a bit of a drop once the individuals have officially committed themselves may be fine. What I feel is a danger is that (a) the drop looks as though it may often be rather large and (b) the level of affectionate behaviour, while it may flatten out for some couples, for others the drop may continue on downwards.

Similarly, non-constructive ways of dealing with conflict might accelerate; and conflicts and problems in the relationship that remain unresolved have the potential to push a couple further and further apart.

A rather strong image of how relationships may become hollow over time is provided by Robert Sternberg's triangular theory, which I discussed earlier – where love is seen as composed of three elements, passion, intimacy and commitment. Each element has dynamic qualities, and so certain types of shift in one or more of them may torpedo the whole thing.

As social psychologist Robert Baron describes it: 'Sternberg's theory . . . suggests that over time the passion component of love generally decreases. This is hardly surprising; most persons know that such strong feelings simmer down over time. More surprising is the possibility that intimacy, too, sometimes decreases. Over the years, many couples stop communicating with one another, since they feel that "they've said it all already". Further, they may be pulled by different careers into different patterns of experience, and each may come to feel there is little to discuss with their mate. If the third component – the couple's decision that they are still in love and are committed to maintaining their relationship – does not increase, the result may be a gradual erosion of love and a deterioration of their relationship.'[7]

Intrinsic to Sternberg's theory is the fact that the reasons for the widening rift may sometimes be less to do with the conduct of the relationship than with changes within one or both of the individuals involved. People can change over the lifespan,[8] and can 'grow apart'. New learning experiences, developing interests, self-discovery may all serve to make the person who was once a good match not quite such an obvious one any more. It may be that the way two people's lives have developed – perhaps they are doing very different jobs, or one is at work and one at home – makes them feel they no longer have much in common. A spouse may simply become gradually disaffected with the other person – perhaps he or she is not behaving as (and/or the relationship is not providing what) the spouse wants and expects. Innumerable difficulties can arise, as we have seen. Boredom, for instance. As Robin Gilmour, a British social psychologist, quite rightly says: 'Couples . . . need to inject variety into their joint experience. Holidays, new ways of sharing sex, exploring new sports, hobbies and studies together are all useful strategies. Change that involves them both can help a couple to avoid, on the one hand, the strain of growing apart through a growing dissimilarity, and, on the other, the boredom of knowing so much about each other that there are no stimulating surprises.'[9]

There are also some individuals who lack social skills, or who have internal problems of some kind – perhaps being clinically depressed, or alcoholic, or violent, or fearful of intimacy. If such a person has nevertheless succeeded in acquiring a partner – or if the problem develops after the relationship has been going for a while – there may come a point when that partner feels that he or she cannot carry on, that the costs are too great. (This is not inevitable, of course, but the couple may need professional help if they wish to avoid breaking up and to improve their quality of life.)

The forces that bind people into relationships are not just those to do with love. There are also, to name a few, companionship (even if the relationship isn't that brilliant), security and familiarity, fear of being unable to find a better alternative, the presence of children, feelings of moral obligation, being bound into a social network of relatives and mutual friends, financial and often property ties. These other forces may be strong enough to keep a couple together, not very happily, for their whole lives (not the ideal fate for a pair of human beings, I must say). But we know that despite the fact that there are numerous barriers to the dissolving of a long-standing relationship, particularly a marriage, many people will do it nevertheless. Individuals may not always recognize the barriers until they are actually contemplating ending the relationship.[10] For some people, though, I suspect it may be that the presence of these barriers lulls them into a false sense of security; the relationship may feel so buttressed that they take its stability for granted.

The British social psychologist Steve Duck thinks that a typical pattern when things are going wrong is for one person to start feeling unhappy with the situation first, and to start brooding;[11] analysing the partner's behaviour, weighing up the rewards and costs of the relationship, assessing alternatives to staying in it. The other person may not fully realize what is going on – although the unhappy partner may 'begin to communicate the problem indirectly at first, by means of hints or "needlings"'.[12] He or she may then start secretly moaning to bar staff and strangers on trains or other third parties who won't rush off and tell the partner all about it. You might know when dating partners are withdrawing from a relationship – they stop phoning when they say they will, they want to spend less time with you, they appear distracted and want to talk about superficial topics.[13] But in a longer-standing relationship, it may be that sometimes communication has dropped to such a low level – in quantity, in expressed affection – and the individual is taken so much for granted, that the extent of his or her disengagement from the relationship may not be as obvious to the partner as one might expect.

But eventually the unhappy person will have to decide what, if anything, to do about it. And he or she won't automatically decide to try to repair it.

Before I look at what people do do, it's worth saying at this point that there are some relationships which (a) are not worth saving and/or (b) cannot be saved. The notion that a committed relationship, once entered, must be clung on to regardless of cost may sound noble but is, in my view, foolish. Equally, committed relationships may sometimes break up when in fact they (a) were worth saving and (b) could have been saved. Some British research on divorced and divorcing men and women found that in 11 percent of one sample of cases *both* the husband and wife said they wished they had remained married.[14] (28 percent of the women and 51 percent of the men in one of their divorced samples said they would have preferred to stay married – this does not mean, however, that many of these marriages could have been rescued.) The researchers also discovered that many people struggle on for a long time in their marriages before finally giving up.

Once someone has become aware that they're no longer happy in the relationship (this could happen even though they still feel they love the partner[15]), what might he or she do?

Reactions to dissatisfaction

A dissatisfied partner has a variety of options. Slinging one's underwear and favourite egg cup with 'a souvenir from Bournemouth' stamped on the bottom into an overnight bag is by no means the only recourse. American psychologist Caryl Rusbult and her colleagues have grouped responses to relationship misery into four main types, two of which they regard as destructive to the relationship and two constructive. 'Exit' and 'neglect' involve actively damaging the relationship or else passively allowing things to get worse; 'voice' and 'loyalty' refer to trying to improve the relationship or waiting for it to get better by itself. The researchers give illustrations of the various types of response:

'*Exit*: Separating, moving out of a joint residence, actively abusing one's partner, getting a divorce, threatening to leave, or screaming at one's partner;

Voice: Discussing problems, seeking help from a friend or therapist, suggesting solutions, changing oneself, or urging one's partner to change;

Loyalty: Waiting and hoping that things will improve, supporting the partner in the face of criticism, or praying for improvement;

Neglect: Ignoring the partner or spending less time together, avoiding discussing problems, treating the partner poorly (being cross with him or her), criticizing the partner for things unrelated to the real problem, or just letting things fall apart.'[16]

Research so far has concentrated more on what makes people likely to choose one option rather than another than on which has the greatest chance of repairing the relationship.[17] Perhaps unsurprisingly, those who felt more satisfied with the relationship before the problems started, who have invested a great deal in it (in terms of, for instance, time, self-disclosure, emotion, shared possessions and friends) and who see the difficulties as fairly severe are more likely to go for the 'voice' alternative. High satisfaction overall, and high investments plus not regarding oneself as having any very good alternatives to staying in the relationship (such as another possible partner, or spending time with friends, or liking the idea of being single again) makes 'loyalty' more likely. Dissatisfaction, lower investments, seeing the problems as serious and that one has attractive alternatives promotes the 'exit' response (which isn't necessarily actually to leave, but could be to think about or threaten it, or to do something else that is actively destructive to the relationship). 'Neglect' occurs more when the person hasn't been feeling very satisfied with or invested in the relationship – and doesn't really know what to do about it and isn't motivated to do much anyway.

People's personal characteristics will affect which option they choose, too. There is evidence that being a woman or else 'psychologically feminine' regardless of sex – that is, being warm to others and concerned with maintaining relationships – makes voice and loyalty more likely. Being 'psychologically masculine', and more focused on instrumental activities such as careers and completing tasks than on relationships, is linked with exit and neglect. Men tend to react neglectfully more often than women – the evidence on whether they are more likely to kick the relationship in the teeth is equivocal.

Clearly, many more factors than these will determine what option an individual chooses at any one moment (and how long he or she spends on it), and indeed a person may go through all of them at various times, or even combine two or more responses at once. What these findings make clear is that 'voice' – the only tactic I would regard as an attempt to repair matters – is by no means certain to occur. Although evidence on effectiveness is sparse, it unsurprisingly indicates that voice and loyalty produce more favourable outcomes than do exit and neglect. Actively harming the relationship or neglecting it until it collapses are by definition not going to do a lot for it.

It may sometimes be, however, that – particularly with a relationship of long standing – the turmoil, disruption, ambivalence and pain as it begins to dissolve may make people have second thoughts. They're suddenly experiencing all this emotion after, perhaps, a long period of feeling nothing much at all. So they think 'Well, perhaps I'm not as sure about this as I thought I was'. At that point they may try to repair matters – if, of course, too much damage has not already been done.[18]

But while 'voice' has at least a chance of mending matters, what Rusbult and her colleagues label as the other constructive act – 'loyalty' – doesn't sound very constructive to me. It's true that they've found that, 'When a partner engages in exit or neglect, couple functioning is enhanced when the individual "bites the bullet" and reacts with voice or loyalty, inhibiting impulses toward exit or neglect. For example, consider an individual who returns home at the end of a tough day and interrupts the partner's attempts at conversation with a rude "just be quiet for a while". Muttering "you're a real joy" is unlikely to improve the situation; it is more adaptive for the partner to react by calmly shrugging it off or asking, "Do you need to talk about your day?"'[19]

Loyalty – 'shrugging it off' – may be fine if the partner behaves badly occasionally because, say, they're under stress at work. But consistent bad behaviour, whether it stems from outside stressors or from unhappiness with the relationship itself, is unlikely to improve by being ignored. Sure, loyalty may keep things on an even keel for a while longer, but, as Rusbult herself recognizes, possibly at some cost to the person keeping quiet. The risk of accumulated resentment, at the very least, seems to me pretty high. Indeed, Rusbult admits that it's too soon to be confident about the value of the various responses – or combinations thereof – for dealing with difficulties.[20] But what started out as minor problems may, in my view, grow with time if not attended to. Weeds in the garden of love have a nasty tendency to grow a bit wild and start choking the more healthy plants.

It is not, of course, the case that people don't have strategies for maintaining and repairing relationships. They do. What is interesting is that nearly all the strategies people list as ones they use for repair purposes they also use for maintenance: talking, spending time together, and so on. In a study of 50 married couples, the only strategy used significantly more for repair than maintenance was 'talk about the problem'.[21]

The trouble is that the repair strategies have to be targeted at the problem, and have to begin before it is too late. The arrival of problems *in itself* is not a reason to think there's no hope. Rusbult and her colleagues' exit/voice/loyalty/neglect model does not assume that the relationship is 'on the road to dissolution . . . this approach deals with normal reactions to periodic and potentially reparable problems'.[22]

Sometimes, however, the relationship *is* heading for the rocks, and may be near enough to bark its shins. If an unhappy partner already feels that he or she no longer loves the spouse and doesn't feel motivated to repair the relationship, then nothing may work. In the study on people's strategies, the researchers found no relation between the number or type of either repair or maintenance strategies used and marital satisfaction. This does not mean that such strategies cannot benefit relationships, but that they will not always. It may be too late, or they may be wrongly targeted.[23] Trying to talk to the partner when he or she doesn't think what you are saying is interesting, or spending more time together going to dinner parties when the partner is bored with your friends, is not going to help.

To have the best chance of repairing a damaged relationship requires understanding of two issues. First, how one's thinking about the relationship can be altered. Second, how one's style of communicating with the partner can be shifted into a mode which will offer a greater chance of sorting things out. This assumes that both partners *want* to sort it out. As I have pointed out, this will not always be the case: the disaffected partner might not wish to. Both partners may be fed up with the relationship, so there's even less momentum in the system to drive people to take positive action. The person who in fact was relatively happy may have difficulty in dealing with the situation once he or she becomes aware of the other's unhappiness. This will be particularly so if the unhappiness is such that the partner makes it clear he or she is thinking of leaving. The more-happy partner may then not feel motivated to try to make a push to save things. 'The mere realization that one's partner doesn't wish to continue creates relational spoilage,' writes one social psychologist, 'that is often sufficient evidence that the relationship is no longer worthy of continued investment.'[24] It may well be a time of considerable difficulty, pain, hurt, guilt and ambivalence all round. But greater love before the problems started to make themselves felt raises the chances of repair attempts – and also makes them worth a try.

Thinking about the relationship

I have concentrated so far very much on what people *do* in relationships. However, a partner's response to a particular action isn't just an automatic reflex: partner A is late, partner B is angry; partner A makes a surprise booking for dinner at that new French restaurant round the corner, partner B is pleased.

How partner B will react depends upon what he or she *thinks* about what partner A has done. There are, for example, several possible ways of reacting to partner A being late for dinner, which now resembles a charred lump more than anything edible. Partner A will provide an explanation – I was held up in an important meeting and couldn't get to a phone, the traffic was terrible, the office gerbil suddenly keeled over and we had to give it an emergency funeral, whatever. Partner B may then proceed to interpret the lateness as, say, *really* a sign that the other is selfish, unreliable, puts work first, doesn't love them any more, or some other internal aspect of the person; or interpret it as a function of external circumstances that aren't destined perpetually to recur. Shame about the gerbil, all flesh is grass; the traffic is sometimes unexpectedly dense; I know what it's like when Scoggins chairs meetings, it's only possible to escape by shouting 'Fire!'

Psychologists have found that there are clear differences between distressed and nondistressed couples in how they regard each other's actions.[25] In unhappy couples, individuals are more likely to attribute the other's negative actions to factors that are internal (due to the person themselves), stable (unlikely to change) and global (likely to affect many other situations in the marriage too – late home from work one day, will forget my birthday the next). In distressed marriages, the spouse is particularly likely to attribute responsibility to the partner for his or her actions (in terms of being worthy of blame, having negative intent and reflecting selfish concerns), such actions having fallen short of the spouse's expectations.[26]

Unfortunately, when the spouse does something nice, like booking that restaurant, in distressed marriages the partner is more likely to attribute it to something external (determined by the situation/outside factors), unstable (temporary) and specific to the situation (and unlikely to influence many other areas of the relationship) – such as 'he/she must have had a particularly good day at work today/there must be a special offer on snails'.

In happy marriages, the reverse pattern of attributions is more likely to occur. So a partner's less-than-wonderful actions will be put down to something external and unstable (and less global) – 'the poor lamb is having a terrible time at work/I think if his mother rings up one more time to remind him to wear his thermal underwear he's going to crack completely'. A partner's positive actions, in contrast, will more often be put down to internal, stable causes, which are beneficial for many aspects of the marriage. He/she booked the restaurant because he/she is thoughtful, kind, considerate, fun-loving, spontaneous, loves me. (Such attributions may occur mainly for positive actions that are unexpected. Routine niceness on the other's part may not be thought much about by the spouse, because such behaviour is expected. So there can be a risk that the partner, even in a happy marriage, begins to feel unappreciated. The occasional 'I know how hard you work to make me happy, and I do appreciate it' might help to prevent such an unfortunate shift . . .[27])

So we can see that in satisfied marriages, partners are thinking about the other's actions in ways that are likely to keep them (the partners) happy. In dissatisfied marriages, spouses are thinking about each other's behaviour in a fashion that means the other person can't win. This helps shed some light on the fact that in unhappy marriages, there are often 'long chains of negative interchanges',[28] and on how couples can gradually feel pushed further and further apart.

Now, of course, we come to the inevitable question in much of this research – what's causing what here? Is the counterproductive style of thinking about what the other does the cause of marital dissatisfaction? Or is it the other way round? Or is some third factor responsible? One can repeat the questions with the benign pattern of attributions and marital satisfaction.

Research is at too early a stage to be sure about the answers. However, it does look as though the counterproductive style of attributions may follow from marital dissatisfaction; *but* may also cause it (and similarly for benign attributions/satisfaction). In one study, how wives made attributions for their husbands' actions predicted how satisfied they were a year later (even after taking into account how satisfied they felt at the beginning of the year).[29] In this research the finding did not hold true for husbands. This may be, the researchers speculate, because women are 'more concerned with issues such as attachment, intimacy, and caring than men are',[30] and are a bit quicker to take the temperature of a relationship. However, there isn't enough evidence to make any strong statements about sex differences in how important different patterns of attributions are. I would be surprised, myself, if future research found much in the way of sex differences. A variety of patterns of attributions are, after all, something both sexes do demonstrate within marriage (and attributions are associated with husbands' *current* satisfaction, even if they didn't – in this study at least – predict later satisfaction).

I don't want to imply that there is just the one pattern of making attributions for a partner's actions. One study has found that a rigid way of making attributions is more characteristic of unhappy marriages.[31] They're more prone to the negative behaviour = bastard/positive behaviour = aberration style of thinking. In happy marriages, partners have more complex patterns. So although overall their patterns of attributions are significantly more benign, that doesn't mean that they won't sometimes think bad action = personal fault/good action = can't rely on that happening again . . .

I do not want to imply, either, that the attributions made may not be perfectly correct. The partner may indeed be a selfish, thoughtless, unloving beast. But the point is that a person's attributions may often be distorted. They can then affect that person's actions, which may have an impact (possibly a negative one) on the partner's feelings and behaviour. If he or she is late, and you are – in the latecomer's view – unjustifiably angry, he or she is not going to be too happy either.

Although the experimental evidence may be in the early stages, many psychologists feel sufficiently confident that they're on to something here to have developed an approach called 'cognitive marital therapy'[32] as part of a variety of therapeutic techniques to help couples in trouble. The view is that getting couples to examine their patterns of thinking about each other's actions, and checking whether or not they are distorted (in any way, not only in terms of attributions), and working on them if so, can be valuable.

Evidence of the effectiveness of helping couples to examine how they interpret each other's actions is sparse. There is a bit of evidence that cognitive therapy by itself can improve marital adjustment.[33] But studies which have compared therapy focusing on a couple's behaviour with therapy centred on behaviour *and* thinking patterns finds both equally effective. Still, one cannot conclude that looking at patterns of thinking adds nothing, because in these studies the couples were assigned randomly to the two types of therapy. In other words, the couples were not matched to type of therapy according to their needs.[34] Distortions of thinking will not be a problem for every couple in distress. As I have said, A might conclude that B is selfish, inconsiderate, uncommunicative, or whatever, and be perfectly correct in this conclusion.

However, given that any action can be interpreted in a variety of ways, that habits of interpreting actions negatively could well be set up, and that interpreting actions negatively could affect one's own feelings and actions which could then impinge badly on the partner, I regard it as highly plausible that for some couples, distorted thinking may play a serious role in the cracking apart of their relationship. Unrealistic expectations of the partner and relationships, for example, could help to set up just such a pattern;[35] failing properly to communicate and explore why a partner has behaved in a certain way, and just *assuming* that one knows why, may well maintain it.

One of the founders of cognitive therapy (which has been used most extensively for treating depression and anxiety), the American psychiatrist Aaron Beck, does – perhaps unsurprisingly – claim that couples can be helped by it.[36] He gives an instance from his own experience of how distorted thinking that remains unrectified can do damage:

'Ken and Marjorie, both busy in their careers (he sold insurance, and she was a secretary in a public relations firm), had decided to spend more time together. One Saturday Marjorie told Ken of her plan to spend the afternoon shopping. Ken, wanting to be close to Marjorie, immediately decided to accompany her. Marjorie, after a particularly frustrating day reviewing the books of a large and complex company, interpreted this as an intrusion (thinking, *"He never lets me do my own thing."*) She nevertheless said nothing to Ken and was quiet during the entire shopping expedition. Ken interpreted her silence to mean that she didn't care for his company, and he became angry at her. Marjorie reacted to his anger by withdrawing even more.

'The facts of the situation were that (1) Marjorie *did* want to spend more time with Ken but wanted to shop alone; (2) she failed to communicate this to Ken; (3) she misinterpreted his overture as an encroachment on her freedom; and (4) Ken misinterpreted her withdrawal as a sign that she did not enjoy his company.

'Numerous, repeated misunderstandings, such as those between Marjorie and Ken, and the resultant mutual anger will erode the foundation of a relationship. I have observed several times that similar misunderstandings escalate to the point of no return. What is remarkable, however, is that if partners catch the misunderstanding and correct it before it goes too far, they can head off the storm. Cognitive therapy is designed to help couples do just that – to clear their thinking and communication so as to prevent the misunderstandings from arising in the first place.'[37]

The Ken and Marjorie example is an excellent illustration of how patterns can be set up that will serve as a rift in the lute. And we know what happens to rifts within lutes.

It is the little rift within the lute,
That by and by will make the music mute,
And ever widening slowly silence all.[38]

Tennyson.
Aaron Beck would have liked him.

Cognitive therapy is a complex process and cannot be self-administered. A couple who wish to repair their relationship may, indeed, often be wise to seek professional help. There is no shame in this. We have seen what a complex, delicate plant relationships are – and we know how frequently they collapse.

It is not my aim to describe in detail everything that might be done in cognitive therapy, but rather to point out the fact that distorted thinking may well have played a role in the onset of trouble in a relationship, and also in maintaining or exacerbating that trouble. One of the aims of cognitive therapy is to show people how their thinking about their partner and the relationship may be problematic.

Beck gives some examples of problems in thinking:

Polarization. This is 'either-or' or 'all-or-nothing' thinking. So if a partner is slightly less loving than usual, say, you conclude they don't love you any more.

Overgeneralization. Making sweeping statements on the basis of a small number of events. 'If your spouse interrupts you, he or she "always" interrupts you. If your spouse shows some disrespect, he or she is "never" respectful.'

Tunnel vision. Picking out one detail of an experience and screening out the rest. One can just imagine it: 'When we went for a walk in the park, once he didn't respond when I spoke to him. He's going off me.' Meanwhile the fact that the rest of the outing was full of chat and hand-holding is ignored. The whole event is interpreted on the basis of that one detail.

Personalization. Considering yourself as the source of your spouse's behaviour when it's nothing whatsoever to do with you. 'She's in a bad mood. It must be because she's angry at me.'

Negative (global) labelling. This is where you apply a global, negative label to a person and not just to that person's actions. Beck gives examples: 'He is a weakling because he did not ask for a raise.' 'She is a nag because she wants me to quit drinking.' People can also apply this form of thinking to themselves, he points out: 'I never do anything properly. I always antagonize people. I'm a failure.'[39]

Although it may be necessary to seek therapy, I believe that knowing how one can slide into certain habits of thought, and that these may be counterproductive to the relationship, may in itself be illuminating. To repair a relationship, it might help simply to start examining what one is doing, and try to test if one's interpretations are accurate. As we know, for example, that in distressed relationships positive and negative actions by the other are interpreted differently from in happy ones, it might then be possible to start checking if one is doing that oneself. And if so, when a partner acts in a certain way, to think of several possible reasons for it, and to assess the evidence for and against each reason, rather than just automatically thinking 'Well, he/she's self-obsessed' or 'I bet those flowers aren't *really* for me, it's just that we've got the boss coming for dinner tomorrow and they'll look pretty on the table.'

Equally, since it takes two to tango, one's own partner may need to examine whether he or she is doing the same thing. It may indeed be the partner who is more deeply submerged in distorted thinking than one is oneself.

Discovering what one's partner is thinking cannot be done by mind-reading. Believing it can is in itself a counterproductive expectation, as we saw earlier. Actually opening one's mouth and trying to explore what is happening with the partner is crucial. The Marjorie and Ken example showed two people trapped by distorted thinking and misinterpretation on both sides, with no communication which might have rectified it. If either of them had said something like, 'Why are you behaving like this? Does it mean that you . . .?', that would have given each side a chance to say what they were doing and why. Often, people may have placed such deep and flawed constructions on things that the partner would be horrified to discover what they were. More open talking might have punctured a positive Zeppelin of mistaken thinking.

To repair a damaged relationship, then, exploring and checking out whether distorted thinking is going on may often be an extremely wise move. The problems of flawed interpretations, as we have just seen, will be greatly exacerbated by a failure of communication. Teaching people to communicate more effectively is, indeed, another vital therapeutic technique for helping couples who wish to repair their relationship.

Shifting psychological patterns

For two people to have a chance of pulling their relationship back from the brink, some straight talking is going to be essential. There is no magical formula for repairing relationships, because of the great variety and complexity of possible causes of the damage. For couples who go for professional help, a range of therapeutic techniques are on offer: not only cognitive therapy, but 'behavioural marital therapy', for instance, which focuses on things such as teaching communication and problem-solving skills. Other therapies focus more on aspects like the emotional and psychological baggage partners have brought to the marriage and which might be causing (or contributing to) the problem.

There are certainly things people can try to do on their own (while accepting that the process may be difficult, painful, unfamiliar, and draw angry and/or defensive reactions from one's partner).

Start examining the possibility that one or both partners have distorted views about each other and the relationship.

Try to increase the rewards of the relationship, not the costs. Being especially thoughtful and caring, say, is better than the silence of terror at what appears to be happening.

Try communicating clearly and directly, but in a non-threatening manner, about one's own expectations (often sadly under-discussed and sometimes quite unrealistic), feelings, needs and desires, and try to get the partner to do likewise.

Try expressing disagreement and exploring the roots of conflicts constructively and without putting the other down, which improves the chances of a positive response from one's partner; treating the other's viewpoint as worthy of fair consideration, and making an obvious attempt to listen and to understand it; and then searching for solutions to problems, negotiating agreements and resolving inequities, rather than allowing oneself to be drawn into an endless spiral of bickering, blaming and answering one complaint with another.

If one's life with a partner seems to consist of nothing but the endless practical routines of life – getting Joanna to school, picking up the dry-cleaning after work, loading the washing machine, mending the kitchen tap, shopping, cooking, eating and washing up, watching television (need I go on?), then the time has probably come to inject some novelty and fun into life. A partner who is psychologically associated with nothing but routine and drudgery – and whose sparkle has been greatly diminished by that same routine and drudgery – may no longer be valued as he or she once was. Joint, pleasurable activities – including sex – are, as we have seen, more characteristic of happy marriages. It's easy to find couples who say the last time they did X (X being something they used to love – feeding each other popcorn in the cinema, paddling at Bognor, going to exhibitions of old egg boxes in modern art galleries), was 'gosh, absolutely years ago, come to think of it . . .'

But couples need to work out what has been going wrong. Simply suggesting a trip to the seaside when the spouse is either totally disengaged from you or hasn't spoken to you without an argument for weeks . . . well, frankly, I wouldn't start booking the second honeymoon.

The social psychologist Steve Duck has speculated that in the early stages of a relationship becoming wobbly, good communication might sort it out. Further down the wobbly line, a person may be sufficiently disaffected with the partner that the attributions he or she is making for that partner's behaviour and the state of the relationship may need close examination before anything further can be done. Each person might find it enlightening to assess their own contribution to the current state of affairs too. At a pretty-firmly-on-the-rocks stage, problems have to be confronted and the whole form of the relationship has to be looked at. Is it to survive or not? If it is to survive, how is it to be recreated to provide the best chance of carrying on?[40]

This theory hasn't been tested yet, but it does re-emphasize the point that repair strategies have to be targeted at the problem, and that different strategies may be needed at different times. If constant rowing has started to become the pattern, say, one partner may have to stop the negative cycles by refusing to retaliate when the other says something negative, instead saying something positive or neutral, and making an obvious effort to understand why the other feels that way. If constant silence is the problem, then one idea might be to think about what the other person enjoys doing which he or she perhaps hasn't done for some time – like visiting the fruit bats at London Zoo – and make sure you both go out and do it. If the partner starts to do some pleasurable things, shared with you, which also offer something to talk about, it might be possible to begin gently to ease back out of a downward spiral of silence, sadness and disengagement before it has gone too far. At least it may make it easier to communicate – and thereby easier gradually to get at whatever is at the root of the difficulty. If the relationship has reached such a disaffected stage that the other partner (or oneself) 'can't do anything right', then it might be worth examining how much that is a function of one's own (or the partner's) skewed thought patterns.

But it may well be that some professional help is needed. Ideally, it's better to seek it before the relationship has been ripped to pieces on the rocks, otherwise it may be far too late for any outside assistance to give it even a chance of survival.

And outside assistance *can* work. Studies comparing different types of marital therapy paint a very unclear picture and controversies abound,[41] but any one of them may be worth a try. The 'success' rates of therapy vary in different studies (depends on what measures of success you take and so on), but seem to average around 55 to 75 percent.[42] That is better than simply leaving couples alone to struggle; there is evidence that, in comparison groups of couples who have not had therapy, in only about 30 percent of cases do they improve on their own.[43] However, even these success rates (and often one does not know how long the improvement in the relationship lasts) still leave a fair number of couples in distress at the end of therapy.

But the bottom line for some relationships is that, even given strong attempts at repair, they will not survive. Both parties will then develop an account of the relationship and its break-up to tell both themselves and the outside world. People want to make sense of it for themselves, and to save face in their social networks of relatives and friends.[44]

Break-ups of what were deep, intimate relationships are inevitably painful. It will be worse for a partner who doesn't want it to happen, of course, but the 'one who leaves' will often suffer a lot of grief and guilt. If the partners have children, there are even more difficulties, both emotional and financial (the latter particularly for women).

At this stage, as Steve Duck puts it, it is time for the repair of the individual.[45]

Here friends and relatives can provide strong social support and help. But most important, in my view, is that the stories people tell themselves about what has happened have two elements. The first is *not* to think that because a relationship has broken up, one might as well crawl into a black plastic bag and wait for the refuse collectors to come. In other words, that one is a worthless human being. Most relationships don't break up because one partner is the pits and deserves only to live alone on a desert island and play with the monkeys. They break up because, as I hope I have demonstrated, a great variety of things can go wrong even if both partners started off with high hopes and bursting with love. One of the important ways of getting over break-ups for many people is to try to boost self-esteem, by spending time with other people who value one, and adding up and focusing on one's good points rather than indulging in self-destructive wallows in one's less wonderful aspects. One is but human.

This brings me to the second element that break-up stories should ideally contain. That is, the person's best attempts to work out what might be learned from what has happened. This means that vital lessons in relationships and in self-understanding will not be lost, and that the person can feel optimistic about the possibility of setting up future relationships with a better chance of success. If one has some notion of what went wrong last time, that provides at least some sense of control and – most vital of all – a feeling that with care, it need not happen again.

Conclusion

The charm of romantic myths is that they make life seem so simple. Find partner (probably first glimpsed through the smoke haze of a party-crammed room), partner returns love, wedding with speeches and Auntie Flo losing her teeth in the avocado dip, live happily ever after.

But, as we have seen, love is far from being a superglue. It's like a rope of crystal threads. Keep rubbing and pushing and wearing away at it, and one day it's gone.

Taking care of one's central relationship is probably the most difficult and complex task any human being can face. Yet we are woefully unprepared for it. While we sit at school learning about the jute exports of obscure islands and the reproductive organs of rabbits, a vast area of human concern lies untouched and unexplored.

There seems to be an unspoken assumption that there's nothing to learn. You just, er, *do* it. The mythical power of love has a very great deal to answer for.

The danger is that once a commitment has been made, there's a terrible temptation to relax. Overt expressions of affection, as we saw, tend to drop off. We may fail to anticipate the extent of the adjustments that have to be made – that there will be conflicts, and difficulties in meshing daily routines, assessing priorities, tackling inequities and reconciling differences. The changing role in society of women, in particular, and their developing perspective on what is involved in being 'a wife' or partner also has to be dealt with. Unrealistic expectations on the part of both sexes may do their insidious work. This other person is now *there*, perhaps even regarded as an extension of yourself, and the occupant of a role – 'wife', 'husband', 'partner'. This makes it easy to lose sight of the fact that the other is a unique individual, one who may, at the time of the commitment, not even be very well known or understood. Not as known and understood as one thinks. What's more, people change. As their life develops, so in some aspects will *they* shift and alter.

Without keeping an eye on the other person *as a person*, not just as 'my partner', the occupier of a static role, it is possible to lose sight of what they may want and need. It is crucial to remain vigilant. Not in an excessive, overanxious, 'what do you mean by that?' every five minutes sort of way, but in the sense that the partner's general state of mind and the relationship's health need to be monitored. Complacency can be a killer. Just as too much predictability in the daily routines of life can lead to progressive emotional deadening in the relationship, so thinking you know the other well can be 'a catalyst for cognitive deadening'. As one social psychologist puts it: 'Familiarity breeds overconfidence which in turn can lead to exaggeration of one's knowledge about the other, [and] reduced vigilance in keeping current on information about the other.'[1]

In happy marriages, the spouses are positive and rewarding to each other, and confront and resolve conflicts. In unhappy ones, such reciprocal positive behaviour trails off and all each gets from the other is negatives. Criticism, complaints, ignoring, interrupting, dominating. This sets up a downward spiral, where the two people spin gradually away from each other into a state of total disengagement; or perhaps descend into a locked battle without respite. Sometimes one withdraws and the other fights on, trying to nag and jibe the partner into a response.

If one is to act on the principle that both partners need rewards, one must know what the other does find rewarding. This requires not only an intimate knowledge of him or her, but effort directed towards making sure that rewards are provided. ('Start interesting conversations', for example, is one of the top five requests even in happy couples, when husbands and wives are asked what changes they'd like in their spouse's behaviour . . .[2]) Then there are one's own rewards to consider: does the partner know what makes you happy and what makes you want to bite your knuckles to quell your irritation?

I find it revealing that even in happy couples, people are more prone to complaining and criticizing each other than they are with strangers, to whom they are polite and considerate. Of course the rules of social intercourse put us on our best behaviour with strangers – but the reverse implication, that the partner will take whatever we hand out, is not so healthy. To say one's bit to a partner without reducing their ego to the size of a peanut is one of the skills nobody should be without.

Focusing some attention on one's relationship is, as we saw earlier, more characteristic of women than of men. The social psychologist Caryl Rusbult sums up relevant research findings like this: 'We can characterize the behaviour of females, relative to that of males, as showing greater direct communication, a more contactful and less controlling style, greater emphasis on maintenance/social-emotional behaviour, greater awareness of relationship problems, a desire to confront and discuss problems and feelings, lesser tendencies toward conflict avoidance, a greater desire for affectional behaviour, less emphasis on instrumental behaviour, and higher levels of intimate self-disclosure.'[3]

It is not that fewer men than women want a good, loving relationship, or that men are less capable of love, it is that they are not brought up to value the skills needed to look after it. We have explored enough research on sex differences in this book to make that rather worryingly clear. It makes the whole process harder for everyone. Although men may eventually be released from the rigid prison of their masculine role, this hasn't happened yet. But the bars of men's cage are bending a bit, and the fact that it is possible to talk about feelings and the nitty-gritty of relationships without losing one's 'manliness' seems gradually to be taking hold.

The happy couples seem to be the ones who intertwine themselves with each other. They are positive, kind, helpful and rewarding more than carping and critical; they express affection and appreciation openly; they sort their daily routines in a way which meshes them together as far as possible and which they find reasonably equitable; they don't just express love verbally and non-verbally, but they do loving *actions*, such as making the relationship a priority and making time to be together.[4] Happy couples do things together which they both enjoy, from sex – and loving sex is another binding force in a happy marriage – to hang gliding. Very importantly, they communicate well – the most frequently experienced problem of couples in marital therapy is poor communication.[5]

The collapse of a loving relationship – whether it's a marriage or not, and however long it has lasted – can be one of the most painful experiences a person will have to endure. It would, in my view, be possible to cut down the quantity of human misery in this area of life significantly if we all knew more about what we were supposed to *do* to look after that love.

I also think, however, that we need to examine what exactly the role of love in our lives is. Do we put too burdensome and unrealistic a weight upon it? A warm, companionable, central relationship is, for most people, a crucial ingredient of a happy and fulfilling life – but love alone will not sustain it. A thriving relationship, as I have argued, rests upon far more than emotion. Just as love is only part of a successful relationship, so we should remind ourselves that having such a relationship is only one facet of our potential as human beings. It's vital for our wellbeing not to let too much of our self-esteem and self-identity rest upon being loved by a specific other person, and to get things in perspective. Friends, work, relatives, interests, abilities – all these matter too. The buttresses of our self-esteem and identity can be widespread, rather than centred entirely on a partner: 'If he/she leaves me, I am nothing and my life is over . . .'

This is not true, not unless one makes it so. A relationship that goes wrong can provide useful pointers for the conduct of future ones. But rather than relying on one's past and the advice and experience of friends, I believe that psychological research has a great deal to offer those who recognize that the love bond needs nurturing, and who want some specific clues in the psychological equivalent of a maze shrouded in fog. I hope this book has uncovered a few.

Notes

INTRODUCTION

1. See e.g. Argyle, M. and Henderson, M. (1985). *The Anatomy of Relationships*. Harmondsworth: Penguin. 124; Buunk, B.P. and van Driel, B. (1989). *Variant Lifestyles and Relationships*. Newbury Park: Sage. 24.
2. Lord Byron, *Don Juan*. c.XIII.st.4.
3. Wodehouse, P.G. (1929). *Summer Lightning*. Harmondsworth: Penguin. 92.
4. Rusbult, C.E. (1987). Responses to dissatisfaction in close relationships: the exit-voice-loyalty-neglect model. Chapter in: Perlman, D. and Duck, S. (eds) *Intimate Relationships*. Newbury Park: Sage. 223.
5. *The Two Gentlemen of Verona*, I.iii.84.
6. See e.g. Beach, S.R.H. and Tesser, A. (1988). Love in marriage: a cognitive account. Chapter in: Sternberg, R.J. and Barnes, M.L. (eds) *The Psychology of Love*. New Haven: Yale University Press. 348–349.

1. WHAT IS LOVE?

1. See e.g. Branden N. (1980). *The Psychology of Romantic Love*. Toronto: Bantam. 14–16.
2. Brehm, S.S. (1988). Passionate love. Chapter in: Sternberg, R.J. and Barnes, M.L. (eds) *The Psychology of Love*. New Haven: Yale University Press. 233.
3. See e.g. Cunningham, J.D. and Antill, J.K. (1981). Love in developing romantic relationships. Chapter in: Duck, S. and Gilmour, R. (eds) *Personal Relationships 2: Developing Personal Relationships*. London: Academic Press. 28, 30-31.
4. See e.g. Branden (1980), 22–24; Cox, G. and Dainow, S. (1988). *Making the Most of Loving*. London: Sheldon Press. 37–38; Tweedie, J. (1979). *In the Name of Love*. London: Pan. 27–28.

5. See e.g. Cunningham and Antill (1981), 28–29; Rubin, Z. (1973). *Liking and Loving*. New York: Holt, Rinehart & Winston. 185.
6. See: Douglas, J.D. and Atwell, F.C. (1988). *Love, Intimacy, and Sex*. Newbury Park: Sage. 180–181, 186–187.
7. See e.g. Cunningham and Antill (1981), 29; Marsh, P. (ed) (1988). *Eye to Eye*. London: Sidgwick and Jackson. 228.
8. Rushton, P.(1985). The broken marriage in early modern England: matrimonial cases from the Durham church courts, 1560–1630. *Archaeologia Aeliana*, 13: 187–196; Rushton, P. (1986). Property, power and family networks: the problem of disputed marriage in early modern England. *Journal of Family History*, 11: 205–219.
9. Rushton (1985), 190.
10. Rushton (1986), 216.
11. Branden (1980), 25–26, 41–42; Buunk, B.P. and van Driel, B. (1989). *Variant Lifestyles and Relationships*. Newbury Park: Sage. 145–146; Rubin (1973), 189–190.
12. See e.g. Argyle, M. and Henderson, M. (1985). *The Anatomy of Relationships*. Harmondsworth: Penguin. 119.
13. Kephart, W.M. (1967). Some correlates of romantic love. *Journal of Marriage and the Family*, 29: 470–474.
14. Simpson, J.A., Campbell, B. and Berscheid, E. (1986). The association between romantic love and marriage: Kephart (1967) twice revisited. *Personality and Social Psychology Bulletin*, 12: 363–372.
15. Television documentary "The Women Who Smile", part of the BBC2 series "Under the Sun". Broadcast 14 June 1990, and reported in *The Listener*, 14 June 1990, 12–13.
16. Levy, R.I. (1973). *The Tahitians*. Chicago: University of Chicago Press. (Cited in Sternberg and Barnes (1988), 173; see also 330–331.)
17. See e.g. Buunk and van Driel (1989), 147; Simmons, C.H., Vom Kolke, A. and Shimizu, H. (1986). Attitudes toward romantic love among American, German, and Japanese students. *Journal of Social Psychology*, 126: 327–336.
18. See e.g. Marsh (1988), 228.
19. Tweedie (1979), 32–38.
20. See e.g. Sternberg, R.J. and Grajek, S. (1984). The nature of love. *Journal of Personality and Social Psychology*, 47: 312–329.
21. See e.g. Branden (1980), 40; Fromm, E. (1957). *The Art of Loving*. London: Unwin. 35, 77–78.

22. See e.g. Branden (1980), 40; Fromm (1957).
23. See: Berryman, J.C., Hargreaves, D.J., Hollin, C.R. and Howells, K. (1987). *Psychology and You*. Leicester: British Psychological Society/Methuen. 99.
24. Quoted in: Rubin (1973), 99.
25. Quoted in: Sternberg and Barnes (1988), 14.
26. *Venus and Adonis*, l. 149.
27. Fehr, B. (1988). Prototype analysis of the concepts of love and commitment. *Journal of Personality and Social Psychology*, 55: 557–579.
28. Hatfield, E. and Walster, G.W. (1978). *A New Look at Love*. Lanham: University Press of America. vii-viii.
29. Rubin (1973), 215–216.
30. Rubin (1973), 213–214, 217.
31. Rubin (1973), 216.
32. Rubin (1973), 215, 219–220.
33. Rubin (1973), 222–225.
34. Dermer, M. and Pyszczynski, T.A. (1978). Effects of erotica upon men's loving and liking responses for women they love. *Journal of Personality and Social Psychology*, 36: 1302–1309.
35. Sternberg and Grajek (1984), 327.
36. Sternberg and Grajek (1984), 325.
37. Sternberg and Grajek (1984), 327–328.
38. Hatfield, E. (1988). Passionate and companionate love. Chapter in Sternberg and Barnes. 193.
39. See e.g. Sternberg, R.J. (1988). Triangulating love. Chapter in Sternberg and Barnes.
40. Sternberg, R.J. (1987). Liking versus loving: a comparative evaluation of theories. *Psychological Bulletin*, 102: 340.
41. Sternberg (1988).
42. See e.g. Hatfield and Walster (1978).
43. See e.g. Hatfield and Walster (1978), 124–126; Hyde, J.S. (1990). *Understanding Human Sexuality*. 4th edn. New York: McGraw-Hill. 357–358.
44. Sternberg (1988).
45. Sternberg (1988), 130.
46. Sternberg (1987), 331–345.
47. Sternberg, R.J. and Barnes, M.L. (1985). Real and ideal others in romantic relationships: is four a crowd? *Journal of Personality and Social Psychology*, 49: 1586–1608; and see Sternberg (1988).

2. ATTITUDES TO LOVE

1. Cochran, S.D. and Peplau, L.A. (1985). Value orientations in heterosexual relationships. *Psychology of Women Quarterly*, 9: 477–488.
2. Cochran and Peplau (1985), 478.
3. Rubin, Z. (1973). *Liking and Loving*. New York: Holt, Rinehart and Winston. 220.
4. See e.g. Lee, J.A. (1988). Love-styles. Chapter in: Sternberg, R.J. and Barnes, M.L. (eds) *The Psychology of Love*. New Haven: Yale University Press.
5. Hendrick, C. and Hendrick, S. (1986). A theory and method of love. *Journal of Personality and Social Psychology*, 50: 392–402.
6. Hendrick, C., Hendrick, S., Foote, F.H., and Slapion-Foote, M.J. (1984). Do men and women love differently? *Journal of Social and Personal Relationships*, 1: 177–195; Hendrick and Hendrick (1986).
7. Hendrick and Hendrick (1986), Study II.
8. See: Hendrick, Hendrick, Foote and Slapion-Foote (1984).
9. Hendrick, Hendrick, Foote and Slapion-Foote (1984), 193.
10. Frazier, P.A. and Esterly, E. (1990). Correlates of relationship beliefs: gender, relationship experience and relationship satisfaction. *Journal of Social and Personal Relationships*, 7: 331–352.
11. Hendrick, C. (1988). Roles and gender in relationships. Chapter in: Duck, S. (ed) *Handbook of Personal Relationships*. Chichester: John Wiley. 438.
12. Hendrick, Hendrick, Foote and Slapion-Foote (1984), 193.
13. E.g. Hill, C.T., Rubin, Z. and Peplau, L.A. (1976). Breakups before marriage: The end of 103 affairs. *Journal of Social Issues*, 32: 147–168; Rubin, Z., Peplau, L.A. and Hill, C.T. (1981). Loving and leaving: Sex differences in romantic attachment. *Sex Roles*, 7: 821–835.
14. Hendrick and Hendrick (1986), 395–396.
15. Hendrick and Hendrick (1986).
16. Cramer, D. (submitted for publication). Nature of romantic love in female adolescents; Hendrick and Hendrick (1986).
17. Sternberg, R.J. (1987). Liking versus loving: a comparative evaluation of theories. *Psychological Bulletin*, 102: 343–344.
18. Lee (1988), 53–54.
19. Bowlby, J. (1969). *Attachment and Loss: Vol. 1. Attachment*. New York: Basic Books; Bowlby, J. (1973). *Attachment and Loss: Vol.*

2. Separation: anxiety and anger. New York: Basic Books; Bowlby, J. (1980). *Attachment and Loss: Vol. 3. Loss.* New York: Basic Books.

20. See also: Collins, N.L. and Read, S.J. (1990). Adult attachment, working models, and relationship quality in dating couples. *Journal of Personality and Social Psychology*, 58: 644–663.

21. Ainsworth, M.D.S., Blehar, M.C., Waters, E. and Wall, S. (1978). *Patterns of Attachment: a psychological study of the strange situation.* Hillsdale, NJ: Erlbaum.

22. Hazan, C. and Shaver, P. (1987). Romantic love conceptualized as an attachment process. *Journal of Personality and Social Psychology*, 52: 511–524.

23. See also: Feeney, J.A. and Noller, P. (1990). Attachment style as a predictor of adult romantic relationships. *Journal of Personality and Social Psychology*, 58: 281–291.

24. See also: Collins and Read (1990); Feeney and Noller (1990).

25. Shaver, P., Hazan, C. and Bradshaw, D. (1988). Love as attachment: the integration of three behavioral systems. Chapter in Sternberg and Barnes.

26. Collins and Read (1990); Simpson, J.A. (1990). Influence of attachment styles on romantic relationships. *Journal of Personality and Social Psychology*, 59: 971–980.

27. Hazan, C. and Shaver, P.R. (1990). Love and work: an attachment-theoretical perspective. *Journal of Personality and Social Psychology*, 59: 270–280.

28. Collins and Read (1990); Simpson (1990).

29. Collins and Read (1990).

30. Collins and Read (1990).

31. Simpson (1990).

32. Shaver, Hazan and Bradshaw (1988), 90.

33. Collins and Read (1990), 660.

3. THE INITIAL CHOICES

1. See e.g. Duck, S. (1988). *Relating to Others.* Milton Keynes: Open University Press. 24–25; Kalick, S.M. and Hamilton, T.E. (1986). The matching hypothesis reexamined. *Journal of Personality and Social Psychology*, 51: 673–682; Aron, A. (1988). The matching hypothesis reconsidered again: comment on Kalick and Hamilton. *Journal of Personality and Social Psychology*, 54: 441–446; Kalick, S.M. and Hamilton, T.E. (1988). Closer look at a matching

simulation: reply to Aron. *Journal of Personality and Social Psychology*, 54: 447–451.

2. Nisbett, R.E. and Wilson, T.D. (1977). The halo effect: evidence for unconscious alteration of judgments. *Journal of Personality and Social Psychology*, 35: 250–256.

3. Mueser, K.T., Grau, B.W., Sussman, S. and Rosen, A.J. (1984). You're only as pretty as you feel: facial expression as a determinant of physical attractiveness. *Journal of Personality and Social Psychology*, 46: 469–478.

4. Feingold, A. (1990). Gender differences in effects of physical attractiveness on romantic attraction: a comparison across five research paradigms. *Journal of Personality and Social Psychology*, 59: 981–993.

5. Baron, R.A. and Byrne, D. (1991). *Social Psychology*. 6th edn. Boston: Allyn and Bacon. 247.

6. Abbott, A.R. and Sebastian, R.J. (1981). Physical attractiveness and expectations of success. *Personality and Social Psychology Bulletin*, 7: 481–486; Feingold (1990).

7. Liggett, J. (1974). *The Human Face*. London: Constable. 274.

8. Cited in: Tysoe, M. (1982). Your face is your fortune. *New Society*, 12 August.

9. See e.g. Baron and Byrne (1991), 250–258.

10. See e.g. Duck (1988), *Relating . . .*, 12; Hewstone, M., Stroebe, W., Codol, J–P. and Stephenson, G.M. (eds) (1988). *Introduction to Social Psychology*. Oxford: Basil Blackwell. 229.

11. See e.g. Baron and Byrne (1991), 254–255.

12. Condon, J.W. and Crano, W.D. (1988). Inferred evaluation and the relation between attitude similarity and interpersonal attraction. *Journal of Personality and Social Psychology*, 54: 789–797.

13. Smeaton, G., Byrne, D. and Murnen, S.K. (1989). The repulsion hypothesis revisited: similarity irrelevance or dissimilarity bias? *Journal of Personality and Social Psychology*, 56: 54–59.

14. Byrne, D., Ervin, C.E. and Lamberth, J. (1970). Continuity between the experimental study of attraction and real-life computer dating. *Journal of Personality and Social Psychology*, 16: 157–165.

15. Dutton, D.G. and Aron, A.P. (1974). Some evidence for heightened sexual attraction under conditions of high anxiety. *Journal of Personality and Social Psychology*, 30: 510–517.

16. Allen, J.B., Kenrick, D.T., Linder, D.E. and McCall, M.A. (1989). Arousal and attraction: a response-facilitation alternative to

misattribution and negative-reinforcement models. *Journal of Personality and Social Psychology*, 57: 261–270.

17. See e.g. Argyle, M. and Henderson, M. (1985). *The Anatomy of Relationships*. Harmondsworth: Penguin. 105; Goodwin, R. (1990). Sex differences among partner preferences: are the sexes really very similar? *Sex Roles*, 23: 501–513.

18. Howard, J.A., Blumstein, P. and Schwartz, P. (1987). Social or evolutionary theories? Some observations on preferences in human mate selection. *Journal of Personality and Social Psychology*, 53: 194–200.

19. Buss, D.M. (1989). Sex differences in human mate preferences: evolutionary hypotheses tested in 37 cultures. *Behavioral and Brain Sciences*, 12: 1–49.

20. Howard, Blumstein and Schwartz (1987), 199.

21. See e.g. Baron and Byrne (1991), 255–258.

22. See e.g. Goodwin, R. and Tang, D. (in press). Preferences for friends and close relationships partners: a cross-cultural comparison. *Journal of Social Psychology*.

23. Duck (1988), *Relating . . .*, 35, 39.

24. See e.g. Earle, J.R. and Perricone, P.J. (1986). Premarital sexuality: a ten-year study of attitudes and behavior on a small university campus. *Journal of Sex Research*, 22: 304–310.

25. Hendrick, S., Hendrick, C., Slapion-Foote, M.J. and Foote, F.H. (1985). Gender differences in sexual attitudes. *Journal of Personality and Social Psychology*, 48: 1630–1642.

26. E.g. Bailey, W.C., Hendrick, C. and Hendrick, S.S. (1987). Relation of sex and gender role to love, sexual attitudes, and self-esteem. *Sex Roles*, 16: 637–648; Hendrick, S.S. and Hendrick, C. (1987). Love and sexual attitudes, self-disclosure and sensation seeking. *Journal of Social and Personal Relationships*, 4: 281–297.

27. I took "neutral" to range from scores 2.8–3.2, the extreme opposite ends of the scale being scores 1 and 5.

28. Ellis, B.J. and Symons, D. (1990). Sex differences in sexual fantasy: an evolutionary psychological approach. *Journal of Sex Research*, 27: 527–555.

29. See e.g. McCabe, M.P. (1987). Desired and experienced levels of premarital affection and sexual intercourse during dating. *Journal of Sex Research*, 23: 23–33.

30. See: Hendrick, C. (1988). Roles and gender in relationships. Chapter in: Duck, S. (ed) *Handbook of Personal Relationships*. Chichester: John Wiley.

31. Knox, D. and Wilson, K. (1981). Dating behaviors of university students. *Family Relations*, 30: 255–258.

32. Christopher, F.S. and Cate, R.M. (1982). Factors involved in premarital sexual decision-making. Paper presented at International Conference on Personal Relations, Madison. Cited in Duck (1988), *Relating* . . ., 70.

33. See e.g. Hendrick (1988); Shotland, R.L. (1989). A model of the causes of date rape in developing and close relationships. Chapter in: Hendrick, C. (ed) *Close Relationships*. Newbury Park: Sage.

34. See e.g. Buunk, B.P. and van Driel, B. (1989). *Variant Lifestyles and Relationships*. Newbury Park: Sage. 17–18.

35. See e.g. Baldwin, J.D. and Baldwin, J.I. (1988). Factors affecting AIDS-related sexual risk-taking behavior among college students. *Journal of Sex Research*, 25: 181–196; Turner, C., Anderson, P., Fitzpatrick, R., Fowler, G. and Mayon-White, R. (1988). Sexual behaviour, contraceptive practice and knowledge of AIDS of Oxford University students. *Journal of Biosocial Science*, 20: 445–451.

36. Hansen, W.B., Hahn, G.L. and Wolkenstein, B.H. (1990). Perceived personal immunity: beliefs about susceptibility to AIDS. *Journal of Sex Research*, 27: 622–628.

37. See e.g. Bruch, M.A. and Hynes, M.J. (1987). Heterosocial anxiety and contraceptive behavior. *Journal of Research in Personality*, 21: 343–360; Siegel, K. and Gibson, W.C. (1988). Barriers to the modification of sexual behavior among heterosexuals at risk for acquired immunodeficiency syndrome. *New York State Journal of Medicine*, 88: 66–70.

38. See e.g. Kelly, J.A. and St. Lawrence, J.S. (1988). AIDS prevention and treatment: psychology's role in the health crisis. *Clinical Psychology Review*, 8: 255–284; Siegel and Gibson (1988).

39. Siegel and Gibson (1988), 68.

4. UNCERTAIN DAYS

1. See e.g. Argyle, M. and Henderson, M. (1985). *The Anatomy of Relationships*. Harmondsworth: Penguin. 164–165.

2. Thornes, B. and Collard, J. (1979). *Who Divorces?* London: Routledge & Kegan Paul. Cited in Argyle and Henderson (1985), 168.

3. See e.g. Blood, B. and Blood, M. (1978). *Marriage*. 3rd edn. New York: Free Press. 144–146.

4. See e.g. Argyle and Henderson (1985), 168–169.

5. See e.g. Argyle and Henderson (1985), 169.

6. See e.g. Auerback, S. and Moser, C. (1987). Groups for the wives of gay and bisexual men. *Social Work*, 32: 321–325; Wolf, T.J. (1987). Group psychotherapy for bisexual men and their wives. *Journal of Homosexuality*, 14: 191–199.

7. See e.g. Kersten, K.K. and Kersten, L.K. (1988). *Marriage and the Family*. New York: Harper & Row. 440–442.

8. Kelly, E.L. and Conley, J.J. (1987). Personality and compatibility: a prospective analysis of marital stability and marital satisfaction. *Journal of Personality and Social Psychology*, 52: 27–40.

9. Caspi, A., Elder, G.H. and Bem, D.J. (1987). Moving against the world: life-course patterns of explosive children. *Developmental Psychology*, 23: 308–313.

10. Hendrick, S.S., Hendrick, C. and Adler, N.L. (1988). Romantic relationships: love, satisfaction, and staying together. *Journal of Personality and Social Psychology*, 54: 980–988.

11. Hendrick, Hendrick and Adler (1988).

12. Simpson, J.A. (1987). The dissolution of romantic relationships: factors involved in relationship stability and emotional distress. *Journal of Personality and Social Psychology*, 53: 683–692.

13. See e.g. Baron, R.A. and Byrne, D. (1991). *Social Psychology*. 6th edn. Boston: Allyn and Bacon. 507–510; Snyder, M. and Simpson, J.A. (1987). Orientations toward romantic relationships. Chapter in: Perlman, D. and Duck, S. (eds) *Intimate Relationships*. Newbury Park: Sage.

14. Snyder and Simpson (1987), 56.

15. See: Clark, M.S. and Reis, H.T. (1988). Interpersonal processes in close relationships. *Annual Review of Psychology*, 39: 609–672.

16. Blaney, N.T., Brown, P. and Blaney, P.H. (1986). Type A, marital adjustment, and life stress. *Journal of Behavioral Medicine*, 9: 491–502.

17. Blaney, Brown and Blaney (1986), 491.

18. Rank, M.R. (1981). The transition to marriage: a comparison of cohabiting and dating relationships ending in marriage or divorce. *Alternative Lifestyles*, 4: 487–506. Cited in Buunk, B.P. and van Driel, B. (1989). *Variant Lifestyles and Relationships*. Newbury Park: Sage. 67.

19. Thornes and Collard (1979). Cited in Argyle and Henderson (1985), 167, 168.

20. See e.g. Buunk and van Driel (1989), 66.

21. See e.g. Argyle and Henderson (1985), 113; Buunk and van Driel (1989), 66–67.
22. See e.g. Buunk and van Driel (1989), 54–56, 67.
23. Buunk and van Driel (1989), 66.
24. Surra, C.A. and Huston, T.L. (1987). Mate selection as a social transition. Chapter in Perlman and Duck.
25. Buunk and van Driel (1989), 66.
26. See e.g. Rusbult, C.E. (1983). A longitudinal test of the investment model: the development (and deterioration) of satisfaction and commitment in heterosexual involvements. *Journal of Personality and Social Psychology*, 45: 101–117.
27. E.g. Rubin's Love and Liking Scales, see Sternberg, R.J. and Grajek, S. (1984). The nature of love. *Journal of Personality and Social Psychology*, 47: 312–329.
28. Hill, C.T., Rubin, Z. and Peplau, L.A. (1976). Breakups before marriage: the end of 103 affairs. *Journal of Social Issues*, 32: 147–168.
29. Hill, Rubin and Peplau (1976), 152.
30. Rusbult (1983).
31. Rusbult (1983), 113.
32. Rusbult, C.E., Johnson, D.J. and Morrow, G.D. (1986). Predicting satisfaction and commitment in adult romantic involvements: an assessment of the generalizability of the investment model. *Social Psychology Quarterly*, 49: 81–89.
33. Rusbult (1983), 102.
34. Rusbult (1983), 103.
35. Simpson, J.A., Gangestad, S.W. and Lerma, M. (1990). Perception of physical attractiveness: mechanisms involved in the maintenance of romantic relationships. *Journal of Personality and Social Psychology*, 59: 1192–1201.
36. Johnson, D.J. and Rusbult, C.E. (1989). Resisting temptation: devaluation of alternative partners as a means of maintaining commitment in close relationships. *Journal of Personality and Social Psychology*, 57: 967–980.
37. Rusbult (1983), 115.
38. Berscheid, E., Snyder, M. and Omoto, A.M. (1989). The Relationship Closeness Inventory: assessing the closeness of interpersonal relationships. *Journal of Personality and Social Psychology*, 57: 792–807.
39. Berscheid, Snyder and Omoto (1989), 802.
40. Hill, Rubin and Peplau (1976).

41. See also: Surra, C.A. and Longstreth, M. (1990). Similarity of outcomes, interdependence, and conflict in dating relationships. *Journal of Personality and Social Psychology*, 59: 501–516.

42. Milardo, R.M., Johnson, M.P. and Huston, T.L. (1983). Developing close relationships: changing patterns of interaction between pair members and social networks. *Journal of Personality and Social Psychology*, 44: 964–976.

43. Duck, S. (1988). *Relating to Others*. Milton Keynes: Open University Press. 74–76; Hill, Rubin and Peplau (1976).

44. Glick, P.C. (1984). Marriage, divorce and living arrangements. *Journal of Family Issues*, 5: 7–26.

45. Huston, T.L., Surra, C.A., Fitzgerald, N.M. and Cate, R.M. (1981). From courtship to marriage: mate selection as an interpersonal process. Chapter in: Duck, S.W. and Gilmour, R. (eds) *Personal Relationships 2: Developing Personal Relationships*. London: Academic Press.

46. Surra, C.A. (1985). Courtship types: variations in interdependence between partners and social networks. *Journal of Personality and Social Psychology*, 49: 357–375.

47. Cate, R.M., Huston, T.L. and Nesselroade, J.R. (1986). Premarital relationships: toward the identification of alternative pathways to marriage. *Journal of Social and Clinical Psychology*, 4: 3–22.

48. See e.g. Cate, R.M. and Lloyd, S.A. (1988). Courtship. Chapter in: Duck, S. (ed) *Handbook of Personal Relationships*. Chichester: John Wiley.

49. Stephen, T.D. (1985). Fixed-sequence and circular-causal models of relationship development: divergent views on the role of communication in intimacy. *Journal of Marriage and the Family*, 47: 955–963.

50. See e.g. Surra (1985); Surra, C.A. and Huston, T.L. (1987). Mate selection as a social transition. Chapter in Perlman and Duck.

51. Thornes and Collard (1979). Cited in Argyle and Henderson (1985), 167–168.

52. Cate, Huston and Nesselroade (1986).

53. Newcomb, M.D. and Bentler, P.M. (1981). Marital breakdown. Chapter in: Duck, S.W. and Gilmour, R. (eds) *Personal Relationships 3: Personal Relationships in Disorder*. London: Academic Press.

54. Huston, Surra, Fitzgerald and Cate (1981); Surra (1985).

55. Duck (1988), *Relating* . . ., 82.

56. Duck (1988), *Relating* . . ., 82.

57. Surra (1985).
58. Surra, C.A. (1987). Reasons for changes in commitment: variations by courtship type. *Journal of Social and Personal Relationships*, 4: 17–33; Surra and Huston (1987).
59. Surra and Huston (1987), 105.
60. Surra (1985).
61. See e.g. Berger, C.R. (1988). Uncertainty and information exchange in developing relationships. Chapter in Duck, *Handbook* . . ..
62. Baxter, L.A. and Wilmot, W.W. (1985). Taboo topics in close relationships. *Journal of Social and Personal Relationships*, 2: 253–269.
63. Baxter, L. and Wilmot, W. (1984). Secret tests: social strategies for acquiring information about the state of the relationship. *Human Communication Research*, 11: 171–201.
64. Baxter, L.A. and Bullis, C. (1986). Turning points in developing romantic relationships. *Human Communication Research*, 12: 469–493.
65. See e.g. Surra and Huston (1987).
66. Holmes, J.G. and Rempel, J.K. (1989). Trust in close relationships. Chapter in: Hendrick, C. (ed) *Close Relationships*. Newbury Park: Sage.
67. Holmes and Rempel (1989), 188.
68. Hatfield, E. (1984). The dangers of intimacy. Chapter in: Derlega, V.J. (ed) *Communication, Intimacy and Close Relationships*. Orlando, FL: Academic Press.
69. Baxter, L.A. (1987). Cognition and communication in the relationship process. Chapter in: Burnett, R., McGhee, P. and Clarke, D.D. (eds) *Accounting for Relationships*. London: Methuen. 209.
70. See e.g. Duck (1988), *Relating* . . ., 55–56.
71. Sprecher, S. (1987). The effects of self disclosure given and received on affection for an intimate partner and stability of the relationship. *Journal of Social and Personal Relationships*, 4: 115–128.
72. Duck (1988), *Relating* . . ., 57.
73. Baxter and Wilmot (1985).

5. MAINTENANCE STRATEGIES

1. See e.g. Argyle, M. and Henderson, M. (1985). *The Anatomy of Relationships*. Harmondsworth: Penguin. 165.
2. Shaver, P., Hazan, C. and Bradshaw, D. (1988). Love as attachment. Chapter in: Sternberg, R.J. and Barnes, M.L. *The Psychology of Love*. New Haven: Yale University Press.

3. Administration on Aging (1984). Aging (US Department of Health and Human Services, Publication No. 347, 2). Washington DC: Government Printing Office. Cited in Weishaus, S. and Field, D. (1988). A half century of marriage: continuity or change? *Journal of Marriage and the Family*, 50: 763–774.

4. Kersten, K.K. and Kersten, L.K. (1988). *Marriage and the Family*. New York: Harper & Row. 226.

5. Simpson, J.A., Campbell, B. and Berscheid, E. (1986). The association between romantic love and marriage: Kephart (1967) twice revisited. *Personality and Social Psychology Bulletin*, 12: 363–372.

6. Landers, A. (1977). If you had to do it all over again, would you marry the same person? *Family Circle*, 90: 2, 52, 54. Cited in Weishaus and Field (1988).

7. Baron, R.A. (1989). *Psychology*. Boston: Allyn and Bacon. 494.

8. Thornes, B. and Collard, J. (1979). *Who Divorces?* London: Routledge and Kegan Paul. Cited in Argyle and Henderson (1985), 165.

9. See e.g. Chester, R. (1985). Marriage in Britain: an overview of research. Chapter in: Dryden, W. (ed) *Marital Therapy in Britain*, vol 1. London: Harper & Row. 20–21.

10. Thornes and Collard (1979). Cited in Argyle and Henderson (1985), 167.

11. Thornes and Collard (1979). Cited in Argyle and Henderson (1985), 167.

12. Buss, D.M. (1989). Conflict between the sexes: strategic interference and the evocation of anger and upset. *Journal of Personality and Social Psychology*, 56: 735–747.

13. Buss (1989), 738.

14. Buss (1989).

15. Smolen, R.C. and Spiegel, D.A. (1987). Marital locus of control as a modifier of the relationship between the frequency of provocation by spouse and marital satisfaction. *Journal of Research in Personality*, 21: 70–80.

16. Perlman, D. (1990). You bug me: some preliminary data and reflections on hassles in close relationships. Paper presented at the International Conference on Personal Relationships, Oxford, July.

17. Eidelson, R.J. and Epstein, N. (1982). Cognition and relationship maladjustment: development of a measure of dysfunctional relationship beliefs. *Journal of Consulting and Clinical Psychology*, 50: 715–720.

18. Bradbury, T.N. and Fincham, F.D. (1988). Individual difference variables in close relationships: a contextual model of marriage as an integrative framework. *Journal of Personality and Social Psychology*, 54: 713–721.

19. See: Epstein, N., Pretzer, J.L. and Fleming, B. (1987). The role of cognitive appraisal in self-reports of marital communication. *Behavior Therapy*, 18: 51–69.

20. Smith, G.T., Snyder, D.K., Trull, T.J. and Monsma, B.R. (1988). Predicting relationship satisfaction from couples' use of leisure time. *American Journal of Family Therapy*, 16: 3–13.

21. See: Smith, Snyder, Trull and Monsma (1988), 12.

22. Holman, T.B. and Jacquart, M. (1988). Leisure-activity patterns and marital satisfaction: a further test. *Journal of Marriage and the Family*, 50: 69–77.

23. Miell, D. (1990). Personal communication.

24. See e.g. Baxter, L.A. (1988). A dialectical perspective on communication strategies in relationship development. Chapter in: Duck, S. (ed) *Handbook of Personal Relationships*. Chichester: John Wiley; Berger, C.R. (1988). Uncertainty and information exchange in developing relationships. Chapter in Duck, *Handbook . . ..*

25. Berger (1988).

26. Baron, R.A. and Byrne, D. (1991). *Social Psychology*. 6th edn. 297.

27. Baxter (1988).

28. Sternberg, R.J. (1987). Liking versus loving: a comparative evaluation of theories. *Psychological Bulletin*, 102: 341.

29. Frazier, P.A. and Esterly, E. (1990). Correlates of relationship beliefs: gender, relationship experience and relationship satisfaction. *Journal of Social and Personal Relationships*, 7: 331–352.

30. Bradbury and Fincham (1988).

31. See e.g. Trotter, R.J. (1986). The three faces of love. *Psychology Today*, September, 46–50, 54.

32. Wills, T.A., Weiss, R.L. and Patterson, G.R. (1974). A behavioral analysis of the determinants of marital satisfaction. *Journal of Consulting and Clinical Psychology*, 42: 802–811.

33. Rubin, L. (1976). *Worlds of Pain*. New York: Basic Books. 147. Cited in Cancian, F.M. (1986). The feminization of love. *Signs: Journal of Women in Culture and Society*, 11: 692–709.

34. Long, E.C.J. and Andrews, D.W. (1990). Perspective taking as a predictor of marital adjustment. *Journal of Personality and Social Psychology*, 59: 126–131.

35. Sillars, A. and Scott, M. (1983). Interpersonal perception between intimates: an integrative review. *Human Communication Research*, 10: 153–176.
36. White, J.M. (1985). Perceived similarity and understanding in married couples. *Journal of Social and Personal Relationships*, 2: 45–57.
37. Davis, M.H. and Oathout, H.A. (1987). Maintenance of satisfaction in romantic relationships: empathy and relational competence. *Journal of Personality and Social Psychology*, 53: 397–410.

6. INTIMACY, COMMUNICATION AND CONFLICT

1. Clark, M.S. and Reis, H.T. (1988). Interpersonal processes in close relationships. *Annual Review of Psychology*, 39: 628.
2. Fitzpatrick, M.A. (1987). Marriage and verbal intimacy. Chapter in: Derlega, V.J. and Berg, J.H. (eds) *Self-Disclosure: Theory, research, and therapy*. New York: Plenum Press.
3. See e.g. Clark and Reis (1988), 609–672; Hendrick, C. (1988). Roles and gender in relationships. Chapter in: Duck, S. (ed) *Handbook of Personal Relationships*. Chichester: John Wiley.
4. Clark and Reis (1988), 636.
5. See e.g. Derlega, V.J., Winstead, B.A., Wong, P.T.P. and Hunter, S. (1985). Gender effects in an initial encounter: a case where men exceed women in disclosure. *Journal of Social and Personal Relationships*, 2: 25–44.
6. Barbee, A.P., Gulley, M.R. and Cunningham, M.R. (1990). Support seeking in personal relationships. *Journal of Social and Personal Relationships*, 7: 531–540.
7. Barbee, Gulley and Cunningham (1990), 537.
8. Collins, N.L. and Read, S.J. (1990). Adult attachment, working models, and relationship quality in dating couples. *Journal of Personality and Social Psychology*, 58: 644–663.
9. Antill, J.K. and Cotton, S. (1987). Self disclosure between husbands and wives: its relationship to sex roles and marital happiness. *Australian Journal of Psychology*, 39: 11–24.
10. Snell, W.E., Miller, R.S. and Belk, S.S. (1988). Development of the emotional self-disclosure scale. *Sex Roles*, 18: 59–73.
11. See e.g. Antill and Cotton (1987); Hendrick (1988), 441.
12. McAdams, D.P. and Vaillant, G.E. (1982). Intimacy motivation and psychosocial adjustment: a longitudinal study. *Journal of Personality Assessment*, 46: 586–593.
13. Fitzpatrick (1987).

14. Collins and Read (1990).
15. Baxter, L.A. (1987). Self-disclosure and relationship development. Chapter in Derlega and Berg.
16. See e.g. Clark and Reis (1988).
17. Hatfield, E. (1984). The dangers of intimacy. Chapter in: Derlega, V.J. (ed) *Communication, Intimacy, and Close Relationships*. Orlando: Academic Press. 215.
18. See: Kersten, K.K. and Kersten, L.K. (1988). *Marriage and the Family*. New York: Harper & Row. 73.
19. See e.g. Boland, J.P. and Follingstad, D.R. (1987). The relationship between communication and marital satisfaction: a review. *Journal of Sex and Marital Therapy*, 13: 286–313.
20. See e.g. Baron, R.A. (1986). *Behavior in Organizations*. 2nd edn. Boston: Allyn and Bacon. 326.
21. See e.g. Boland and Follingstad (1987); Burgess, R.L. (1981). Relationships in marriage and the family. Chapter in: Duck, S. and Gilmour, R. (eds) *Personal Relationships 1: Studying Personal Relationships*. London: Academic Press; Dindia, K. and Fitzpatrick, M.A. (1985). Marital communication: three approaches compared. Chapter in: Duck, S. and Perlman, D. (eds) *Understanding Personal Relationships*. London: Sage.
22. Boland and Follingstad (1987), 304.
23. Markman, H.J., Floyd, F.J., Stanley, S.M. and Storaasli, R.D. (1988). Prevention of marital distress: a longitudinal investigation. *Journal of Consulting and Clinical Psychology*, 56: 210–217.
24. Markman, Floyd, Stanley and Storaasli (1988), 215.
25. Duck, S. (1990). Relationships as unfinished business: out of the frying pan and into the 1990s. *Journal of Social and Personal Relationships*, 7: 5–28.
26. Buunk, B.P., Schaap, C. and Prevoo, N. (1990). Conflict resolution styles attributed to self and partner in premarital relationships. *Journal of Social Psychology*, 130: 821–823.
27. See e.g. Christensen, A. and Heavey, C.L. (1990). Gender and social structure in the demand/withdraw pattern of marital conflict. *Journal of Personality and Social Psychology*, 59: 73–81; Gottman, J.M. and Krokoff, L.J. (1989). Marital interaction and satisfaction: a longitudinal view. *Journal of Consulting and Clinical Psychology*, 57: 47–52.
28. Gottman and Krokoff (1989).
29. Gottman and Krokoff (1989), 49.
30. Argyle, M. and Furnham, A. (1983). Sources of satisfaction and

conflict in long-term relationships. *Journal of Marriage and the Family*, 45: 481–493.

31. Epstein, N., Pretzer, J.L. and Fleming, B. (1987). The role of cognitive appraisal in self-reports of marital communication. *Behavior Therapy*, 18: 51–69.

32. Kersten and Kersten (1988), 268.

33. For a discussion of anger, see e.g. Kersten and Kersten (1988), 262–265, 269.

34. Gottman and Krokoff (1989), 50.

35. See e.g. Boland and Follingstad (1987).

36. Smith, D.A., Vivian, D. and O'Leary, K.D. (1990). Longitudinal prediction of marital discord from premarital expressions of affect. *Journal of Consulting and Clinical Psychology*, 58: 790–798.

37. Smith, Vivian and O'Leary (1990), 796.

38. Aida, Y. and Falbo, T. (1991). Relationships between marital satisfaction, resources, and power strategies. *Sex Roles*, 24: 43–56; and see Falbo, T. and Peplau, L.A. (1980). Power strategies in intimate relationships. *Journal of Personality and Social Psychology*, 38: 618–628.

39. See: Christensen and Heavey (1990); Gottman and Krokoff (1989).

40. For discussions of spouse abuse, see e.g. Gelles, R.J. (1987). *The Violent Home*. Newbury Park: Sage; Giles-Sims, J. (1983). *Wife Battering*. New York: Guilford Press; Horley, S. (1988). *Love and Pain*. London: Bedford Square Press; Kersten and Kersten (1988), 439–445, 449–450.

41. Andrews, B. and Brown, G.W. (1988). Marital violence in the community: a biographical approach. *British Journal of Psychiatry*, 153: 305–312.

7. NEGOTIATING IMBALANCES

1. VanYperen, N.W. and Buunk, B.P. (1990). A longitudinal study of equity and satisfaction in intimate relationships. *European Journal of Social Psychology*, 20: 287–309.

2. See e.g. Hatfield, E., Traupmann, J., Sprecher, S., Utne, M. and Hay, J. (1985). Equity and intimate relations: recent research. Chapter in: Ickes, W. (ed) *Compatible and Incompatible Relationships*. New York: Springer Verlag; VanYperen and Buunk (1990).

3. See e.g. Hatfield, E., Utne, M.K. and Traupmann, J. (1979). Equity theory and intimate relationships. Chapter in: Burgess, R.L. and

Huston, T.L. (eds) *Exchange Theory in Developing Relationships*. New York: Academic Press.

4. Buunk, B.P. and VanYperen, N.W. (in press). Social comparison, equality, and relationship satisfaction: gender differences over a ten-year period. *Social Justice Research*.

5. See also: VanYperen, N.W. and Buunk, B.P. (1991). Equity theory and exchange and communal orientation from a cross-national perspective. *Journal of Social Psychology*, 131: 5–20.

6. See e.g. Cate, R.M., Lloyd, S.A. and Long, E. (1988). The role of rewards and fairness in developing premarital relationships. *Journal of Marriage and the Family*, 50: 443–452; Martin, M.W. (1985). Satisfaction with intimate exchange: gender-role differences and the impact of equity, equality, and rewards. *Sex Roles*, 13: 597–605.

7. See e.g. Argyle, M. and Henderson, M. (1985). *The Anatomy of Relationships*. Harmondsworth: Penguin. 130; Lee, G.R. (1988). Marital satisfaction in later life: the effects of nonmarital roles. *Journal of Marriage and the Family*, 50: 775–783.

8. Moss, P., Bolland, G., Foxman, R. and Owen, C. (1986). Marital relations during the transition to parenthood. *Journal of Reproductive and Infant Psychology*, 4: 57–67.

9. Moss, Bolland, Foxman and Owen (1986), 65.

10. Moss, Bolland, Foxman and Owen (1986), 66.

11. See e.g. Kersten, K.K. and Kersten, L.K. (1988). *Marriage and the Family*. New York: Harper & Row. 331.

12. See e.g. Lee (1988).

13. See e.g. Morgan, S.P., Lye, D.N. and Condran, G.A. (1988). Sons, daughters, and the risk of marital disruption. *American Journal of Sociology*, 94: 110–129.

14. Byrne, D. and Murnen, S.K. (1988). Maintaining loving relationships. Chapter in: Sternberg, R.J. and Barnes, M.L. (eds) *The Psychology of Love*. New Haven: Yale University Press. 301.

15. Buunk, B.P. and van Driel, B. (1989). *Variant Lifestyles and Relationships*. Newbury Park: Sage. 15.

16. Morgan, Lye and Condran (1988), 110.

17. See: Marsh, P. (ed) (1988). *Eye to Eye*. London: Sidgwick and Jackson. 224.

18. See e.g. Lewis, S.N.C. and Cooper, C.L. (1988). The transition to parenthood in dual-earner couples. *Psychological Medicine*, 18: 477–486.

19. See e.g. O'Hara, M.W. and Zekoski, E.M. (1988). Postpartum

depression: a comprehensive review. Chapter in: Kumar, R. and Brockington, I.F. (eds) *Motherhood and Mental Illness*. London: Wright.

20. See e.g. Lewis, C. (1986). *Becoming a Father*. Milton Keynes: Open University Press. 133.

21. See e.g. Baruch, G.K. and Barnett, R.C. (1986). Consequences of fathers' participation in family work: parents' role strain and well-being. *Journal of Personality and Social Psychology*, 51: 983–992; Kersten and Kersten (1988), 241–243.

22. See e.g. Lewis and Cooper (1988).

23. Ruble, D.N., Fleming, A.S., Hackel, L.S. and Stangor, C. (1988). Changes in the marital relationship during the transition to first time motherhood: effects of violated expectations concerning division of household labor. *Journal of Personality and Social Psychology*, 55: 78–87.

24. Goldberg, W.A., Michaels, G.Y. and Lamb, M.E. (1985). Husband and wives' adjustment to pregnancy and first parenthood. *Journal of Family Issues*, 6: 483–503.

25. Croghan, R. and Miell, D. (1991). Accounts of intimate support relationships in the early months of mothering. Chapter in: Harvey, J., Orbuch, T. and Weber, A. (eds) *Attributions, Accounts and Close Relationships*. Berlin: Springer Verlag.

26. Lewis (1986), 82.

27. See e.g. Lewis (1986), 81.

28. Lewis (1986), 184.

29. Russell, G. (1983). *The Changing Role of Fathers?* St Lucia, Queensland: University of Queensland Press.

30. Russell, G. (1989). Work/family patterns and couple relationships in shared caregiving families. *Social Behaviour*, 4: 267.

31. Russell (1989), 265–283.

32. Russell (1989), 276.

33. Baruch and Barnett (1986).

34. Emler, N. and Abrams, D. (1989). The sexual distribution of benefits and burdens in the household. *Social Justice Research*, 3: 137–156.

35. See e.g. Lewis and Cooper (1988).

36. For more on assertiveness, see e.g. Tysoe, M. (1988). *All This and Work Too: the psychology of office life*. London: Fontana/Collins. 83–88.

37. Block, J.H., Block, J. and Morrison, A. (1981). Parental agreement-disagreement on child-rearing orientations and gender-

related personality correlates in children. *Child Development*, 52: 965–974.

38. Cooper, C.L. (1981). *Executive Families Under Stress*. Englewood Cliffs, N.J.: Prentice-Hall. 114, 116.

39. See e.g. Lewis, S.N.C. and Cooper, C.L. (1987). Stress in two-earner couples and stage in the life-cycle. *Journal of Occupational Psychology*, 60: 289–303.

40. For further discussion of the dual-earner lifestyle, see e.g. Lewis, S. and Cooper, C.L. (1989). *Career Couples*. London: Unwin; Vannoy-Hiller, D. and Philliber, W.W. (1989). *Equal Partners*. Newbury Park: Sage.

41. Kersten and Kersten (1988), 246, 247.

42. Kersten and Kersten (1988), 247.

43. Fontana, D. (1989). *Managing Stress*. Leicester/London: British Psychological Society/ Routledge. 82.

44. See e.g. Spitze, G. (1988). Women's employment and family relations: a review. *Journal of Marriage and the Family*, 50: 595–618.

45. Spitze (1988).

46. See e.g. Cooper, C.L. (1986). Job distress: recent research and the emerging role of the clinical occupational psychologist. *Bulletin of the British Psychological Society*, 39: 325–331.

47. Tysoe (1988), 175.

48. See e.g. White, L.K., Booth, A. and Edwards, J.N. (1986). Children and marital happiness: why the negative correlation? *Journal of Family Issues*, 7: 131–147.

8. SEX

1. James, W.H. (1983). Decline in coital rates with spouses' ages and duration of marriage. *Journal of Biosocial Science*, 15: 83–87.

2. See e.g. Brecher, E.M. and Brecher, J. (1986). Extracting valid sexological findings from severely flawed and biased population samples. *Journal of Sex Research*, 22: 6–20.

3. See e.g. Doddridge, R., Schumm, W.R. and Bergen, M.B. (1987). Factors related to decline in preferred frequency of sexual intercourse among young couples. *Psychological Reports*, 60: 391–395.

4. Greenblat, C.S. (1983). The salience of sexuality in the early years of marriage. *Journal of Marriage and the Family*, 45: 295.

5. See e.g. Bancroft, J. (1989). *Human Sexuality and Its Problems*. 2nd edn. Edinburgh: Churchill Livingstone. 287, 291; Hyde,

J.S. (1990). *Understanding Human Sexuality*. 4th edn. New York: McGraw-Hill. 335–336, 339–340.

6. See e.g. Bancroft (1989), 287–288; Hyde (1990), 337.
7. Hyde (1990), 340.
8. Kersten, K.K. and Kersten, L.K. (1988). *Marriage and the Family*. New York: Harper & Row. 389.
9. Bancroft (1989), 288.
10. Bancroft (1989), 296.
11. Blumstein, P. and Schwartz, P. (1983). *American Couples*. New York: William Morrow. Cited in e.g. Hyde (1990), 322.
12. See e.g. Duck, S. (1988). *Relating to Others*. Milton Keynes: Open University Press. 44.
13. See e.g. Kersten and Kersten (1988), 311.
14. See e.g. Reamy, K.J. and White, S.E. (1987). Sexuality in the puerperium: a review. *Archives of Sexual Behavior*, 16: 165–186.
15. See e.g. Alder, E.M. (1989). Sexual behaviour in pregnancy, after childbirth and during breast-feeding. *Bailliere's Clinical Obstetrics and Gynaecology*, 3: 805–821.
16. Moss, P., Bolland, G., Foxman, R. and Owen, C. (1986). Marital relations during the transition to parenthood. *Journal of Reproductive and Infant Psychology*, 4: 57–67.
17. See e.g. Morokoff, P.J. (1989). Sex bias and POD. *American Psychologist*, 44: 73–75; Wakefield, J. (1989). Manufacturing female dysfunction: a reply to Morokoff. *American Psychologist*, 44: 75–77.
18. For detailed discussions, see e.g. Bancroft (1989); Cole, M. and Dryden, W. (eds) (1988). *Sex Therapy in Britain*. Milton Keynes: Open University Press; Dodd, B.G. and Parsons, A.D. (1984). Psychosexual problems. Chapter in: Broome, A. and Wallace, L. (eds) *Psychology and Gynaecological Problems*. London: Tavistock; Hyde (1990), ch. 20; Yaffé, M. (1981). Disordered sexual relationships. Chapter in: Duck, S. and Gilmour, R. (eds) *Personal Relationships 3: Personal Relationships in Disorder*. London: Academic Press.
19. Frank, E., Anderson, C. and Rubinstein, D. (1978). Frequency of sexual dysfunction in 'normal' couples. *New England Journal of Medicine*, 299: 111–115.
20. See e.g. Dodd and Parsons (1984).
21. Jehu, D. (1984). Sexual inadequacy. Chapter in: Howells, K. (ed) *The Psychology of Sexual Diversity*. Oxford: Basil Blackwell. 136.

22. Spector, K. and Boyle, M. (1987). Erectile problems in a non-clinical sample: remission rates and perceived factors in remission. *Sexual and Marital Therapy*, 2: 65–71.
23. Baker, C.D. and De Silva, P. (1988). The relationship between male sexual dysfunction and belief in Zilbergeld's myths: an empirical investigation. *Sexual and Marital Therapy*, 3: 229–238.
24. See e.g. Frank, Anderson and Rubinstein (1978).
25. Hyde (1990), 533.
26. See e.g. Bancroft (1989), 493–502; Cole, M. (1985). Sex therapy – a critical appraisal. *British Journal of Psychiatry*, 147: 337–351.
27. Yaffé (1981), 121.
28. Argyle, M. and Henderson, M. (1985). *The Anatomy of Relationships*. Harmondsworth: Penguin. 139.
29. Duck, S. (1988). Enjoying a sexual relationship. Chapter in: Marsh, P. (ed) *Eye to Eye*. London: Sidgwick and Jackson. 215, 216.
30. See e.g. Bancroft (1989), 258–259; Dodd and Parsons (1984).
31. Spector, K.R. and Boyle, M. (1986). The prevalence and perceived aetiology of male sexual problems in a non-clinical sample. *British Journal of Medical Psychology*, 59: 351.
32. Spector and Boyle (1986), 357.
33. Yaffé (1981), 119.
34. See e.g. Rust, J., Golombok, S. and Collier, J. (1988). Marital problems and sexual dysfunction: how are they related? *British Journal of Psychiatry*, 152: 629–631.
35. Rust, Golombok and Collier (1988), 631.
36. Rust, Golombok and Collier (1988), 630.
37. See e.g. Duck (1988) in Marsh.
38. Rust, Golombok and Collier (1988), 631.
39. Argyle and Henderson (1985), 139.
40. Margolin, L. and White, L. (1987). The continuing role of physical attractiveness in marriage. *Journal of Marriage and the Family*, 49: 21–27.
41. Duck (1988) in Marsh, 217.
42. Margolin and White (1987), 26.
43. See e.g. Jehu (1984).
44. Spector and Boyle (1986), 351–358.
45. Spector and Boyle (1986).
46. Hyde (1990), 247–258.
47. Markman, H.J., Floyd, F.J., Stanley, S.M. and Storaasli, R.D. (1988). Prevention of marital distress: a longitudinal investigation. *Journal of Consulting and Clinical Psychology*, 56: 210–217.

48. Ross, J.L., Clifford, R.E. and Eisenman, R. (1987). Communication of sexual preferences in married couples. *Bulletin of the Psychonomic Society*, 25: 58–60.

49. Cole (1985).

50. Cole (1985), 348.

51. See e.g. Argyle and Henderson (1985), 149.

52. Sanders, D. (1985). *The Woman Book of Love and Sex*. London: Sphere; Sanders, D. (1987). *The Woman Report on Men*. London: Sphere.

53. See e.g. Lawson, A. (1988). *Adultery*. Oxford: Basil Blackwell. 77–78; Roscoe, B., Cavanaugh, L.E. and Kennedy, D.R. (1988). Dating infidelity: behaviors, reasons and consequences. *Adolescence*, 23: 35–43.

54. See e.g. Argyle and Henderson (1985), 148–149; Buunk, B.P. and van Driel, B. (1989). *Variant Lifestyles and Relationships*. Newbury Park: Sage. 96–97.

55. Taylor, C.J. (1986). Extramarital sex: good for the goose? good for the gander? *Women and Therapy*, 5: 289–295; see also Lawson (1988), 74.

56. Taylor (1986), 294, 295.

57. See e.g. Kersten and Kersten (1988), 315; Roscoe, Cavanaugh and Kennedy (1988).

58. See e.g. Thompson, A.P. (1984). Emotional and sexual components of extramarital relations. *Journal of Marriage and the Family*, 46: 35–42.

59. Spector and Boyle (1986).

60. See e.g. Buunk, B. (1987). Conditions that promote breakups as a consequence of extradyadic involvements. *Journal of Social and Clinical Psychology*, 5: 271–284.

61. Cunningham, J.D. and Antill, J.K. (1981). Love in developing romantic relationships. Chapter in: Duck, S. and Gilmour, R. (eds) *Personal Relationships 2: Developing Personal Relationships*. London: Academic Press.

62. Cunningham and Antill (1981), 50.

63. See e.g. Buunk and van Driel (1989), 110–111.

64. See e.g. Meyering, R.A. and Epling-McWherter, E.A. (1985–87). Decision-making in extramarital relationships. *Lifestyles*, 8: 115–129.

65. See e.g. Bancroft (1989), 259–260.

66. See e.g. Buunk and van Driel (1989), 103.

67. Meyering and Epling-McWherter (1985–87).

68. See e.g. Lawson (1988), 78–79.

69. See e.g. Buunk and van Driel (1989), 100–101.
70. See e.g. Meyering and Epling-McWherter (1985–87).
71. Baron, R.A. (1989). *Psychology*. Boston: Allyn and Bacon. 512.
72. Lawson, A. and Samson, C. (1988). Age, gender and adultery. *British Journal of Sociology*, 39: 428; see also Lawson (1988), 102–104.
73. Lawson (1988), 231–232.
74. See: Schaap, C., Buunk, B. and Kerkstra, A. (1988). Marital conflict resolution. Chapter in: Noller, P. and Fitzpatrick, M.A. (eds) *Perspectives on Marital Interaction*. Clevedon, Avon: Multilingual Matters.
75. See e.g. Buunk, B. and Bringle, R.G. (1987). Jealousy in love relationships. Chapter in: Perlman, D. and Duck, S. (eds) *Intimate Relationships*. Newbury Park: Sage.
76. See e.g. Berscheid, E. (1983). Emotion. Chapter in: Kelley, H.H. et al., *Close Relationships*. New York: W.H. Freeman.
77. Buunk (1987).
78. Gagnon, J.H. (1977). *Human Sexualities*. Glencoe, Ill.: Scott, Foresman. Cited in Argyle and Henderson (1985), 151.
79. Buunk (1987), 281.
80. Buunk (1987), 283.
81. Goodwin, R. (1990). Needs, roles and relationship alternatives. Paper presented at the International Conference on Personal Relationships, Oxford, July. 7.
82. See e.g. Buunk (1987); Buunk and van Driel (1989), 113.
83. VanYperen, N.W. and Buunk, B.P. (1990). A longitudinal study of equity and satisfaction in intimate relationships. *European Journal of Social Psychology*, 20: 287–309; VanYperen, N.W. and Buunk, B.P. (1991). Equity theory and exchange and communal orientation from a cross-national perspective. *Journal of Social Psychology*, 131: 5–20.
84. Buss, D.M. (1989). Conflict between the sexes: strategic interference and the evocation of anger and upset. *Journal of Personality and Social Psychology*, 56: 735–747.
85. See e.g. Richardson, L. (1986). Another world. *Psychology Today*, 20(2): 22–27.

9. REPAIRING RELATIONSHIPS

1. See e.g. Duck, S. (1988). *Relating to Others*. Milton Keynes: Open University Press. 12–13, 112; McFarland, C. and Ross, M. (1987). The relation between current impressions and memories of self

and dating partners. *Personality and Social Psychology Bulletin*, 13: 228–238.

2. See e.g. Duck, S. (1981). Toward a research map for the study of relationship breakdown. Chapter in: Duck, S. and Gilmour, R. (eds) *Personal Relationships 3: Personal Relationships in Disorder*. London: Academic Press; Duck (1988), *Relating . . .*, 105–111.

3. Rusbult, C.E., Verette, J., Whitney, G.A., Slovik, L.F. and Lipkus, I. (1991). Accommodation processes in close relationships: theory and preliminary empirical evidence. *Journal of Personality and Social Psychology*, 60: 53–78.

4. Birchler, G.R., Weiss, R.L. and Vincent, J.P. (1975). Multimethod analysis of social reinforcement exchange between maritally distressed and nondistressed spouse and stranger dyads. *Journal of Personality and Social Psychology*, 31: 349–360.

5. See e.g. Byrne, D. and Murnen, S.K. (1988). Maintaining loving relationships. Chapter in: Sternberg, R.J. and Barnes, M.L. (eds) *The Psychology of Love*. New Haven: Yale University Press.

6. See: Marsh, P. (ed) (1988). *Eye to Eye*. London: Sidgwick and Jackson. 222.

7. Baron, R.A. (1989). *Psychology*. Boston: Allyn and Bacon. 493.

8. See e.g. Baron (1989), 509–511.

9. Gilmour, R. (1988). Breaking up. Chapter in Marsh, 233.

10. See e.g. Cate, R.M. and Lloyd, S.A. (1988). Courtship. Chapter in: Duck, S. (ed) *Handbook of Personal Relationships*. Chichester: John Wiley.

11. See e.g. Duck (1988), *Relating . . .*, 114–116.

12. Duck (1988), *Relating . . .*, 115.

13. See e.g. Marsh (1988), 234.

14. Davis, G. and Murch, M. (1988). *Grounds for Divorce*. Oxford: Clarendon Press.

15. See e.g. Beach, S.R.H. and Tesser, A. (1988). Love in marriage: a cognitive account. Chapter in Sternberg and Barnes.

16. Rusbult, Verette, Whitney, Slovik and Lipkus (1991), 54.

17. See e.g. Rusbult, C.E. (1987). Responses to dissatisfaction in close relationships: the exit-voice-loyalty-neglect model. Chapter in: Perlman, D. and Duck, S. (eds) *Intimate Relationships*. Newbury Park: Sage.

18. See e.g. Beach and Tesser (1988); Duck (1988), *Relating . . .*, 117.

19. Rusbult, Verette, Whitney, Slovik and Lipkus (1991), 54.

20. Rusbult (1987); see also Rusbult, Verette, Whitney, Slovik and Lipkus (1991).

21. Dindia, K. and Baxter, L.A. (1987). Strategies for maintaining and repairing marital relationships. *Journal of Social and Personal Relationships*, 4: 143–158.
22. Rusbult, C.E., Morrow, G.D. and Johnson, D.J. (1987). Self-esteem and problem-solving behaviour in close relationships. *British Journal of Social Psychology*, 26: 293.
23. See e.g. Baxter, L.A. (1988). A dialectical perspective on communication strategies in relationship development. Chapter in Duck, *Handbook . . ..*
24. Baxter, L.A. (1987). Cognition and communication in the relationship process. Chapter in: Burnett, R., McGhee, P. and Clarke, D.D. (eds) *Accounting for Relationships*. London: Methuen. 206.
25. See e.g. Baucom, D.H., Sayers, S.L. and Duhe, A. (1989). Attributional style and attributional patterns among married couples. *Journal of Personality and Social Psychology*, 56: 596–607; Bradbury, T.N. and Fincham, F.D. (1988). Individual difference variables in close relationships: a contextual model of marriage as an integrative framework. *Journal of Personality and Social Psychology*, 54: 713–721; Fincham, F.D. and Bradbury, T.N. (1987). The impact of attributions in marriage: a longitudinal analysis. *Journal of Personality and Social Psychology*, 53: 510–517.
26. See e.g. Bradbury and Fincham (1988); Fincham and Bradbury (1987).
27. Baucom, D.H. (1987). Attributions in distressed relations: how can we explain them? Chapter in Perlman and Duck.
28. Fincham, F.D., Beach, S.R. and Baucom, D.H. (1987). Attribution processes in distressed and nondistressed couples: 4. Self-partner attribution differences. *Journal of Personality and Social Psychology*, 52: 746.
29. Fincham and Bradbury (1987).
30. Fincham and Bradbury (1987), 515.
31. Baucom, Sayers and Duhe (1989).
32. See e.g. Epstein, N. (1986). Cognitive marital therapy: multilevel assessment and intervention. *Journal of Rational-Emotive Therapy*, 4: 68–81.
33. See e.g. Baucom, D.H., Epstein, N., Sayers, S. and Sher, T.G. (1989). The role of cognitions in marital relationships: definitional, methodological, and conceptual issues. *Journal of Consulting and Clinical Psychology*, 57: 31–38.
34. See e.g. Baucom, D.H. and Lester, G.W. (1986). The usefulness of cognitive restructuring as an adjunct to behavioral marital

therapy. *Behavior Therapy*, 17: 385–403.

35. See e.g. Fincham and Bradbury (1987).
36. Beck, A.T. (1988). *Love Is Never Enough*. New York: Harper & Row.
37. Beck (1988), 2–3.
38. Alfred, Lord Tennyson. *Merlin and Vivien*, l.388.
39. Beck (1988), 210, 211.
40. Duck, S. (1984). A perspective on the repair of personal relationships: repair of what, when? Chapter in: Duck, S. (ed) *Personal Relationships 5: Repairing Personal Relationships*. London: Academic Press.
41. See e.g. Snyder, D.K. and Wills, R.M. (1989). Behavioral versus insight-oriented marital therapy: effects on individual and interspousal functioning. *Journal of Consulting and Clinical Psychology*, 57: 39–46; Snyder, D.K., Wills, R.M. and Grady-Fletcher, A. (1991). Long-term effectiveness of behavioral versus insight-oriented marital therapy: a 4–year follow-up study. *Journal of Consulting and Clinical Psychology*, 59: 138–141; Jacobson, N.S. (1991). Behavioral versus insight-oriented marital therapy: labels can be misleading. *Journal of Consulting and Clinical Psychology*, 59: 142–145; Snyder, D.K., Wills, R.M. and Grady-Fletcher, A. (1991). Risks and challenges of long-term psychotherapy outcome research: reply to Jacobson. *Journal of Consulting and Clinical Psychology*, 59: 146–149.
42. See e.g. Snyder and Wills (1989).
43. Hahlweg, K. and Markman, H.J. (1988). Effectiveness of behavioral marital therapy: empirical status of behavioral techniques in preventing and alleviating marital distress. *Journal of Consulting and Clinical Psychology*, 56: 440–447.
44. See e.g. Duck (1988), *Relating . . .*, 118–119.
45. See e.g. Duck (1988), *Relating . . .*, 122.

CONCLUSION
1. Baxter, L.A. (1988). A dialectical perspective on communication strategies in relationship development. Chapter in: Duck, S. (ed) *Handbook of Personal Relationships*. Chichester: John Wiley. 268.
2. Birchler, G. (1979). Communication skills in married couples. Chapter in: Bellack, A. and Hersen, M. (eds) *Research and Practice in Social Skills Training*. New York: Plenum.
3. Rusbult, C.E. (1987). Responses to dissatisfaction in close relationships: the exit-voice-loyalty-neglect model. Chapter in: Perlman,

D. and Duck, S. (eds) *Intimate Relationships*. Newbury Park: Sage. 223.

4. See e.g. Duck, S. (1988). *Relating to Others*. Milton Keynes: Open University Press. 124.

5. See e.g. Smith, D.A., Vivian, D. and O'Leary, K.D. (1990). Longitudinal prediction of marital discord from premarital expressions of affect. *Journal of Consulting and Clinical Psychology*, 58: 790–798.

Index

Men and Divorce

John Abulafia

Divorce is traumatic for everyone involved. It is no different for men, but whereas practical advice is readily available, the emotional side is too often ignored. The truth is it *hurts*, just as much for men as for women.

This is the first book to look at the emotional side of the divorce trauma from the man's point of view. It looks at *why* it hurts, and how to get through the bitterness, loneliness and shattering life-change divorce gives rise to – for those who left as well as those who were left.

Through the experiences of the many men he interviewed, John Abulafia shows not only the various ways in which men cope or don't cope, but also how the path to a new life can be made easier, and how to learn from the situation.

Written with sensitivity and understanding, *Men and Divorce* will prove helpful not only to divorcing men but also to the women on the other end.

FONTANA

The Cinderella Complex

Women's Hidden Fear of Independence

Colette Dowling

A book in which – whether she likes it or not – every woman will recognize herself.

'*I found that what I really wanted was to be taken care of. It was not just a question of having someone else pay the bills. I wanted full-time emotional protection, a buffer between me and the world.*'

For Colette Dowling, single parent and successful journalist, this discovery was a shocking one. She found that the same desire lies at the heart of millions of other women's lives. Yet the Cinderella complex is a phenomenon the women's movement has not yet confronted.

The conflict between wanting to be independent, and the need to be taken care of, can be a destructive one. '*The fear is that if we really stand on our own feet, we'll end up stranded – unwomanly, unlovely, unloved.*' This book helps women face up to that fear, and work towards real independence.

A FONTANA ORIGINAL

Jealousy

Nancy Friday

Author of *My Mother My Self*

Jealousy is a major breakthrough on a very important subject, written by Nancy Friday with honesty and a willingness to reveal her own experiences, based on meticulous research and told with the skill and suspense of a thriller.

Jealousy is one of the most common emotions, however much we may all deny it. It propels us in deeply unconscious ways, influencing our actions much more than we realize. Nancy Friday asks – and convincingly answers – us, her friends, psychologists and writers a whole list of questions. Why are some people more jealous than others? Are women more jealous than men? Have they always been? What is the difference between envy and jealousy? Should one try to control jealousy? Is sibling rivalry the most prevalent and dangerous of all jealousies?

Nancy Friday shares with the reader an often painful, sometimes funny, always ruthlessly honest examination of her own jealous feelings both in the past and present, and investigates every aspect of the subject, presenting us in the end with the hope that we may be able to come to terms with jealousy, and so curb the havoc it creates in our lives.

Fontana

The Successful Self

Freeing Our Hidden Inner Strengths

Dorothy Rowe

Is it possible to be truly successful as a person? Or must we, as most of us do, continue to live our lives feeling in some way trapped and oppressed, frustrated, irritable, haunted by worries and regrets, creating misery for ourselves and others?

In *The Successful Self*, leading psychologist Dorothy Rowe shows us how to live more comfortably and creatively within ourselves by achieving a fuller understanding of how we experience our existence and how we perceive the threat of its annihilation.

She demonstrates how to develop the social and personal skills we lack, retaining the uniqueness of our individuality while becoming an integral part of the life around us and learning how to value and accept ourselves.

With characteristic originality, clarity and unfailing wisdom, Dorothy Rowe enables us to revolutionize our own lives and the lives of others in the process of becoming a Successful Self.

'Dr Dorothy Rowe, seer, has qualities which to my mind place her somewhere between sainthood and genius.'   FAY WELDON

'A very brightly written book that intriguingly makes you question something most of us discuss: do we really like ourselves? Then it goes on to help us do so.'   MAVIS NICHOLSON

Fontana